Michael Rutherford is a founding member of Genesis. He also formed Mike + The Mechanics in 1985. He was inducted into th ꓴock and Roll Hall of Fame as a member of Genesis in Mike lives with his family in West Sussex.

The Living Years

Mike Rutherford

Constable • London

CONSTABLE

First published in Great Britain in 2014 by Constable
an imprint of Constable & Robinson Ltd.

This paperback edition published in 2014 by Constable

A CIP catalogue record for this book
is available from the British Library.

ISBN 978-1-47211-696-3 (paperback)
ISBN: 978-1-47211-035-0 (ebook)

Typeset in Bembo by SX Composing DTP, Rayleigh Essex

Printed and bou

To
Angie, Kate, Tom and Harry

PREFACE

I was in a hotel room in Chicago when the phone rang at 3 a.m. It was Angie: 'I've got some bad news – Dad's died.' Time really does freeze at moments like that and your heart plummets. Mum had called her: 'Angie, darling, Dad's dead. I've poked him with my stick and he's not moving: he's definitely gone.' Mum was in a wheelchair and very immobile – she and my father slept in twin beds – and the phrase was exactly like her. I could almost hear her voice.

At that moment I couldn't think of anything to say or to even begin to discuss arrangements. I was too much in shock. After I hung up I stood by the hotel window and looked down at the car headlights. I was on the thirty-fifth floor and it suddenly seemed incredibly quiet and very lonely. I felt very distant from anything that was happening down on the street – I just didn't feel part of the world.

We were in the middle of a six-show run in Chicago, playing to 20,000 people a night, and less than a month into our year-long tour. If I'd wanted to fly back to England I knew that the band and our manager, Tony Smith, would have supported me, just as we had always accommodated each other musically. But I also knew that there was nothing I could really do in Farnham. Mum had Angie and my sister Nicky to look after her, and my father had taken care of all the funeral arrangements. So Tony Smith and I sat down and made a plan. In two weeks' time I would fly overnight to England for the funeral, and after the service I would fly straight back by Concorde to California for a show at the LA Forum.

The next two weeks were surreal. I found I could go on stage and get lost in the music for two-and-a-half hours, but then the show would end and the realization of what had happened would hit all over again. There was a sense of security, of safety, playing with Tony and Phil, but my own emotions and my father's death were things we didn't discuss.

There were times in my life when I felt guilty not talking about my feelings, but that was just how I was brought up. I think public school was a large part of it but it was also generational: my father and I belonged to a time when sons didn't tell their fathers they loved them. I'd never told my dad that I loved him, and my biggest regret was not telling him what a wonderful man he'd been in my life.

I arrived in England on 13 October 1986 and went home briefly to see the children. I then drove with Angie to the funeral service in Aldershot. The night before I'd been on stage in front of thousands of people, and now I was in a car on the way to an English church to say goodbye to my father for the last time. After that, I would be flying back to LA – I knew then I needed some help. I asked Angie if she would fly back with me just for one night. Someone drove to our house to pick up her passport while we were in the church and then it was straight to Heathrow, where we boarded Concorde for the first leg of our journey. Angie was still in her funeral dress and only had her handbag.

We arrived in New York and a car was waiting on the tarmac to take us to the private jet that would fly us to LA. I think it was then that the enormity of it all really struck me. As we flew west, keeping up with the sun, the day seemed endless and yet all the time I was aware of leaving that church in Aldershot further behind, while LA was getting closer. It seemed very still on that plane – it was just us and a couple of crew – and the sun still wasn't setting. I felt as though I'd lost my compass point.

I found out later that two of the people in the audience that night in LA were Elton John and Gary Farrow, his PR. They both knew what was happening and spent the time before the show discussing whether I was going to make it back or not. The band were trying to decide which songs they could play without me or even if they would have to cancel the show. I arrived with twenty minutes to spare thanks to a police escort from the airport.

It may sound self-serving to say that I played that show for my father, but when I heard those eerie chords to 'Mama', that primal, basic beat, that's what I felt I was doing. My father had always taught me that if you had an obligation, you fulfilled it – it was as simple as that. That night I was giving something of the right spirit, and I think he would have approved.

When I went to bed and Angie eventually fell asleep, I couldn't stop thinking about how bizarre the whole thing was. I'd buried my father in the morning and then travelled backwards in time to play the show. Somehow I also felt that my father had gone on a journey too – I wasn't quite sure where either of us were at that point.

★ ★ ★

My father's death hit me the most six years later, following my mother's death in 1992. My sister Nicky cleared out their house and sent me three weathered, leather-bound trunks belonging to my father.

I was still reeling from my mother's death and the fact that we had to sell my parent's first and only home in Farnham. It was the end of an era and I didn't really feel ready to look into the trunks in case they stirred up emotions I wasn't sure I could handle. I've always been one to keep my emotions hidden away. I put the trunks in the attic above my studio and that's where they remained untouched for a few years.

I'm not sure when the time is right to deal with the past, but it wasn't a calculated thing – I was in my studio a few years later having a writer's block sort of day, and my mind started thinking about the trunks. The next thing I was up there wondering which one to open first, as there was also one belonging to my grandfather. I decided to open my grandfather's trunk and one of my father's at the same time. The thing that startled me the most when I lifted the lids was the military precision – the way everything was so neat and tidy. In my grandfather's case all of the papers and files were bunched together with elastic bands, while in my father's case all of his paperwork was neatly put in plastic folders. I had a shock of recognition, as I've always surrounded myself with plastic folders – and I've never even been in the military.

In these plastic folders was a mixture of naval histories from Dartmouth, memorabilia from the wars, his medals, CBE, Distinguished Service Order certificates and his medical history, and his sword was also in the trunk. In my grandfather's trunk there was similar stuff, but I also found two of the books he had written: *Soldiering with a Stethoscope* and *Memoirs of an Army Doctor*. There were great reviews amongst his papers, praising Colonel Rutherford and the publishing deal he had landed. My father's trunk contained a manuscript of his own memoirs along with a very positive and generous letter from David Niven, from whom he'd obviously sought an opinion (my father was a fan of Niven's memoir, *The Moon's a Balloon*). However, there was also a publisher's rejection letter saying there was 'not very much demand for military history these days and so I am sorry we cannot accept it'. I felt my father's disappointment.

Last year my sons took my father's manuscript and had it made into a beautiful leather-bound book. They gave it to me for Christmas – I was completely overwhelmed. I may hide my emotions pretty well but it was hard on that day. I sat down and started piecing together my father's life, and read his memoir from cover to cover. I felt so proud not only of my father's naval career, but of the legacy he left me.

CHAPTER ONE

In May 1906 I was born in a London nursing home, my father then being stationed in Chelsea Barracks as Medical Officer. Having joined the Royal Army Medical Corps from private practice, he had gone off to the South African War, at the end of which he had married my mother who belonged to one of the old Cape families, the Cloetes, who had arrived in 1652 in South Africa and had lost no time in increasing their numbers.

My father was born into the age of empire: archdukes, emperors, a map of the world that was coloured pink. The seas were ruled by Edward VII's Navy, which 'had countenanced no rival since the Battle of Trafalgar', and households like my father's were ruled over by iron-fisted nannies.

My father's travels began aged ten when his father, my grandpa, returned to South Africa. Nanny came too – although I'm not sure how happy she was about it:

We arrived at Durban and, disembarking, I had my first delighted ride in a rickshaw, a two-wheeled vehicle drawn by a Zulu between the shafts. He wore decorative clothing, though not much of it, and a headdress of horns. From time to time he leapt in the air with a blood-curdling yell, almost spilling his passengers over the back. I could not have enjoyed anything more but Nanny, who shared the general national view in those days that the black races began at Calais, was most put out by such goings on.

Three decades later my father was back in Durban again, which is where he met my mother, Anne: at the time he was Acting Captain of the heavy cruiser *Suffolk*, which had docked there for a refit. He saw my mother at a charity dance and they got married six weeks later: given that my mother was always the impulsive one, it seems odd that it was all so quick. In any case, the happy couple enjoyed a six-day honeymoon before my father sailed off again, this time for Trincomalee in Sri Lanka. They didn't see each other again for ten months.

My parents were reunited in England after VE Day, my mother having sailed over on a troop ship and my father having been appointed to a position in the Admiralty, which was situated on Horse Guards Parade in Whitehall. However, by the time my mother was expecting my sister Nicolette in 1947, my father had been appointed Chief of Staff to the Naval Representative of the Joint Chiefs of Staff in Australia. It was decided that my mother should go back to Durban for Nicky's birth and only travel the rest of the way to catch up with my father afterwards. This meant that Dad didn't know he had a daughter until a cable message was rushed up the gangway of his ship in Adelaide.

When my father's term of duty ended in 1949 my parents and

sister moved back to England. My father returned to his job in Admiralty and found a house to lease in Chertsey, Surrey, and that was where I was born on 2 October 1950. They chose not to go for the less-is-more option when choosing my names, so I was christened Michael John Cloete Crawford Rutherford. Less than two years later Dad was off again, this time to the Korean War.

My father was eight years old when he watched his own father go off to the First World War carrying field glasses, a sword and a revolver. Being eighteen months old I don't remember what Dad was carrying when he left for the Far East, but I do remember the day, two years later, when he came back: he asked how many teeth I had and then let me crawl all over his car – good opening moves, I thought.

In fact, it was all going well until bedtime, when I began to get a bit suspicious: where was this strange man's home? Surely it couldn't be with us?

Apparently, it was.

I can clearly picture my father coming into my room at dusk to say goodnight to me, his silhouette at the end of the bed. He was a big man – not quite as tall as I ended up, but big – yet he didn't seem scary.

I still had my doubts about whether he would disappear again overnight, though, and so kept getting up to check on his where-abouts. Eventually my parents gave in and moved my bed into their room so that they could get some sleep.

My father was always smart and he always had good posture: even out of his Captain's uniform it was his posture, his presence, which impressed people about him. Wherever he went – into a restaurant or a shop or a stationer – he commanded respect:

people were polite and courteous. He was also always punctual, methodical and orderly.

As a boy I mostly took after my mother.

My mother had wanted to go to art college but girls didn't in her day; she'd also wanted to be a ballet dancer but had grown too tall. She was very aware of sounds and energy, and a sunset or a blue sky would set her off every time: 'Darling! The colours!'

She was a wonderfully, beautifully dotty woman. I think my father enjoyed the way she was her own person, but he was also quite long-suffering: when they were living in Melbourne, for instance, my mother had got carried away collecting wattle flowers, which she loved because they were bright yellow and reminded her of home in South Africa. What she didn't know was that, unlike in South Africa, wattle was a protected species in Australia. One day she filled my father's car with wattle equivalent to a £200 fine. He had to drive to the beach in the middle of the night, dig a hole and bury it.

Mum was a widow, although her previous marriage wasn't something that my parents spoke about. It wasn't until I was thirteen and we were on a family holiday in Italy that I began to wonder out loud why every single piece of silver on our dining-room cabinet at home had the name 'Captain Woods' engraved on it. There was a startled hush and Mum went completely white. In those days there was still a stigma attached to being married more than once; plus, 'Captain Woods' had died of cancer, which no one ever talked about. I think it must have been Mum's idea to sweep her history under the carpet, because my father was too direct to hide things.

Maybe they also kept it quiet because they were genuinely

worried that it would have an effect on me – although if they were really concerned about it, perhaps they shouldn't have had all that engraved silver lying around. Of course, it made no difference to me whatsoever.

I was five years old when my father was appointed Commanding Officer of Whale Island in Portsmouth Harbour. Dad had trained as a naval gunnery officer there twenty years earlier; now, in 1955, he was returning to take charge.

It was the pinnacle of his naval career and he was soon installed in the Captain's house, as were my mother, Nicky and I. The arrangement was a bit unusual. Until the end of the Second World War, the Captain's house had been very much bachelor territory (wives and families were expected to stay at home on shore). Also, most officers, by the time they reached the rank of captain, had children who were grown up and at university. My father, who was forty-nine in 1955, had a seven-year-old daughter and a five-year-old son – although it seems that Nicky and I learned to fit in pretty quickly:

> *Both children took their appointed station in the establishment and there was no child psychology or anything like that. Their tricycles, when not in use, were placed between their own little white lines in the tricycle park outside the Captain's house, gear was replaced in a seamanlike manner after every playtime and if they ever asked: 'Is that an order?' and the reply happened to be: 'Yes – right turn – double march!' that was all there was to it.*

Like my father when he was a child, I had a nanny, at least while we were living on Whale Island. She was the daughter of a lieutenant and could run like the wind, which came in handy whenever I cycled off. My aim was always to get to the beach – rumour had it there were pieces of eight buried there – but I never got very far. What's more, on the rare occasions when I did manage to out-pedal Nanny, I was thwarted by the island's public-address system, which would inform everyone that I was on the loose: 'Anyone sighting the Captain's son is requested to report position, course and speed, intercept and return him to base.'

Disappointingly, they always did.

I still managed to have plenty of adventures on Whaley. I delivered the pigswill with the head stableman, Mr Brown – a clean bin was kept on his horse-drawn cart so that if it rained I could be put inside and the lid put on. In our second year on the island I also joined the HMS *Excellent* boy cadets. I was five by this time but still underage; however, my father was the Commander so no one was going to argue. According to Dad's book, I fell in a goldfish pond before one parade and bawled my eyes out in a 'most unseamanlike manner' when I wasn't allowed to carry on in my wet trousers. I do wonder if he came to regret bending the rules.

There was also the time when one of the island's guns was fired unexpectedly:

Michael was riding Joey the pony on the upper lawn supervised by Mr Brown. At the sound of the gunfire Joey bucked and unseated Mike who hung upside down suspended by one leg and held up by the stirrup.

When remounted his morale was quite unaffected as he

assumed that it was all part of riding and that to hang upside
down occasionally like a Cossack was quite normal.

A highlight of our time on Whaley was the time a Russian
naval squadron visited Portsmouth and my father was given the
job of looking after a Sverdlov-class cruiser and its crew. After
the Captain had been for tea at our house, I was invited to spend
the next day aboard his ship in return. I duly came back loaded
with presents so it was a great success from my point of view,
although I think my father was a bit disappointed that I hadn't
also managed to glean some Cold-War secrets while I was at it.
In the end the only thing I learned was the Russian word for
'thank you': I realized that the more I said it, the more chocolates
I got. They were enormous things – about the size of my hand
– but I still thank you-ed my way through six of them. Then I
went home and was sick.

What I remember most about Whaley is how big everything
was: the pageantry was huge, there were vast spaces to run around
in, the parade ground seemed to go on forever. And at the centre
of it all was my father. Every ceremony revolved around him,
everyone saluted him wherever he went. (I loved saluting, it
seemed very grown up: something only men did. I would always
be trying to get away from Nanny and my sister because nobody
ever saluted them.)

Walking around the island with my father, I can remember
puffing out my chest to be as big as possible, feeling the importance of being by his side.

★ ★ ★

It was a letter from the Admiralty that changed everything for my father. Instead of bringing the news that he was promoted to the position of Rear Admiral, as he'd hoped, the letter told him instead that he'd be expected to retire from the Navy in two months' time.

At the time this letter arrived Dad had been in the Navy for thirty-six years, gained two Mentions-in-Despatches in the Second World War and a Distinguished Service Order earned off the coast of Korea in the early fifties. Suddenly he was out of work. With a wife and two young children to provide for, retirement was out of the question. For the first time in his life he had to go job-hunting, and the signs didn't look good:

I was […] given an official booklet giving advice upon the transition to civilian life. This I read one evening. It was the most depressing thing I have ever read and by the end of it, I needed a couple of stiff whiskies to restore my morale. It appeared that I was virtually valueless to the labour market and must adopt a humble and low profile ready to accept a modest job in the hope of climbing the ladder once more if I was lucky enough to get on the ladder at all.

In the words of today's young people it was dead dreary.

Quite a few rejections followed but then my father applied for a job working on the Blue Steel missile defence system that was being developed by Hawker Siddeley (which later became part of British Aerospace). He was successful, but the job meant moving to the opposite end of the country, Cheshire, where Hawker Siddeley had their headquarters. My father always believed in the right outfit for the occasion, and on the day he left for Wilmslow he did so in his new uniform: a bowler hat, rolled umbrella and pigskin gloves.

Mum, Nicky and I followed not long after and moved into a Manchester hotel, the Dean Water, while my parents were looking for a house. The hotel used to have dances on a Saturday evening and my sister and I, dressed in our pyjamas, would look over the banisters at the dancers going past in their smart evening gear. It was like a glimpse into another world: very exciting.

Far Hills, the house that my parents found, was a detached, brick-built 1930s house about four miles from the Hawker Siddeley base. This meant that whenever the black, triangular Vulcan Bombers flew overhead, the whole place shook, which impressed any guests we had staying. I was more impressed by the fact I could use the base's runway as a go-Karting track.

I had a yellow 30cc go-Kart – very cool – and we would put it in the back of our big red-and-white Austin and drive to the base with it sticking out of the boot. My main memory is of me trying to start the damn thing, but when I did get it going, I went flying.

Mum would always drive me to the airbase and she'd also drive Dad to work each day. Her style was probably best described as colourful. On one occasion we were late going to the train station and we hurried to the car, which was parked in the garage. Nicky and I in piled into the back and were looking out of the rear window in anticipation when Mum went full throttle straight through the garage wall in front.

Driving up to visit our relatives in Scotland was also a drama. One year we hired a caravan and Nicky and I went with Mum to collect it the night before. By the time she'd negotiated it back through our narrow gates into the driveway I was already hoping that Dad would take the helm the next morning. We would be manoeuvring out straight on to a main road which, with Mum at the wheel, was the kind of thing that left you afraid for your life.

Mum's objection to Dad's driving was that he did it as though he was steering a ship. He'd leave the garage as if he were leaving the harbour, set sail down the road at a very respectable pace and be totally unaware of fellow motorists flashing him, shaking their fists and trying to overtake. He'd be completely in his own world, which would drive my mother to distraction. Mum, by contrast, didn't have a problem with speed: we'd hit the motorway and she'd hit the gas, pushing the car to the limit of the maximum speed it could do. It would shake and rattle, and my father would hang on to the loop above his window with white knuckles. He knew that if he attempted to despatch any orders, he would be ejected immediately. Reaching our destination intact was always a relief.

I particularly enjoyed Scotland and visiting my Great-aunt Jean (from my mother's side of the family). The Biggars had three farms and bred Galloway cattle, and I think it was there that I developed a desire to become a farmer. I loved the lifestyle, the open spaces and especially being around the cows: they felt kind and safe, and hearing them munching their hay in the quiet of the evening was very satisfying.

Generally, though, there wasn't much love lost between my parents' families and siblings. There was an Aunty Rosie who lived in Southsea and was artistic and slightly eccentric – especially when helped along by a glass of wine or two – but we only visited her a couple of times. Strange, given that on Whale Island we'd been so nearby. It didn't end well between Aunty Rosie and me: Mum rang me one day when I was in my twenties and told me that Auntie Rosie had recently got married. I told Mum to give her my congratulations, as you would, but that didn't go down too well.

'Not married, darling! *Buried!*'

I saw even less of my mother's brother, Uncle Berners – in fact I only met him once. When his name was mentioned it was always in lowered tones, when my parents thought I was out of earshot. This might have been because he'd acted badly and opted out of looking after his mother, my 'Jean Granny', as we used to call her. But it might also have been because Uncle Berners, who was the vicar of Eton for many years, changed his name later on in life to something double-barrelled, which really bugged my parents. My father wasn't very tolerant of pomposity.

Because of Uncle Berners, Dad ended up paying for the upkeep of both grannies – Jean Granny and his own mother, Granny Malimore – who both lived into their nineties. Granny Malimore (who was called Malimore because that was the name of her house in Farnham) was very bright but not very active. Jean Granny, meanwhile, was very active but not very bright. They'd meet at family occasions and Jean Granny would always find some stairs to rush up and then say things like, 'Oh, am I going too fast for you, Roberta?' And Granny Malimore would get her own back by memorizing all kinds of historical facts and embarrassing Jean Granny by asking her questions she couldn't answer.

I don't know how Jean Granny managed to live so long, but I think Granny Malimore did it by refrigeration. You'd go to her house in Farnham, breathe out, and see your breath in the air. And her fire would be on. It was one of those little smokeless fires, the size of an acorn. The minute a glow got going and a bit of heat started coming out, she'd jump up, bung on a scuttle-full of coal and nearly extinguish the thing.

Granny Malimore had a TV – quite rare in those days – which she'd been given by a wealthy cousin from Cape Town. She watched everything but preferred it if you thought that she only ever read *The Times*. We would go into the room and find her feigning to read the newspaper, but if we put our hand on the telly it would always be boiling hot. It probably gave off more heat than the fire.

Meanwhile, Jean Granny lived in a slightly threadbare 'residential hotel for the elderly' in Farnham called Morris Lodge Hotel. Morris Lodge played a big part in our family life. While my father had been away during the Korean War my mother had moved there with my sister and me, and I'm sure it was one of the reasons why she was able to cope. Nicky and I were always under surveillance, usually by some colourful character or other. It was run by a Colonel and Mrs Crosse, accompanied by a couple of rather bossy sisters. It's probably why *Fawlty Towers* later became a favourite of mine: I felt I could identify.

Even after we moved to Cheshire we'd often go back to Morris Lodge for holidays. We'd also spend occasional weekends fishing in the Derbyshire hills. I loved being outdoors, and even today rivers move me.

The river at Hartington has a beautiful meander that was always serene and calm, although generally became less so after the Rutherfords and dog had descended. The serious fishermen that used to go there were appalled, not least because my mother had a top-of-the-range Hardy rod but still used a worm for fly-fishing.

Dad wasn't a great fisherman at all and I think I caught only two fish in my entire career, but Mum had more of a feel for it. When she was young in South Africa she'd been quite sporty: she'd ride horses and sail in races, and she used to shoot too. But those days were gone by the time I appeared.

★ ★ ★

Mum was game for anything and would try to loosen Dad up, but there was a stiffness and formality about my father. He always had a sense of humour – it was very dry and lots of people missed it, but it was definitely there – but as far as I was concerned Dad was very reserved, although I always felt loved and secure.

My father had grown up with my grandpa's tales of the Boer War but he never told me a single war story, although he clearly had plenty to tell. When war was declared in 1939 his first mission was to sail to Canada with a million pounds of gold bullion, which was being sent from France for safekeeping. In 1940, after France had fallen to Germany, he'd been in charge of seizing two French ships in Plymouth harbour, and in 1941 he'd been on the *King George V* when it helped sink the *Bismarck*. But as a child I always sensed that he didn't want to talk about the war, and it didn't feel appropriate to ask.

Ours was never an unhappy household but it was serious. I had seen my dad practising yoga, which he'd picked up while he was in the Far East, but he would never kick a ball on the lawn with me and we'd never just chat. From a very young age I was also aware that he had incredibly high standards: I knew that his job on Whale Island had been to decide who passed exams and who failed.

One image I have of us together doesn't quite fit: my dad and I used to share baths when I was very little. I would have a plastic submarine – one of those funny things you got in a cornflake packet and put baking soda in to make it go up and down – and I'm sure Dad, watching me play with it, thought it was only a matter of time until I started my own naval career.

We weren't really together very much. By the time he came home from work I would often be in bed and then, when I was seven-and-a-half, I was packed off to boarding school. Maybe it was because my father wasn't a big part of my everyday life that the occasions when we were together felt so important.

As for my mother, I have no idea what she did all day but, whatever it was, she always seemed to be in a rush – my main memory of Mum is of her rushing into a room, smelling of the cold air she'd brought in from outdoors, dropping something off and rushing back out again.

Neither of my parents had many friends and, thinking about it now, I can see what a shock it must have been for both of them having to learn to deal with the real world outside the services at quite a late stage in their lives. Not only had my father never owned a house before – as a captain, he'd always been on the move and wherever he'd hung his cap, that was home – he'd never even paid a bill. Nor had Mum ever needed to cook a meal or worry about domestic chores: captains' wives didn't.

Perhaps that was why they didn't quite know how to make a home for Nicky and me. We didn't really have friends, either: my best friend was our cleaning lady's son, who I used to play with on the landing at Far Hills.

While we were on Whale Island, the naval carpenters there had made me a beautiful wooden trunk full of oak bricks, which the cleaning lady's son and I used to make forts from so that we could then fire things at each other. It was great fun, but one day I must have thought he was cheating because I threw a brick at his head. There wasn't much blood but that was the only time my father ever slippered me.

It may sound like a lonely life but I didn't feel lonely. I was quite self-sufficient. I even provided myself with my own pocket money: half-crowns, which I would take off my father's dresser. They were big, chunky things – they looked substantial – and I'd generally spend them on sweets or model kits: planes, not boats, which I thought were a bit dull. Talk about adding insult to injury. It was only when I got to prep school that I realized what I had been missing out on socially. And there was another discovery, too: music.

CHAPTER TWO

'Now, Michael, you're the son of a naval officer, you must behave like a naval officer and be strong at all times.'

I'll never forget my father's words to me as he left me, aged seven, at my prep school, The Leas in Hoylake, for my first term: he was wearing a smart tweed jacket, cavalry twills, brown suede shoes – and I was terrified.

Lying awake in my dormitory that night, boys either side whimpering and crying, a cold bath looming in the morning, I remember repeating Dad's words to myself – 'You're the son of a naval officer: be strong, don't show your feelings and you'll be all right' – and sure enough I was. For about three weeks. Then, one morning when I was having my milk in the big gym hall, it suddenly dawned on me: my parents had left me and I wouldn't see them for another six weeks. I was trapped. I'd been done.

With my milk bottle still in my hand, I burst into tears and then howled all the way through the rest of the break. The other boys had got over it all weeks ago, of course, and were no doubt thinking, 'What's wrong with Rutherford?' But I always was a bit slow getting there emotionally.

My father had also been to a prep school. It was in Rochester and, with its 'chipped desks, cracked inkpots, primitive lavatories, characteristic smell and regimen of porridge, cottage pie, sausage rolls, suet roll and rice pudding', was typical of its kind. That was in 1914, and things hadn't changed much by the time I got to The Leas. The only real difference was that Dad had to wear an Eton jacket and white kid gloves for dancing lessons, whereas I wore plimsoles – which wasn't ideal because my partner, Jones Minor, always trod on my feet. He always had a runny nose, too.

I had only asked my parents for one thing before leaving for The Leas and that was that they'd promise me I wouldn't have to do dancing lessons. Waltzing my way painfully round the gym a few weeks later I can remember feeling very let down.

I didn't feel angry at being sent away but I did feel rather sorry for myself. After my first term at The Leas I'd made up my mind: there was no way I was going back for more. My parents were very clever about the situation, though. They never tried to sell the school to me. I think they knew I would smell a rat. Instead, Mum would say, 'Now, Mikey, we're already in January, so we don't count January. You're coming home in March, so there's only February. Four weeks!' And I would think, 'Oh, yeah! What am I worrying about?'

It's amazing what the passage of time does and how you can just get used to things. Looking back The Leas really wasn't so bad: it was a big, four-storey building with creeper on it, grand front doors for the headmaster and lots of wings sticking out. Down an avenue of trees were the science blocks, playing fields and an indoor swimming pool (unheated, typically). There was also a roller-skating area – not exactly a rink – and in the evenings the light from the classrooms lit it up so that for about an hour after the bell went you could still skate. That was almost like freedom.

The food was generally disgusting – that was one thing that definitely hadn't changed since 1914 – but there was a fruit hut, which was a bit like a cross between a Nissen hut and a refrigerated greenhouse. Every morning at elevenses we'd go there to choose something to have with our milk, and the smell inside was fantastic.

Fruit was encouraged at The Leas and boys coming back from visits home would often bring baskets of oranges, apples and pears. My mother, who was quite eccentric on a food level, as well as on every other level, would send me back with pomegranates and lychees. (Bananas were a whole other story. During the holidays, if she ever saw me about to eat one with a brown bit in it, she'd take one look and say, 'Oh, darling, that's off. Give it to Dad.')

I was a scout at The Leas, the leader of Squirrel Patrol. We'd have treasure hunts in which we would be sent into Hoylake to collect a list of various odd items against the clock. As I found out one day, this didn't mean that you were allowed to take the bus. I thought I'd shown great ingenuity but it wasn't appreciated by the master, who beat me with a very hard slipper afterwards.

Scouts also meant scout camp every summer, which I loved. My father lent me his Captain's cap – an incredibly trusting thing for him to have done – and off we'd go to Wales, miles away from anywhere. We'd walk up Cader Idris and down scree slopes and do all kinds of other outward-bound type things. I thought the scoutmaster, Mr Waring, was great, although looking back now I slightly wonder whether his behaviour would be deemed appropriate these days. He had a lovely old Rolls-Royce with huge fenders and he'd drive round Wales with boys hanging off the sides.

I was never particularly sporty at school but I did excel at swimming and golf. I was always trying to beat a Malaysian boy at swimming: he was far superior to me, and the only time I would manage it was when he wasn't feeling well. There were a couple of times when I thought about dirty tactics – spiking his food and so on – but when I won a few rounds of golf and was made school Golf Captain, I decided I would concentrate on being superior at that. (Admittedly, there weren't too many other candidates fighting for the position but I was still proud of myself.)

I knew my father had a set of clubs somewhere, as he would occasionally recount stories of playing golf with various dignitaries on his travels round the Empire and try to convince whomever would listen that his prowess was on a global scale too. The truth, however, was that he'd only played once since the Second World War. It was in 1952 and he was in Singapore at the time, staying with an RAF commander who co-opted him into his 'Flying Boat Wing Team'. Realizing he might be a bit rusty, Dad tried to wriggle out of it, but it was too late:

As a guest I could hardly make a run for it and an idea of pretending to strain a back muscle during a practice swing was too blatantly transparent.

In due course, I stood on the first tee before an expectant crowd but I did not feel nervous – the drinks and lunch saw to that – and a carefree mood swept over me. If I was to make a ghastly ass of myself – the hell with it!

As it was a short hole I selected an iron club with a head like a shovel and avoiding any practice swing lest I gouged a chunk out of the turf, I addressed the ball and swung.

My guardian angels, the drinks and the lunch ensured that I did not raise my head too soon and the ball screamed straight as a die up the fairway to appreciative murmurs from the onlookers.

So often on these occasions performance exceeds expectations.

As I did not care who won and had not the faintest idea of the score as my amiable opponent marked the card I adopted a relaxed style with no anxieties or inhibitions, my approach shots were confident and my putting deadly – my guardian angels being still in charge to the extent that one of my drives which shot off at a tangent towards some buildings hit a tree and returned to the fairway.

Suddenly, after I fluked a long putt which hit the back of the hole hard, jumped into the air and fell in, my opponent said, 'Jolly good – your match!' and on return to tea I found that I had defeated the opposition's ace player. People said, 'If you haven't played for fourteen years you must have been a scratch or plus handicap player' and I spent the rest of my time at Singapore avoiding offers of games from people who could really play golf.

I did not play again for another ten years when, then retired, I took part in the fathers' match at my son's prep school . . .

On the day of that fathers' match, I wasn't aware that I should have somehow got my father drunk before he stepped on to the course. We were standing on the first tee when Dad pulled out a rusty-looking wood-shafted driver that, to my eyes, hardly resembled a golf club at all it was so prehistoric. Especially as everyone else had steel-shafted clubs. When he took his first swing with such gusto that he managed to miss the ball completely, I just wanted a hole to appear next to me so that I could putt myself into it.

Unfazed, my father had another attempt and carried on, totally oblivious to my embarrassment. Luckily for me, he also got better after that and by the end, even though we didn't win, I was thoroughly enjoying it.

★ ★ ★

Sundays were the real highlight of my time at The Leas, though: lunch out with my parents followed by *Pick of the Pops*.

Leaving prep school on a Sunday always felt like getting out of prison: outside the colours looked brighter, the air smelled better . . . plus you got roast beef. My mother and father would arrive early in the morning to come to chapel – Dad in his cavalry twills, erect and composed, Mum waving and coo-eeing enthusiastically. Then we'd all drive into Hoylake and have lunch at a hotel. After that, Dad would patiently settle down with *The Times* and I would huddle up to the radio in the sitting area, still in my grey school shorts and blue cap, jostling for position with any other Leas boys who might be there too.

It's hard to explain what an event *Pick of the Pops* was back then. Now, you can listen to anything you want at any time you want; there's music in every single restaurant, every shop, every airport, every lift. In 1963 pop music was limited to three hours on a Sunday afternoon, and the sense of anticipation was amazing. You would be counting the days until a Beatles album was released, and when Alan Freeman finally played 'She Loves You' or 'Please Please Me' the buzz would be tremendous – I can still feel it now. (The guitar riff from 'You Really Got Me' by the Kinks was the same. Nothing that great has ever dated.) It was a blank canvas, pop music. There were no precedents so everything was new and unique and exciting, and I loved it all: the Who, the Stones, the Small Faces, Joan Baez, Arthur Brown . . . although my first hero was, without question, Cliff Richard.

It was my sister Nicky who got me into Cliff.

My parents weren't really musical, although my father loved theatre and musical hall. At home I would often see him watching *The Good Old Days* with Leonard Sachs and pretending to conduct along to the songs. But they didn't own any records (having moved around so much while Dad was in the Navy, they didn't have many possessions generally), so the gramophone in our house was in Nicky's bedroom. Which always bugged me.

Nicky mainly listened to Tommy Steele and Elvis – ballad Elvis – which didn't get me going. It was only when I heard 'Move It' by Cliff and the Shadows – that wild, guitar-based sound – that I got a real body-charge of excitement. And then there was Cliff himself: his sharp suits, his quiffed-back hair, his moves . . . with that raw sound as well, he had it all.

My first gig, which I persuaded my parents to take me to, was Cliff and the Shadows at the Apollo in Manchester. A few days before, I would manage to buy some Brylcreem, and just as we were getting ready to leave I greased my hair into some sort of quiff so that I could look as cool as Cliff did. My mother didn't think I looked very cool at all, marched me upstairs and stuck my head under the tap.

Funnily enough, it didn't dampen the experience. Cliff was wearing a white jacket and black shirt and was as good as I'd hoped, although the idea that I could do what he was doing never occurred to me: he was so grown up and beyond my world.

As well as the sound, it was the shape of the guitar that appealed to me. I'd seen pictures of a red Hofner with double cutaways and I liked the symmetry of it. This meant that my first guitar – a cheap nylon-stringed acoustic – was a bit of a disappointment. As was Bert Weedon's manual *Play in a Day*, mainly because that was what I was expecting to do. And I didn't. The book had a picture of Bert on the cover wearing a suit and holding a jazz guitar, but by page three he'd lost me.

I wasn't entirely put off: I could still practise posturing with a record on. At Far Hills there weren't any mirrors that worked properly. Nicky had a dressing table mirror that angled, but if I wanted it to stay where it got me looking good, I had to wedge it into position with a book. Worse, I could only go into Nicky's room if she wasn't there. But when we went down to stay at Morris Lodge there was a huge, old, dark wooden wardrobe with two full-length mirrors on the doors. I spent quite a lot of time in front of them.

Dad must have taken pity on me at this point because he decided to send me for some lessons with a guitar teacher in Bramhall. Education, and learning in any form, was something that he considered worthwhile. Unfortunately, as far as I was concerned, this wasn't much better than Bert Weedon. I didn't want to learn about scales and notation from a guy in a tweed sports jacket: I wanted to learn songs. I stopped going after a couple of weeks, which I'm sure upset Dad.

The thing about being a guitarist – even a not-very-good one – was that it automatically made you stand out at The Leas. Everyone else played the piano or the recorder.

My first live performance was at a school assembly in my third year, where I performed a solo version of 'Michael Rowed the Boat Ashore'. (The bill also included 'Dry Bones – A Negro Spiritual' and ended up with the school song, 'Deo Parere Libertas'.)

I was in the school choir but my voice wasn't great and, to make matters worse, my guitar, which a master had tuned for me, had been knocked over by some idiot just before I went on stage. It remained painfully out of tune for the whole performance. I wasn't an outgoing guy but luckily I was too young to be fazed. I battled on regardless and then, feeling flushed with success, decided to form a band.

There were five of us in the Chesters, although only two of us could play instruments: me and Dimitri Griliopoulis. He was a drummer so it was a no-brainer that we'd bond instantly, but I don't think we minded that the others were only along for the ride. The main thing was being able to say you were *in* a band – we all understood that. Playing something was not the point.

The thinking behind our name was that The Leas was fifteen minutes from Liverpool, which was the place where everything was kicking off musically. The Liverpools didn't sound very good, though, so we decided to go for the Chesters, Chester being the nearest city that worked.

We'd hold our rehearsals in the main hall and every so

often the music teacher would insist that we let some flautist or recorder player join in, which didn't help with our image – although neither did the cricket jumpers that Dimitri and I wore in our promotional photos. During one school holiday, in desperation, we persuaded Nicky to pose with us. She looked like she should be in a band, which was more than you could say about Dimitri and me.

Dimitri and I wrote a couple of songs together – 'We used to be so happy / We said one day we'd mar-ry' – but I didn't blame Dimitri when he started moonlighting with The Leas' other band, the Echoes. I was too busy learning to play my new electric guitar to mind.

It probably wasn't the greatest look, having Mum with me in the guitar shop. She was wearing a tweed skirt and a headscarf, but then again, I was wearing shorts and Start-rite sandals. Mum always dressed me smartly and also kept a brush in her handbag, which she'd whip out to do my hair before we went anywhere.

I hadn't got a clue what kind of guitar I wanted and the shop itself was a bit overpowering. I was a bit too intimidated by the coolness of the instruments hanging on the walls to look around. The guy could have sold us anything he wanted, which is exactly what he did. I left with a Fender jazz guitar, which had strings about quarter of an inch off the fretboard: the last kind of thing you'd want to get if you were a beginner. I also ended up with a Selmer Little Giant amp – impressive name, teeny little thing. It was only about a foot by a foot-and-a-half. The fact that I would need an amplifier had never occurred to me before that day. Newspapers at the time were full of cartoons of long-haired guys playing electric guitars in their bedrooms while their parents – usually their fathers – screwed up their eyes in agony, and the guitars would always be plugged straight into the mains socket. That seemed fair enough to me.

Just seeing my light-blonde guitar lying in its crushed green-velvet lined case was exciting. As soon as we got back to Far Hills I rushed up to my bedroom and started strumming away in a very unmusical fashion. Even to me the sound seemed loud – beautifully loud – but I can't imagine what it must have been like for my father: amplified music was such a complete unknown for his generation.

On my father's side there was a link to the romantic poet Percy Bysshe Shelley (my great-great grandmother was sister to Shelley's mother) and so I think my mother expected me to have an artistic streak. 'Darling,' she'd say, 'it's in the blood: Shelley's line!' But Dad, although he never put the brakes on me, must have been worried – not least about our house. Every time I started playing he'd stride round the house and start tapping the walls. He thought I was shaking the cement out of the brick-work (as I might have been, slightly). He never said anything to me, though – and, needless to say, our house never did fall down.

★ ★ ★

As well as Dimitri, I had also made friends with a boy called David Sandford at The Leas. David came from Ireland, and in my last term I was invited to go over and stay with him. It was the first time I had ever flown and David Sandford's father, who was a turkey farmer in Strangford, picked me up at Belfast airport in his beaten-up old Land Rover.

I suppose Mr Sandford thought he'd make the most of the

opportunity because David and I were put to work feeding his turkeys and helping with the harvest. There were some other older boys there too and we all stayed in a caravan on our own behind the barn. It was free labour for David's dad but freedom for me: I was twelve and felt very grown up.

By this point I'd smoked the odd Player's No. 6 but for those ten days I could (and did) smoke as much as I wanted. I also found that the cider the older boys were drinking was bearable. Growing up I had always aspired to my parents' sherry at Christmas. I wasn't interested in their gin and tonics or gin and vermouths. Sherry was the one that appealed to me: that lovely colour. Then one year they gave me a glass and I discovered that it was disgusting, although of course I couldn't say that to them. 'Mm! Lovely!' I said, forcing it down. Cider was definitely an improvement.

The only real downside of the whole trip was that the caravan was just yards away from 17,000 turkeys. I still get a lingering whiff of ammonia in my nostrils at the very thought of Strangford. What with that and the sherry, Christmas dinner hasn't been the same since.

Bar a few incidents at prep school and this rather heady Irish holiday, I was a rather well-behaved boy. My father had always impressed on me the importance of politeness, trust and honour, and I felt that these were among the things for which he'd fought the war. In 1941 his ship, *Excellent*, had returned to Portsmouth for a refit the day after the first big blitz and he'd been appalled to see 'the smoking ruins of our home port':

I went ashore for a look and had a rather disproportionate flash of anger at the damage done to the pubs where we had spent many rather cheerful hours and whence we had taken out the barmaids after closing time for a spot of dancing at the local Assembly Rooms (known generally by the less decorous name of the Arse and Belly Rooms). It seemed so spiteful and un-gentlemanly to bash a man's pub — rather like smashing his golf clubs or damaging his children's bicycles.

The ethos of The Leas was clearly one that my father approved of because when I left the school in July 1964 he wrote to the headmaster:

We are glad that Michael has acquitted himself as a Leasian by achieving reasonable distinction in the fields of games and the social life of the school, by becoming a house prefect and by passing satisfactorily into Charterhouse.

We are also glad that Michael has been able to be with you for these vital early years, subject to the examples and influences that make up the school's personality.

It is not easy, these days, to find an environment founded on the basic simple virtues and cemented by a forthright religious life. Such things tend to be regarded by the self-styled progressives as corny and old hat but one would respect their views the more did they but offer adequate alternatives.

Sent with the letter was also 'a small contribution to the organ fund. I think this appropriate as Michael has done his bit over the last six years in helping to wear the old one out!' It was true, I had.

I don't know if Dad really thought I had passed 'satisfactorily' into Charterhouse. Situated in Surrey, it was one of the top public schools in the country and had fees to match. In my last term at The Leas my father entered me for a naval scholarship that would have covered the cost of my time there. It was decided on the basis of an interview, and things appeared to be going well – I seemed to be impressing the four medalled members of naval top brass sitting across the room. But then one of them asked if I had read any naval histories.

'Oh,' I said, 'I've read lots.'

'Really? Which ones?'

Silence.

With that, my scholarship was history too.

CHAPTER THREE

'The guitar,' said Mr Chare, 'is a symbol of the revolution. And there'll be no revolution starting in my house, on my watch.' And he banged his fists down on his desk.

Chare (pronounced 'Char') was my Charterhouse house-master and my nemesis. His eyebrows were about an inch long and stuck out as far as his chin, and he walked around with steel tips on his heels so that you hear him coming like some sort of Nazi commander. He spoke through his teeth, too. All the boys were frightened of him but he particularly had it in for me. He thought that the youth revolution was going to start in his house and that I was going to be the instigator.

★ ★ ★

Charterhouse had been founded in 1611 and got stuck some-where in Dickensian times. Boys were assigned to one of eleven houses, some of which had been modernized, but not mine (of course). Lockites was a dump. The loos were outside – you'd have to dash through the rain and snow in winter. I can still picture the trails of slipper prints. The house itself had been built too close to the hill behind so it was always dark and damp. When I think back to my prep-school days, there's a feeling of space about the memories: the links golf course and beyond that the sea and Hilbre Island, where once a term you'd go for the day and get crabs out of rock pools. When I think about Charterhouse, the memories are all grey and black.

The first one or two years at Charterhouse were spent in dorms. You then moved on to 'cubes' – basically ceiling-less hospital cubicles – which at least allowed semi-privacy when masturbating. Only in the final year did you get a study bedroom, by which time you were too broken to appreciate it.

There were endless archaic rules and regulations on everything from how long your hair could be (it couldn't) to how many jacket buttons you had to have done up. Everybody spoke the school slang. Work was called 'hash' so classrooms were 'hash-rooms' and terms were 'quarters' (Oration, Long and Cricket; Long was the shortest, obviously). And then there was fagging: the good old British public school tradition whereby older boys terrorize younger ones while masters look on fondly, remembering their own youth.

I was fag to a guy called Tony Lorenz, who was known as Bubbles because he was small and round. In later life, Bubbles would become a successful London estate agent. He wasn't terrible to me: I was his skivvy but it didn't generally go beyond fetching him a bit of toast or taking his stuff to the washing room. However, the fags weren't just answerable to the boy to whom they'd been allotted. If a prefect called 'fag', all of you had to go chasing after them. You had to run – no dawdling – but the trick was to go missing on the way. That was where the outside lavatories came in useful. I passed quite a lot of time there.

Strange as it may seem, I never really questioned fagging. It just was the way it was and, to be honest, I was even half-looking forward to having a fag of my own. Then, just as I got to my Senior year, Charterhouse scrapped the fagging system.

Even 350-year-old public schools weren't completely safe from the sixties and the changing mood in the country. A couple of years after I'd left, I passed Charterhouse and, incredibly, there were even boys with semi-long hair. But that was typical of the miserable hand fate dealt me at Charterhouse. The only ray of sunshine was music.

★ ★ ★

Charterhouse was a famous school for music: Ralph Vaughan Williams, one of the few classical composers I like, had been there, and it had a hymn book that made a particular impact on me and another boy called Tony Banks. It was modern but melodic, and I thought the drama of some of the hymns' big chords and chord sequences was fantastic.

This meant that Chapel was a double-edged sword. The music was great and it was an attractive building: stained-glass windows and very tall. The flipside was the religion: forty minutes a day and twice on a Sunday. It was murder trying to stay awake during Sunday Evensong. Many a boy could be seen still 'praying' with their eyes shut when everyone else had stood up.

I didn't usually have a problem staying awake to listen to Radio Luxembourg, though. Radios were banned but somehow I'd managed to smuggle in a little transistor that I'd listen to under my pillow after lights out. I got away with it for quite a while but then one night I must have drifted off. I woke to the sound of the approaching footsteps of the music master, Geoffrey Ford.

Geoffrey was so openly gay it was accepted. There was nothing hidden and predatory about him. I was more worried by the masters who'd gone to university and come straight back to the school: I thought that was a definite sign something was wrong. Geoffrey wasn't one of those more unreasonable types but I still didn't want to be caught. Unfortunately, being half asleep, I turned the knob of my radio up, not off, as Geoffrey got closer. The sudden blast of volume catapulted me upright, at which point the radio fell out from under my pillow and clattered on to the floor.

It seems ironic that it was the music master who confiscated my radio but Charterhouse was like that: nothing about it made sense. The effect it had on me was to give me a lasting hatred of authority and petty bureaucracy. If I see there's reason behind it, I can take it, but silly rules and regulations just piss me off. It's why I never would have lasted in the Navy.

Tony Banks, Peter Gabriel and Anthony Phillips were all in a different house to me, Duckites not Lockites, and weren't undesirable elements like I was. Ant had dangerously long hair but he was good at cricket so was forgiven. More importantly as far as I was concerned, he was great at the guitar.

The first time I saw Ant was in the basement meeting room of the 'Rock Soc'. (Thinking about it now, the name sounds surprisingly advanced: it wasn't until the seventies and America that I was really aware of anyone talking about 'rock', although of course there it was 'rawk'.) Ant had a red Stratocaster and a Vox AC30 amplifier, which was what the pros used. It was way beyond what anyone else in the school had. He was skinny, with white-blond hair and a nose a bit like Pete Townshend's. And his fingers looked right on the guitar. It's funny, you can often tell if someone's going to be any good at an instrument before they've even played a note.

Ant had been to see a session by the Swinging Blue Jeans (who'd had hits with 'Good Golly Miss Molly' and 'Hippy Hippy Shake') and he knew far more chords than I did. He even played a bit of lead guitar. Because he was in a different house and a year below me, our paths shouldn't really have crossed, but he took me under his wing and taught me everything Bert Weedon hadn't.

★ ★ ★

When I first went to Charterhouse my parents were still living 230 miles away in Cheshire – which didn't help with the settling-in process – but in my final year my father retired and my parents moved down to Farnham. My parents' new house, Hill Cottage, was a three-bedroom, white-plastered 1940s house on a hill at the top of crossroads on the Frensham Road. It was smaller than Far Hills, and while my parents were moving they gave me some of their furniture for safe-keeping. It wasn't much – a three-piece sofa, a couple of rugs, a couple of standard lamps – but when Chare walked into my study-bedroom I heard him gasp. 'What is THIS, Rutherford?' He made my parents take it all away – rugs were the height of decadence as far as Chare was concerned.

After my parents moved to Farnham we'd regularly go as a

family to the Officer's Club in Aldershot and have a curry for Sunday lunch (I think Dad always felt he could be anywhere in the Empire when he ate a curry, plus at the Officer's Club it was the only thing on the menu). He must have felt a distance opening up between us because at some point he also decided to take me sailing on Hawley Lake. Whether this was his way of bonding or of trying to steer me back towards a naval career, I'm not sure.

I arrived at the lake in full mufti gear – blazer, yachting shoes, cravat – to find that my father, even though he wasn't in uniform, was still revered as a captain by the retired folk from the services who ran the yachting establishment. They couldn't have been more helpful: the dinghy was present and correct, my father was given a respectful helping hand getting in and off we went. With everyone watching. Ready for a show.

I still think it was an unreasonably windy day.

Hawley Lake might sound an unthreatening kind of place but it was pretty bloody choppy that afternoon and, as I set sail, I already knew there was only one way that it was going to end. As the canvas rattled and rolled, my father did his best to help me out.

'Hold the jib!' he yelled.

'I am!' I yelled back.

I wasn't, mainly because I hadn't got the faintest idea what a jib was. But at least I knew how to swim. Which turned out to be useful that day.

Maybe this episode was another reason why my father didn't object to me going into the music business eventually, but my naval career wasn't quite dead in the water yet.

Military service was compulsory at Charterhouse: Army, Air Force or Navy.

About 80 per cent of the boys were in the Army because that was where you had to start your stint and most couldn't be bothered to change to one of the more interesting forces later. The culmination of Charterhouse Army service was the march, which was surprisingly scenic – you went via Haslemere and the Devil's Punchbowl – but it was also fifty miles long. When it came to my turn I finished it all right, but then I was made to do it again. I don't know what happened – there may have been a taxi involved – but after that I left and joined the Navy.

In retrospect, this was a no-brainer. In winter we'd sit around indoors tying knots – seriously – and in the summer we'd go sailing on Frensham Ponds. (Sailing got much easier the minute my father wasn't watching.) Best of all was the day each Cricket Quarter when the Army lot went off for a trek in full Army gear and backpack in the boiling sun. It was a day I would generally spend lying on top of the Frensham Ponds boatshed drinking cider with Ant, who'd also sussed out how best to spend his time.

Charterhouse was a different school if you were good at sport. I knew that golf was never going to be on a par with rugby or football – if you were good at those, you were in a different league popularity-wise – but I thought I could build on my golfing success at The Leas. Then Chare banned me. He thought golf was dangerously individualistic and anti-establishment, particularly for a rebel like me.

'Rutherford, you are banned. You must play more team sports.'

What could you do? After that, sport at Charterhouse for me was cricket – which, in Division C, Fourth Team, was a real team effort. You'd arrive at a far-off part of a far-off field, away from the masters, sit on the grass in the sun and work out together what the score should be. The funny thing was, by the end of the day you'd be so into it that you'd believe you really *had* scored those fifty runs. You'd go back to the house feeling quite heroic.

I could live without golf – after all, you had to wear some weird nerd kit in those days – but I couldn't live without music.

And so Chare banned me from playing my guitar.

At the time I was in the upper house, a kind of recreation room, playing my guitar to *Sgt. Pepper*, which had just come out and was the most exciting thing I'd ever heard. I think Chare must have had a bad housemasters' meeting because he stormed in, raving, and grabbed me by the collar. 'Rutherford,' he hissed through his teeth. 'you are banned. You are not playing the guitar anymore, Rutherford.' He then bent me over and caned me. It was eight o'clock at night and I was in my dressing gown. After that, obviously, there was no way I was going to stop. Not least because the biggest concert of my Charterhouse career was only a few weeks away.

The band that I'd joined were the Anon. Ant was the driving force behind them but it was their singer, Richard Macphail, who'd come up with the name. He'd originally wanted it to be 'Anon', like an unknown poet, but nobody could cope with not having an article.

Rich was great. He could sing, he looked the part and he had the moves: we called him Mick Phail because he could do a bit of a Jagger act. He was also terribly up, just a very positive guy. Once he left school he grew his ginger hair down to his elbows and I would often see him at gigs with no shoes on.

The rest of the line-up was Rob Tyrell on drums – God, he was good – and Rivers Job, who had been to prep school with Ant, on bass. Rivers Job – have you ever known a cooler name? He was very short and his bass guitar looked too big for his body, but it seemed to work on him somehow. (Rivers left Charterhouse after O-levels and I saw him next at a pub in Guildford playing with the Savoy Blues Band, who were quite a successful thing in those days. I remember looking up at him on stage and thinking: he's actually doing it!)

It was after Rivers had left the school that I picked up the bass. Ant was better than me at guitar so it was an obvious move and not at all a demotion. However, something must have annoyed me because, not long after, I threw a huff and left the band. I think the problem might have been that Ant was being selfish about something or other – his way or no way. Ant probably thought it was because I couldn't take the discipline, which was also possible. Anyway, I do remember flouncing off slightly. The result was my new band, the Climax, who lasted two terms and whose name was the best thing about us. Ant would come into the hall where we were practising, laugh and walk straight out again.

It was during one of those two terms that the Charterhouse school magazine ran an article called 'Why not pop?' The Climax were described as making 'a reasonable sound', although we were 'more of a shadow than a reality' (probably a fair assessment). The Anon (minus me) got double the column inches:

Their music is of a Rhythm and Blues type, featuring numbers from The Stones, Yardbirds, John Mayall's Bluesbreakers and The

Cream, together with a very reasonable number of their own
compositions . . . The group's outlook is interesting: they deny
energetically that their music interferes at all with their work . . .
'After all, it's us who should know whether it does or not, we've
had a lot of trouble about that.' Their reaction to the difficulties
which they have to face as a group is one of hope for more freedom
in the future; at present, feelings on the part of their parents are
only lukewarm, money for new equipment is sorely needed, and the
fact of their being at school makes holiday dates difficult to arrange
·. . . But such frustrations are, they agree, more than compensated
for by the moments when the group is together and playing well.

I'm sure that my parents were 'only lukewarm', too, but they
didn't show it. When my mother came to collect me for the holidays I would pile my gear into the car and she wouldn't turn a
hair, even though I'd now got a couple of 4×12 speakers as well
as a Hofner Verythin guitar, for which Jean Granny had given me
the money. ('Anything you want, just ask me,' she'd always say
when we visited her in Morris Lodge, although when I took her
up on it she almost fell out of bed she got such a shock. Bed was
where a lot of the people at Morris Lodge hung out during the
daytime – the downstairs rooms were quite formal.)

I think Mum quite liked loud noise but, even so, I must have
made a horrible racket practising. What was worse was that I
was a night-time person in those days. It was only after they'd
gone to bed that I would go into the dining room, light the
candles in Captain Woods's candelabras to get a bit of a vibe,
and start playing. Although they never complained once, I knew
my father was concerned at the direction my life seemed to

be taking. My school reports would often say things like 'He returned this Quarter to the old habit of doing no work' (Maths) and 'He has made no effort at all this quarter in this subject. He will inevitably fail' (Physics). Dad also knew about the problems with Chare.

My father would never discuss things with me for the first few days after I had arrived home: he'd always give me a bit of time while he prepared and made notes. Then, when he'd had time to think about what he was going to say, he'd call me into the dining room, shut the door and say, 'Now, tell me how it's going.'

It'd be an official interview, not a casual chat, and he'd have his notepads and pens laid out in front of him. I could imagine him preparing in just the same way for some young sub lieutenant who'd been misbehaving.

Deep down, I respected my father's authority – unlike the rules and regulations at Charterhouse, I could see there was sense behind the things he said – but mainly I was aware that he was everything I didn't want to be.

Until my generation, boys aspired to the same cavalry-twill trousers and brown suede shoes their dads had. Sons of my father's generation were often told, 'You'll never be as fine a man as your father'. When my dad was told just that, as he wrote in his memoir, he 'found it very dampening'.

Dad wanted to be like my grandpa but I couldn't think of anything more depressing. With the Beatles, a new era had come in and all kids my age wanted to be the absolute oppo-site of everything their parents were. The weird thing is that it happened so fast – the Beatles only really lasted six years and Hendrix's career was even shorter – and yet in that time everything changed. The newspapers were full of stories about the scandalous behaviour of the youth of today – the end was nigh. When I would drift into the room while my parents were watching Reginald Bosanquet read the TV news, the stories always seemed to be about the revolution that kids my age were leading.

I played it up, of course. I was sixteen: I didn't want my dad to *get* me. 'You don't understand, you just don't get it.' Sometimes I said it more for effect than because I felt it, but the truth was that although kids had always thought their parents were old-fashioned, this time there really was a huge gulf opening up.

Did Dad think the world was coming to an end? I'm sure he didn't: he'd lived through two world wars and been round the world several times. He understood what was going on. Maybe he'd also realized that because my generation didn't have real wars to fight, we had to find other battles. In any case, his attitude was never like some of the other old captains at his club in London: 'Damn young hooligans!' It was more that he was just completely lost as the world changed around him.

★ ★ ★

The Climax and the Anon weren't the only bands at Charterhouse. There was also the Garden Wall, who the school magazine reckoned were: 'the only true exponent of Soul Music in the school. With a distinctly earthy quality to their work, they gave some spirited performances in last quarter's Charity Beat Concert, Peter Gabriel's vocalizing being a major feature.'

Ant was part of the Garden Wall as well as the Anon, and Tony Banks was their piano player (although he spent quite a lot of his time fighting over the keyboard with Peter). The Garden Wall also had a trumpet player, which said it all as far as I was concerned. My band had guitars and amplifiers; the Garden Wall had a trumpet and an upright piano.

I must have done two or three concerts – calling them gigs would be stretching it – at Charterhouse, but it wasn't just about the performing. Half the fun in those days was simply talking about it. The camaraderie, the preparation and the planning was as important to me as the playing. I would even get a kick out of carrying Ant's Vox amp to the classrooms for rehearsals, me on one side and Ant on the other. Leading it through the old stone cloisters felt so clandestine: a real two-fingers up to the masters.

That said, it wasn't planning but an accident that got me round Chare's guitar ban. Having rejoined the Anon, on the day of the big end-of-term concert I made my way to the main hall: wooden floors, galleried ceiling, a balcony about two-thirds of the way back, 600 or so boys in the audience and the headmaster in the front row with Chare beside him. And only then did I realize my guitar lead was broken.

In a panic I scrabbled around in the wings and managed to find a replacement, but it was only four-feet long, which meant that I was four feet away from my spotlight. I'm sure the rest of the Anon thought that this was a deliberate ploy – lurking in the darkness – but I would have been out front, belting out Stones covers to Chare given half a chance. Not that it mattered: the gig was a huge success and I managed to avoid expulsion at the same time.

★ ★ ★

Music was a lifesaver at school but so too was the highly illegal Honda 50 motorbike that I'd managed to acquire. I kept it at a local garage where I paid a monthly rent, which doubled as hush money because the garage owner knew exactly where I was from.

It wasn't a cool motorbike, the Honda 50, and I never managed to convince myself that it looked good, which made it more painful. But it gave me the freedom I needed, and the fact that it was so completely against the rules made riding it feel even better. It often didn't matter where I went. It was just the fact that I could start it up and escape the clutches of the whole suppressive regime.

One afternoon I was heading for Guildford, and as I looked in my wing mirror I recognized one of the masters' cars on my tail. Not that it had 'Master' written all over it, but there was a certain type of car parked in the staff car park and this one definitely fell into that category. However much I tried to lose him by turning down various lanes, he was right behind me. Eventually I realized there was nothing for it but to bail out.

Having made a sharp and dangerous turn into a driveway I leapt off the bike and ran across the garden with my helmet firmly in place. I then managed to jump the fence into the next garden – nearly taking the clothes line with me. Having clambered back over another fence and on to the road, I was relieved to find that the car had disappeared from sight. I can't say it was one of my coolest moments.

It never really occurred to me not to go back, to ride off for good on my motorbike. Occasionally word would come down the wire about runaways – two boys from Harrow or someone from Eton – but even while I was busy rebelling it seemed para-mount not to embarrass my father. What I did do was skip classes to go to the pub in Godalming and drink gin and lime – even though I still didn't like the taste of gin – and I would regularly get beaten for sneaking off to smoke cigarettes with Ant. The worst thing about this was that it wasn't the master who spotted you coming out of the bushes who did the beating: they'd report you to your housemaster who'd then drag you in for interroga-tion. And that meant Chare.

'Have you been smoking, Rutherford?'

'No, sir.'

'Bend over.'

It was the lack of transparency that really rankled.

Amazingly, I never got caught skiving off school to go to gigs at the Marquee Club in London. I took great care not to be seen: I would wait until it was dark and then climb out of the window in my mauve platforms.

I would either ride my Honda 50 to Guildford station or walk down the hill to Godalming station, a school mac disguising my velvet flares, and wait anxiously for my friends Chris Piggott and Andy Dunkley to turn up. (Dunkley was the brave one: he wanted to get expelled. As for Chris Piggott, I was surprised he was still talking to me because early on in my musical career I'd blown up his amplifier. 'DC' socket on the amp stood for 'Direct Current', and anything direct – so I thought – was obviously going be louder than anything that wasn't. I had plugged in my guitar and smoke had come billowing out.)

The Marquee Club in Wardour Street was the home of everything that meant anything to me back then. It's funny but I never found Soho threatening, although it was seedy enough in those days. It was full of strip shows and dirty bookshops. (You'd wander in and wander out of those quite quickly: the fact you'd been in was the main thing. Strip clubs were a bit more intimidating. There'd always be a guy on the door trying to entice you in – 'Come on in, young man'.) The funky buildings, the red and yellow and green neon lights at night, the cool London people with their scarves and hats: it all felt slightly forbidden but never scary. Maybe it was because there was so much music happening there that I didn't feel intimidated. There were folk clubs, the 100 Club up the road at Oxford Street and, best of all, the Marquee, which felt like a real musos' place and not just some nightclub with a disco.

The Marquee Club was where I saw the Nice with Keith Emerson, the Herd with Peter Frampton, the Cream, the Action and the Sands (Chris Squire had a fantastic Rickenbacker bass sound: he wasn't just playing low notes, he was playing lead lines; I remember being very impressed by that). And I loved the harmonies – in those days every band seemed to have about three people doing backing vocals.

The volume was mind-blowing and the heat was amazing. The Marquee Club was on ground level, but you felt underground as everything was dark and dripping with sweat. No one ever took their Afghan coats off, although if you were sensible you'd got an Afghan waistcoat and were wearing that over your tie-dye T-shirt. Everyone was in boots and flares, which made trying to tell the girls and boys apart difficult. At least I was in a room with the opposite sex which, after Charterhouse, was wonderful. The only girls most Charterhouse boys ever met would be at friends' parties in the holidays: you'd find yourself trying to be the cool guy, which in reality meant shuffling from foot to foot and mumbling incoherently.

Chris, Andy and I would travel down to London, go to a gig and then get the milk train back at 5:30 in the morning, something that – thinking about it now – still gets me hot round the collar. There was such great pleasure in escaping to London, feeling part of the scene, but I was also terrified of getting caught and letting my father down. I never, ever told anyone what I was up to – whispers had a habit of getting round at Charterhouse. By the time I left school, the pinnacle of my ambition was to play the Marquee Club. I thought that if you could play there, you really were somebody.

Ant and I were quite close by now and we'd often stay with each other in the holidays. At my parents' house we'd play guitar late into the night, and my mother would usually come down in the morning for breakfast and say things like, 'Darling! Loved that tune!' It was more difficult at Ant's house. Ant's father was a top banker who ran the finances for the Marylebone Cricket Club and I could tell he did not approve of our music: I always felt slightly uncomfortable. Ant's mother was much more supportive, laughing and joking, and she also transported the Anon's equipment to the Tony Pike Sound Studio in Putney when we went to a session there. She drove our gear in the back of her Mercedes while Ant, Rich and I had to take the bus.

Tony Pike's studio was in the back of a small house and Tony was an old-school kind of guy. We could tell he had no understanding of our music and noise. He had a slight West Country accent too, which didn't quite work when he started complaining about the damage he thought we were causing to his equipment: 'You just mind my comprezzorz . . .'

'Silly old fucker,' I would mutter, not realizing that the whole point of control rooms was that you could hear everything when you were standing in them. As he was.

'Oi! You mind your language down there.'

The song we'd recorded, 'Pennsylvania Flickhouse', was very much Ant's – a sort of Godalming 'Route 66'. Rich had worked out that, because our songs were three minutes long, we could easily record six in an hour. When we found we'd only managed one we immediately started making plans for a return visit, but soon after that Rich's father took him out of Charterhouse and sent him to Millfield in Somerset: he thought Rich was mixing with a bad lot in the Anon. He might have been right – at least, as far as I was concerned – but that left us without a singer, at which point Ant decided it should be me.

I didn't like the idea of being a front man. It might have been different if I'd had a voice. I've always thought that 60 per cent of the world have an okay-enough voice to be a singer of some sort, and some great singers don't have a great voice but still find a way to make it work. I wasn't in that category (although neither was Ant). It was when Ant got me to sing the Rolling Stones' 'Mercy Mercy' and I felt something happening in my Adam's apple area (it was quite worrying: my vocal chords seemed to slip out of place) that I really knew I wasn't meant to sing. However, in those days if you could sing a bit, that meant you were a singer, so we dropped any songs with high notes in them from the repertoire instead.

Meanwhile, the tension was building between my father and

me. He wrote me letters (of course, I didn't keep them) and during the holidays I would argue with him constantly about the length of my hair and my clothes, most of which came from Kensington Market. I would go there at weekends and look round the stalls, see a band in the evening and get the train home afterwards, always making sure just to miss the one that I was expected on. On other occasions I would stay with Nicky, who now had a flat in Hamilton Gardens that she shared with a couple of other girls. I would go there and be slightly overpowered by these wonderful, long-legged and rather awe-inspiring women walking around the place.

Nicky had been to boarding school too, the Royal Naval School for Girls in Haslemere, and was now working as a secretary at the *Guardian*. She'd always been less scatty than Mum and me. Even at twelve she'd been grown-up, which must have made it easier for my parents, especially as they were older than usual themselves. As far as my dad was concerned she could do no wrong. She was bright, she wrote my parents letters, she visited them and now she was a young lady working in London while I was sloping off with Chris Piggott to anti-establishment events like the Windsor Jazz and Blues Festival. (Not a great experience: it was July, cold, wet and the sound was crap. Plus, the Small Faces only played for fifteen minutes, which really pissed me off. But I was there!) I'm sure Dad thought that I was a waste of space in comparison with Nicky. The only good thing was that he didn't know half of what I was doing. But it was only a matter of time before things came to a head.

Dad and I had often argued about Chare in the past, but my father thought it was me who was the problem. However, when

Chare threw me out of the school just before my O-levels I think it finally dawned on my dad that something odd was going on: the timing was so bloody stupid as I had only one term left. Perhaps I'd been right and the old bugger really did have it in for me.

It was still term time when my father was called down to meet with Chare to discuss my future. I only found out what happened later: apparently Chare lost it completely with Dad, ranting and raving and scolding him like a pupil. That wouldn't have impressed Dad. He had a word for people like Chare: 'uncharming'. More than that, when Dad asked for a list of all the terrible things I'd done, Chare couldn't come up with anything: I hadn't killed anyone, I hadn't maimed anyone, I hadn't burned down the school.

My father had been paying my school fees for the past three years and, as far as Dad was concerned, Chare was not behaving correctly. Dad wrote to the headmaster to say as much, no doubt quoting precisely the figure he'd paid for me to be at his school. At that point the headmaster must have decided to overrule Chare, who was not a popular figure. A deal was cut: I could go back for my O-levels but would have to leave to do my A-levels somewhere else.

This was a great outcome for me – vindication at last – and it also led to the start of a slow improvement in my relationship with my father. But there were other important events also now occurring. The Anon had petered out, but a new band was taking shape . . .

CHAPTER FOUR

I hadn't really come across Tony Banks and Peter Gabriel that much at Charterhouse: we were in different houses and boys didn't tend to mix. Sometimes I would see them in Record Corner, the record shop in Godalming, listening to music through headphones in one of the little booths, but because Record Corner was strictly off limits – you needed a chit even to walk into town – it wasn't really the place to bond. (Charterhouse boys always got jeered a bit in Godalming but it didn't bother me: I would see the town boys with their long hair and feel we were all in the same game. Music seemed to me to do an important job in bridging divides.)

Everything about Peter Gabriel in those days was soft and round. You could tell he wasn't a sportsman. He had a circular, slightly chubby face and his school jacket always seemed too small for him, but although he was quiet, he had an air of confidence about him. At Charterhouse there were guys who were trying to be cool, those who were cool without trying, and those who were never going to get there. Pete was none of those. He was comfortable in his skin. He made his own hats and dyed

T-shirts in sinks; he was quite free-spirited, but very worldly too.

Tony was also quiet, but he was edgy and skinny and had a quick, worried step – he'd never stride anywhere. He came from a classical background, whereas Pete loved R&B, Nina Simone and Otis Redding. As well as the piano, Pete played the drums at Charterhouse. He was never destined to be a great drummer but he had a very strong feel for rhythm. His drum kit was his pride and joy and he'd lend it to anyone who managed to twist his arm, but he'd always stand alongside with his eyebrows furrowed while it was being played.

It was during the 1967 Easter holidays that Ant and I, together with Pete and Tony, recorded a demo tape in the attic of another Charterhouse boy, Brian Roberts. He was the kind of guy who you knew from a young age would be a BBC technician in later life. A boffin. He always had a white shirt with a stain on it and greasy hair.

Brian had transformed the attic of this house into a recording studio. It just had egg boxes on the walls and a two-track tape recorder in the corner, but it was still pretty cutting edge in those days. It was more than enough for our purposes.

Ant, who had been planning to sing on the tape, had invited Tony to come to Brian's and play keyboards. Tony had then invited Pete to come because he knew Pete had a better voice than Ant. (Funnily enough, I don't remember Ant having a hump about being replaced as singer: he knew it was for the common good.)

Given that Ant and I were into the blues – John Mayall and Eric Clapton – as well as the Stones and the Beatles, we were quite a diverse lot. I've always thought that half the point of being in a band is that the guys you're playing with are different to you: they bring something to the music that you can't.

We recorded five songs that afternoon, four by me and Ant, and one, 'She Is Beautiful', by Peter and Tony. Theirs was definitely the best. It had a moody sadness to it, a hint of darkness – probably because it had been written for Peter's voice, which always had that feeling.

Sometimes you just need a lucky break. That first tape we made in Brian Roberts's attic had our best songs on it, but if you took away Pete and Tony's song it wasn't as good. Yet Jonathan King must have heard there was something there.

Jonathan had been at Charterhouse a few years before us and had come back to the school for an old boys' day. At the time he'd just had a huge hit with 'Everyone's Gone to the Moon' and had written and produced another hit, 'It's Good News Week', for Hedgehoppers Anonymous, which was released on Decca. He was also a bombastic self-promoter who talked the talk and wore noisy, very flamboyant clothes. I'm also sure he fancied Pete – we all thought that. But he did have an ear for a song.

I don't know why it got left to our friend John Alexander, another school friend, to put the tape in Jonathan's car while he was down at Charterhouse – I think in the end John Al was the only one who had the nerve. He was one of those lucky boys who'd got away with long hair because nobody realized it was long. It was thick, black and curly, and he had a chunk of it that he could tuck behind his ear and pull out when the masters weren't around. He undertook the clandestine operation on Jonathan's car and managed to leave the tape along with a note: 'These are Charterhouse boys, have a listen.' And Jonathan must have done because soon after that he invited us up to London to meet his business partner, Joe Roncoroni.

Joe was an old-school music publisher: a well-built Jewish guy who'd been publishing cabaret and vaudeville songs when suddenly pop appeared. We were naturally extremely impressed that he and Jonathan liked our songs, but we were less sure about Jonathan's idea that our next step should be to form a band. Until then our plan was to be songwriters and let someone else do the performing, something that wasn't unusual back then.

Songwriting was (and is still) the area in which I measure success: I've seen many guitarists who can play fantastically well but can't write an original song. We wanted to be original from the word go but, unfortunately for us, Jonathan King didn't like our kind of originality. We recorded another couple of demos for him but he was losing interest fast, so then we forgot about trying to be original and did something we knew he'd like.

'The Silent Sun', our first single, was written by Pete and Tony and was basically a Bee Gees pastiche. Ant wasn't convinced by it but I thought it was a great song, and Jonathan liked it as well – so much that he tried to sign us up for the rest of our lives.

I'm not sure that the contract he got us to sign with Decca was more binding than most contracts were back then, but as we were minors we shouldn't have been signing it in the first place. That alone was enough to raise our parents' suspicions. Between them they called in Goodman, Derek and Co. – top lawyers who had represented the Beatles – to redraft the contract.

This certainly cost our parents quite a bit of money, but perhaps they were happy to help us out because they felt that this was their world – contracts and lawyers as opposed to gigs and guitars. A contract was something my father knew how to handle and could form an opinion on, whereas I'm not sure that would have been true for 'The Silent Sun'. In any case, I didn't feel worried about him going off to London in his bowler hat to meet Jonathan King. It was the school holidays and, when Dad came home and hung his coat up in the hall afterwards, I knew it'd gone well. Of course, I still had to wait for the official debriefing, for which he called me into the dining room the next day. Not that I really cared at the time: contracts, man, whatever.

Now that we were a band, we needed a name. Jonathan came up with Genesis and, although I wasn't mad about the name, it stuck. We had wasted so many hours on lists of names (Pete had come up with Band of Angels and Ant had something flowery like Champagne Meadow) that Genesis was a bit of a relief.

We also needed a look. Pete, who, like my father, believed in the right outfit for the occasion, suggested that we should all go to Carnaby Street to buy clothes for *Top of the Pops*. Pete was more aware of image than the rest of us, who hadn't even realized that we needed an image. The fact that *Top of the Pops* hadn't asked us on yet didn't really come into it: it was obviously only a matter of time.

Swinging London was then at its height and Carnaby Street was the centre of the fashion world. There was something about turning the corner off Regent's Street, going left and seeing that sign that was exciting.

Pete's plan was that we should all have black-and-white outfits, and the look is preserved for posterity in Genesis's first publicity shot. I look dopey, if you ask me. Chris Stewart, our drummer, is the moody one, but all of us look like we seriously think it's about to take off.

And, of course, we'd spend the next few years selling fuck all.

'The Silent Sun', our first single, was released on Decca in February 1968. Soon after, Kenny Everett played it on the BBC, which was wonderfully legitimizing – the BBC was official, the real thing, the voice of authority. God, it sounded fantastic. I'm sure Jonathan must have had a word with Kenny – 'Play this for me, mate.' But when I first heard us on the radio, standing in Ant's kitchen, I was convinced it was all about to happen. Here we go, boys, I thought. Stand back.

By this time I'd left Charterhouse, although Ant had stayed on to do A-levels. We were also without a drummer. One of my last jobs at Charterhouse was to fire Chris. (Which was probably a good career move, seeing as he would later write the bestselling *Driving over Lemons*.) The plan had been that Ant and John Al would come with me as backups. When I opened the door to Chris's study bedroom and started with 'Chris: Ant, John, Al and I think . . .' I looked over my shoulder to discover that they'd pissed off.

New Musical Express called 'The Silent Sun', 'a disc of many facets and great depth', although 'it might be a bit too complex for the average fan'. We also got a good review in *Melody Maker*, which was the one we really wanted to be in. *Melody Maker* had a quality to it – musicians read it and believed it.

Sadly, our next single, 'A Winter's Tale', generated zero interest. The only way it was going to be played on Radio 1 was if someone took an acetate up to Broadcasting House and shoved it in Tony Blackburn's hands as he came out. Which is exactly what Pete suggested doing. Somehow it was Tony Banks who ended up being the one standing outside the door in Portland Place. Unfortunately, Tony gets a bit aggressive when he gets nervous and I think Blackburn thought he was going to be beaten up.

★ ★ ★

I was seventeen in 1968 and growing up fast. In the spring Cliff had performed 'Congratulations' at the Eurovision Song Contest and he now definitely looked dated to me. (To be fair, I still think he has a great voice: give him the right song. But I wasn't ten anymore. Cliff who? It was like we'd never known each other.) I was also a year into my A-levels at Farnborough Tech, studying English (which I enjoyed), French (which might come in handy) and Economics (which I didn't understand).

By my age, my father had finished his training at the Naval College in Osborne on the Isle of Wight and, later, Dartmouth. He'd already undertaken two tours on the training battleship HMS *Thunderer* and had joined the battleship *Revenge*, part of the Atlantic Fleet, as a Naval Cadet. Eight months later he was promoted to Midshipman and joined the cruiser *Danae*, which was based at Malta.

By the time he was twenty-one he'd sailed along the Suez Canal on his way to Singapore and Hong Kong, and was back on land to study for further exams at the Royal Naval College in Greenwich. It wasn't all work:

The glittering London season was underway. With my parents on occasions I did various events such as the Royal Academy, Chelsea

Flower Show, the Derby, Royal Tournament, Varsity and Eton and Harrow match and so on.

To take part in these splendid events a suitable wardrobe was essential.

If going around town in daytime, a bowler hat and rolled umbrella were needed. If going out informally or to the West End at all in the evening a dinner jacket with boiled shirt, wing collar and black tie was worn. This was surmounted by an opera hat, a cunning device like a conjuror's top hat which could be collapsed and put under a theatre seat and at a flip of the wrist sprung out into shape.

He'd also got himself a car, a two-seater Morris Cowley, which had a canvas hood and one door. On the passenger side. This meant that, 'If the passenger was a lovely girl in long evening dress and satin shoes . . . it could be the end of a beautiful friendship.' (When I was his age I had a yellow Ford Anglia with brown rust weeping down the right wing and was stuck in Farnham.)

After my father had finished his two terms in Greenwich, he went to train in Gunnery, Torpedo and Navigation at Whale Island, where he would take command thirty years later.

[Training] ended with a nightmare three weeks of exams ranging from abstruse mathematics to drilling a company or instructing a fifteen-inch turret's crew.

These surmounted, I was appointed to the junior staff of the Gunnery School at Chatham which, unlike Whale Island, was not an independent command but an integral part of the Royal

Naval Barracks. Besides being instructors at the School, we were also Barrack's Officers.

I was made parade training officer so – basilisk-eyed and all boots, black gaiters and silver-plated whistle chain – marched myself about the parade ground bringing alarm and despondency to the classes going through the hoop thereon.

Regarding my own future career, I'd tried to get my dad to let me study for A levels in London, but after being thrown out of Charterhouse by Chare (albeit with ten O-levels) my stock wasn't high. Like most boys leaving the school I had also been sent for an aptitude test at King's College, Cambridge, to see what kind of career might suit me. The results probably hadn't impressed Dad much either:

Rutherford, M. J.

A fluent and perhaps rather disorderly boy, distinctly below average in IQ. If he has talents they seem likely to emerge on the arts side rather than in the sciences. My impression is that he might do much better outside the confines of conventional education.

Meanwhile, Pete was studying at Davies, Laing and Dick in Notting Hill Gate, the coolest crammer in the country, and generally leading the life I wanted to lead. He'd bought a London taxi and wore a long black coat and a big scarf. His persona was changing. He was becoming more outgoing and looked part of the cool London set. As for Jonathan King – who was only a few years older than us – he was driving around London in a white Rolls-Royce and living in a mews house. (I used to wonder about his bathroom: it was all mirrors so that when you sat on the loo seat, you saw yourself going on forever and ever. We all thought he might be gay, but in those days that kind of thing wasn't discussed.) Tony, who was a year ahead of Pete and me, was finishing his A-levels at Charterhouse and getting ready to study Chemistry at Sussex University. And there I was, out in the sticks.

I did at least have some freedom in Farnham. Mum had found me some smart digs – she wasn't going to have me living in a bedsit – although the downside was that the odd character who ran the place was way too sharp for me to sneak my girlfriend past him. I think he'd been in service as a butler somewhere once, but he was now silver-haired with permanently brown, nicotine-stained fingers. There'd often be a tap on the door if he thought something funny was going on: 'Is everything all right in there?' He'd then lean on the door post, leering at you slightly. Fortunately my girlfriend Josie's digs were owned by a deaf old lady so I could sneak through the front door without being heard.

Josie was pretty, blonde and also a student at Farnborough Tech. When I wasn't having long lunches in the pub (I had no intention of doing any work after Charterhouse), I spent most of my time with her. We even went away for a week in Wales together. I didn't think my parents would miss me now that I was living away from home but, to be on the safe side, I told them I was going away with Ant. Unfortunately, Ant then rang Hill Cottage one day, which slightly blew that one.

'Hello, Captain Rutherford, is Michael there?'

'He's with you. Isn't he?'

'Oh . . .? Yes!'

My father summoned me into the dining room the next time I went home. 'Your mother and I are very disappointed to learn you've lied to us.'

Dad would always say 'your mother and I' in situations like this. Perhaps he felt it made more of an impact because Mum and I were closer.

You always think you can pull the wool over your parents' eyes and I was planning to busk my way out of it. I quickly realized it wasn't going to work this time. Dad would never shout but he was furious: the morality of it he wasn't going to get into, but the lying was a very serious thing as far as he was concerned.

I had an enjoyable, carefree time for the first year that I was with Josie. Her own father had either died or left when she was younger and I think she saw me as a bit of a father figure. Then the band started to take off and I would spend the next two years trying to figure out ways of bringing the relationship gently to an end.

★ ★ ★

From Genesis to Revelation, the first Genesis album, was made in three days working non-stop. We were staying at the flat of a friend, David Thomas, in Earl's Court and didn't see light the whole time.

By this point Pete had found us a new drummer, John Silver, who was a good jazz drummer, but when we all went into Regent B studios off Charing Cross Road none of us really had any idea what we were doing. We were trying to hang on and play our parts just about well enough, which was quite a struggle in those days. I could barely play my bass. In fact, I was without doubt the least-good musician in the band but at the time I was more concerned with wanting to be part of the scene than necessarily getting the music right. To be making an album at seventeen felt so up there that it didn't matter that Regent B studios was basically a basement off the Charing Cross Road. It felt like a government building – there was a sense that you might be marched off for interrogation at any moment. As for what was going on in the control room, none of us had a clue.

Looking back now, *From Genesis to Revelation* seems surprisingly dark: it's folky and poppy but the atmosphere grabs you. While Ant and I were writing hippyish lyrics about trees and leaves and boats and albatrosses, Pete was already writing songs like 'The Conqueror':

> *He climbs inside the looking glass*
> *And points at everything he hates.*
> *He calls to you 'Hey, look out, son,*
> *There's a gun they're pointing at your pretty face.'*

He was painting pictures with words that would capture an emotion and, without your thinking about them, go straight into your body.

Although all the songs were credited to us as a band, the truth was we were more like two gangs of friends, Ant and I, and Tony and Peter. Neither Ant nor I had really got going as songwriters at this point. Our attitude was always 'One for all and all for one', but *From Genesis to Revelation* was mostly Peter and Tony.

We were all too insecure to tell Jonathan King to piss off when he suggested basing the album around a religious theme – had it been the following album, we probably would have done. At the time, though, the idea seemed like something cohesive to work with, so we went along with it. Legend has it that *From Genesis to Revelation* ended up being shelved in the religious music section of record shops as a result, but the fact is we only sold 600 copies so it can't have been in many record shops in any case. I can't remember ever seeing it, and I did look.

★ ★ ★

Although I wasn't yet committed to the path we were taking, Ant had never had any doubt. His life was music, nothing else: it was all-consuming. As a result he was more susceptible than the rest of us to the ups and downs. When Jonathan King got Arthur Greenslade to put some weak string arrangements on the album, I was pretty annoyed. But it just about killed Ant.

Not that Ant or I bought records ourselves: we'd go up to Rich Macphail's flat in London and listen to his. After Millfield, Rich had gone on to live on a kibbutz in Israel, where he'd spent the past few months doing the cooking, listening to music and getting stoned. (He was eventually busted and fined, and had sailed to England via Cyprus, Piraeus, Athens, Naples, Genoa and Marseilles.)

It was at Rich's flat that I first heard a song in stereo. It was 'A Salty Dog' by Procol Harum. I put the headphones on and it was like your skull opening up: an extra dimension; a huge, pastoral picture in strings. It would have been intense even without the dope we were both smoking.

Rich's flat was also where I had my first acid trip, although unlike the dope, that was completely unintentional.

I hadn't really encountered any drugs at the Marquee Club when I'd skived off from Charterhouse to see gigs there. I'm sure all kinds of things were happening at the back but I was always at the front.

On this particular night I'd been to the Marquee to see the Cream, who'd been fantastic: the volume alone blew my head off. I was wearing my jeans and Afghan but must still have looked liked someone trying a bit too hard to be cool because someone spiked my Coca-Cola.

It didn't hit me until I got back to Rich's flat. Then it really hit me. At some point in the early hours I tried to crawl from my bedroom to the bathroom, but the problem was that the corridor between the two kept getting longer and longer. Years and years passed while I was on my hands and knees, and every time I looked up, I was never any closer.

That was bad but what was worse was to come. I was due to meet my parents at eleven o'clock the next morning at the Station Hotel in Victoria: we were all going off for a family weekend in Paris.

I arrived just a few minutes late but completely out of my tree, still dripping in sweat and shaking. Mum took one look at me and knew straightaway what the problem was.

'Mikey! Darling! You poor boy! What terrible flu!'

I'm pretty sure Dad had an idea what was going down but Mum was convinced that I needed to be put to bed with hot water bottles. Whether or not these helped I don't know, but I had recovered enough by the morning to make the trip.

My parents' idea was that it would be an educational, sight-seeing tour. We'd go to the galleries, the Sacré-Coeur, Montmartre and so on. What they didn't know was how much my mind had already been expanded in the past twenty-four hours.

★ ★ ★

I finished my A-levels in 1969 and applied to Edinburgh University to read English. It was so far away I thought no one else would want to go there so I'd stand a chance of getting in. Pete was planning to go to the London Film School, Tony was wondering whether to take a year out from his degree at Sussex University and John Silver was going off in the autumn to study in America. Only Ant was totally committed to our music but his enthusiasm was enough to inspire us to spend the summer rehearsing as a band.

Ant and I had previously rehearsed together in Granny Malimore's house. She was quite fierce, a tough old thing, but she'd bring Ant and me marmalade sandwiches while we took the chairs and table out of her dining room to make space. (I'm sure Dad sold it to her: 'It's all right, it's just a hobby. He's going to university in September.')

Luckily for Granny Malimore, during the summer most of our Charterhouse friends' parents were away, so we were able to work our way round their empty houses instead.

We normally had a two-week stint in each because that was how long our parents were away for. We spent two weeks in David Thomas's house in South Marlborough – a stunning white mansion with a swimming pool; two weeks in Ant's house, which was hung-tiled and covered in creeper; and two weeks at Peter's house, in Chobham. There's a picture of us outside Ant's house loading our gear into Pete's sister's horsebox, which I think rather

sums up Genesis at this point in time. Other bands were rehearsing in north London basements, while we were moving our stuff
around in a horse trailer still full of straw and horse shit. No one
had thought to clear it out.

The house of Brian Roberts's granny, where we also spent
two weeks, was on a gated estate in East Grinstead. While we
were there we all watched the moon landings on a tiny TV in
a huge wooden frame. Brian also got a journalist from the *East
Grinstead Courier* down to write a story about us for the paper:

> *With a curious combination of all-acoustic sounds and vocal
> harmonies they have so far had three singles released on Decca and
> one album 'From Genesis to Revelation' produced by singer and
> controversial 'pop' columnist Jonathan King.*
>
> *Brian Roberts, now an assistant cameraman, said: 'We all
> met at school at Charterhouse and began writing together. A
> group was formed from this. I began to record work and have
> continued to do so.'*
>
> *So far all their work has been done from the recording studio.
> But thinking very seriously of becoming professional, they are
> looking for the type of work where audiences are prepared to sit
> down and listen – as on the present college circuits. Their music is
> essentially for the listener, not the raver.*

True: you really couldn't get anything out of the music we
were making back then unless you sat down and went on the
journey. Although, of course, we hadn't actually performed for
an audience at all yet. The *East Grinstead Courier* covered that up
rather nicely, I thought.

In all the houses in which we were staying, the noise we were making seemed scarily loud. And sometimes you'd be aware of another strange sound, too, coming from down a corridor. When you went to investigate you'd find Pete tucked up in a telephone alcove, playing the flute.

A lot of the time you felt that Pete's brain might have been somewhere else, whereas Tony always lived in the now. He liked everything to be organized, planned and perfect. Pete was also a perfectionist but he was happy to get there the meandering way. He could deal with chaos and mismanagement, and things going wrong – such as the moment when we were at Chobham and his parents suddenly rang to say that they were coming back early. He remained calm even though we only had a couple of hours to tidy up and be off the premises. Somehow we got the house cleared and were just thinking that we'd made it, when Tony's bloody car wouldn't start.

My Ford Anglia may not have been a cool car but it was at least slightly cooler than Tony's. He had an Austin 35, which was the kind of car your granny would drive, even in 1969. It looked like a kid's drawing of a car – a round bubble car – and the indicators were things that would pop up between the front and back doors. They never worked. Whenever we stopped at traffic lights, one of us would have to stick an arm out of the window and physically force the indicators out. The only good thing about the Austin was that it was so small you could push it easily, which was how we got it down Pete's parents' drive and cunningly pushed the car left, not right, which was the direction Peter's parents would be coming from at any minute . . .

★ ★ ★

We were in the yellow Formica kitchen at Ant's house when Tony asked the fateful question: 'Are we going on?' It was getting towards the end of summer and we had to decide what we were going to do.

I used to think Tony only stayed in the band because he was worried he'd miss something: he couldn't bear the thought that if he left and we were a success, he wouldn't have been part of it. Pete was still weighing up whether to go to film school – even then he was thinking about other options – but I didn't really want to go to Edinburgh. So when Ant turned then to me and said, 'Well, are we going on?' I said yes.

It's only now that I realize that Ant may actually have meant, 'Are *we* going on?', i.e. him and me. We were very close at that moment and I think that's what Ant might have preferred. But in any case it was decided: Genesis were going professional. It didn't mean that I thought I would still be a musician in ten years' time, let alone forty. I was eighteen – even two years is a lifetime at that age.

Naturally, I tried to sound a bit more convincing when I broke the news to my father. I told him we were all so passionate about what we'd produced over the holidays that we couldn't just leave it there.

Would I have defied him if he'd tried to stop me? No question – how could I be a teenage grump if he was on my side? Since I'd left Charterhouse I wasn't huffing around, slamming doors anymore, but things still weren't great between us. But Dad had the wisdom to realize that if he fought me, it would only make me more determined. He also had the ability to take the long view, which I'm sure was the result of thirty-six years in the Navy and a world war. In fact, I think it was because our parents' generation as a whole were still in shock that mine got away with doing what it did. They wanted a quiet life after the bombing and fighting and, after all they'd been through, our misdemeanours probably didn't seem that bad.

But for my father to actively support me, which is exactly what he did . . . I still don't quite understand it. He'd sent me to good schools to give me the very best education he could, and then let himself be persuaded that my future lay in being in a band.

CHAPTER FIVE

Christmas Cottage in Dorking was where Genesis spent the winter of 1969 and where we really became a band. If we had been in London, we'd have been going out to see other bands all the time, comparing ourselves, thinking about what everyone else was doing. Instead we were in a beautiful but incredibly remote part of the country, determined to find out where we could go musically. This involved lots of long improvising sessions.

Rich had secured the cottage for us – it belonged to his parents, who were trying to sell it – and we moved there in November 1969. We parked at the bottom of the drive and then had to climb up about a hundred earth steps in the cold to get to the cottage – not great given that we were laden down with our new gear. Ant, because he'd been ill with bronchitis, got away with carrying two microphone stands, but the rest of us had to deal with Tony's organ.

The organ had been bought with money from our parents, something that my father had organized. Our parents hadn't had much contact with each other since the renegotiation of the

Decca contract, but my father had rung them up when we'd decided to turn professional:

'Now listen here, we should have a conversation about helping these young boys.'

'Listen here' was how he always began.

I'm not sure exactly what he said next but my father would have wanted to talk about the best way to help us go forwards: planning and organization were his things. And whatever he did say must have been persuasive because our parents agreed to contribute £200 each to help us buy equipment, so not only could we get Tony an organ, we could also buy a PA so you could actually hear Pete's vocals. We also got a bass guitar and amp for me (I'd been borrowing until then). Transporting the lot down to Dorking hadn't been easy. I was in Pete's taxi, driving behind Tony in his Austin 35, and there'd been a speaker cabinet completely filling Tony's rear window.

We argued like fuck in that cottage. It was a mixture of love and hate with probably a bit of murder as well. Tony, Ant, Pete and I were all incredibly strong-willed, all determined to prove ourselves musically and to get our own way. To make matters worse we were crushed inside the small cottage. Rich, now officially our roadie, had to sleep on the floor in the living room: he couldn't sleep in his old bedroom because Tony and Pete were in there.

There was no furniture except the beds and it was always dark because we rehearsed in the living room with a blanket over the window even though we were miles from anywhere. When you're not very good – which we weren't – you tend to turn the volume up to compensate.

Someone would always be storming off upstairs or out of the front door and we'd have to regroup. Being a Libran I tended to be a bit calmer but I think we would have killed each other without Rich. Or starved. As well as being the peacemaker Rich was our cook, which meant trying to keep all of us fed on a virtually non-existent budget. Occasionally I would go home and Mum would slip me £10 and send me back with a fruit box (being the son of a sailor she might have thought I had a tendency towards scurvy), but none of us wanted to ask our parents for more money. This meant we lived on sausages, potatoes and yoghurt, which Pete always kept in a bowl in the airing cupboard. There was one occasion when Ant's mother sent us sweetbreads. Rich took one look at them and said, 'What the hell am I going to do with those?'

God knows what John Mayhew, our new drummer, made of it all.

After John Silver had left for America, Pete had, once again, found us a replacement drummer, and a professional one at that. The new John had been a carpenter but had given it up to go touring with bands. It showed. When we started doing gigs, John would arrive backstage with a little bag containing fresh clothes to change into after he'd got sweaty playing. We were incredulous. We would all go onstage in what we were wearing. I would write all day in T-shirt and jeans, go and play, and then go home.

The problem was that while John was a good carpenter (he made a couple of Leslie speakers for Tony's organ), he was possibly better at carpentry than drumming. Pete would often have to show John how his part should go – not that Pete could play it either but he'd explain the feel. Which was pretty frustrating for both of them.

Pete often found it hard to put across what he was thinking musically. He'd sit down at the piano and play us a piece and then at the end of it say, 'No, no, that's not right. What I meant was this.' Each of us had to get the others to use their imaginations to see what something could become, to transport them and make them understand how it sounded in our own head – but Pete never managed to sell things very well. There'd be lots of ums and ers.

Pete composed on the piano but he wasn't allowed to play it: that was Tony's territory. If Pete wrote something, Tony would have to learn to play it himself. In many ways they were the best of friends, but Tony was competitive and there was a friction between them that didn't exist between Ant and me. With our two twelve-string guitars we were busy creating a distinctive, unusual sound, coming up with new, interesting chords and experimenting with tunings. (A new tuning would be a great way of finding inspiration: it'd be like turning over a new page.) We were taking folk music and developing it into another area, I felt, and we'd often carry on when the others had finished for the day.

We had a strong work ethic, undoubtedly – we were very serious about everything back then. We simply realized that if you worked until 4 a.m. one morning you probably wouldn't start work until midday the next day. Better to get going by ten in the morning (although none of us were early risers) and finish for supper at around eight. Occasionally we'd try and work after that but because we were tired and full up, we never really achieved anything. Rich, Ant and I had usually smoked a bit of grass by then, too, which had an effect.

Our blackout of other music wasn't intentional either – we'd hear of other bands 'getting it together in the country' but we weren't deliberately trying to keep ourselves pure. We listened to King Crimson's *In the Court of the Crimson King* endlessly, which made us want to get a mellotron, and *Days of Future Passed* by the Moody Blues. Ant and I also listened to Crosby, Stills & Nash. However, now that I'd started writing I found I didn't really want to listen to other bands. The music I'd heard between the ages of eight and fourteen – the Kinks, the Small Faces, Joni Mitchell and the Beatles, most of all – would always have the biggest impact. I knew that was where I would find my inspiration.

★ ★ ★

It wasn't all work. Occasionally I would escape from the cottage for the night to visit Josie in Brighton, where she was now living. This was a drag because I'd recently got rid of my Ford Anglia so was back to a motorbike, a Triumph 250. That motorbike and I were never meant to be as one and riding it down to Sussex on a wet, windy winter's night was pretty grim. Especially the time, after not having seen Josie for weeks, I got there and found someone else in her bed.

Things didn't improve when Josie came to stay at the cottage and there were endless me-or-the-band ultimatums. A group is a very selfish sort of being: it soaks you up and doesn't leave time for much else. People on the outside suffer.

Pete had a very attractive girlfriend called Jill, who was more forgiving than Josie. Pete would sometimes disappear off to go and see her. This caused some resentment, although we tolerated it as long as it didn't get in the way.

Ant also had a girlfriend – a dancer in the Ballet Rambert – but she had broken up with him in the summer. I've never known anyone take a split so badly. But musically, if not emotionally, Ant was far ahead of the rest of us: the songs he was writing – such as 'Let Us Now Make Love' – were by comparison so grown-up melodically and lyrically. Something changed about Ant after Lucy, although I didn't see it at the time. I just felt that there was no room in his life for anything apart from music.

★ ★ ★

Dad probably felt somewhat alarmed whenever the band had a weekend off and I turned up back at Hill Cottage. I never saw my father without a jacket and he usually wore a tie as well, whereas in 1969 the look I was aiming for was something between a Rastafarian and the Beatles. I'm not sure I got the hairstyle right (it was extremely long and messy) but my wardrobe was spot on: flares and a Second World War military jacket which smelled as though an entire battalion had worn it at one stage or another. That my father could have seen this jacket as an insult never occurred to me – I wasn't even trying to rebel at this stage, I was just being a typical teenager. With his usual forbearance Dad refrained from ever saying anything – although it was at around this point that he summoned me to his club in London for a talk about my future.

There'd always been an open invitation to meet Dad at his club, the Royal Naval and Military Club in St James's, and I'd always put it off. I wasn't sure how well things were going with the band so I had been deliberately keeping him at arm's length. Now I knew I couldn't avoid it any longer.

The club was in a very austere building with very austere residents and a very austere code. I'd been told to wear a jacket and tie but decided on an imaginative interpretation and arrived wearing my mauve platforms together with a blue velvet suit I'd bought from Kensington Market. The look of horror on the doorman's face when I handed him my Afghan coat was absolutely priceless – he couldn't hold it far enough away from him. The smell never went from those coats. Ever.

I met my father, who was dressed in a Savile Row three-piece suit, in a vast room filled with leather chairs and endless portraits of admirals. Like the other residents of the club, the waiters tried hard to ignore me and carry on as normal. I remember thinking my appearance must have shocked my father but I never sensed for one minute that he was embarrassed. This was extraordinary given that, if roles had been reversed, I would have probably kicked myself straight back outside.

I was expecting a grilling as we sat down for lunch but instead we had a real, proper, grown-up conversation for what felt like the first time. Dad had obviously come to terms with any regret he'd felt over my failure to follow him into the Navy, and although he laid the Foreign Office down as an alternative career, he didn't sell it that hard. I think he'd realized it was a different era and that the Commonwealth was going to shrink. Privately, I didn't consider the civil service for even a second, which might have been why I suggested journalism as a fallback plan.

I wonder now if maybe Dad just wanted to show me his world over luncheon: he always looked right in London with his suit, polished shoes and his umbrella over his arm. In any case, I didn't come away depressed. In fact, as the doorman handed me back my coat (pinched between the very tips of his fingers), I think I was feeling quite positive.

★ ★ ★

By this time, we'd been shut away for a bit too long. You could tell because when we played our first proper gig at Brunel University in January 1970, it took us forever to work out how to set up: who should go on the left, who should go on the right. At one point we had Tony at the front, then Ant behind him, then John and his drums behind that: three deep. I have no idea where Pete and I ended up. The problem was partly that we'd seen so few bands play we had no idea how you were supposed to do it; it was also because we'd always sat round in a circle while we were at the cottage. The idea that you should be facing outwards, towards an audience, was quite a novelty.

Our next gig was at a works do for a company in Wolverhampton that made screws. The audience had wanted a dance band and hadn't got a clue what we were about. We'd be playing a song in straight 4/4 time and then suddenly go into 7/8, at which point the mood would collapse and everyone would have to stand around awkwardly for a couple of bars, shuffling their feet, until we got back into 4/4 so that they could start dancing again. It didn't really faze us but we were very conscious that it couldn't have been much fun for anybody else.

After the gig we slept on the floor of the staff changing rooms, and I woke up in the middle of the night dripping with sweat because the underfloor heating had come on. It was uncomfortable, but not as uncomfortable as the next evening when we played at a youth club in Bramhall and spent the night in a squat in Buxton. It was January and half the windows in the place were gone: guys were chopping up furniture to keep the fire going.

Our transportation at this point consisted of a blue-and-white Rank Hovis McDouggal bread van, which was a gift from Rich's father. He had worked for Hovis until he retired and, given Rich's parents' hostility towards the music scene, it was somewhat ironic how in debt to the Macphails Genesis now were. The only problem was that Rich himself couldn't drive and so I ended up having to teach him. To give him his credit he was a quick learner: he only hit a car once. Fortunately it happened the day after one of our better-paying gigs. We were paid £50 and Rich did exactly £50 of damage.

The bread van wasn't comfortable. Until John Mayhew put his carpentry skills to use and made some back seats, someone would always have to sit on the battery, and by the time we'd packed the gear in, it was incredibly cramped. Then, perhaps as a result of the Wolverhampton and Buxton misery, Pete decided he wanted to take his mattress with him to our next gig. We sat and watched him drag it down the steep hill from the cottage and wondered how on earth he thought it was going to fit in the back with the gear. Looking back, maybe we were a bit jealous too. I mean, who said you couldn't bring your bed on the road?

Pete always did think outside the box. Unlike the rest of us, he also thought about the business side of things. At the cottage he'd sit by the phone for hours with a list of agents to ring up and then cross them off one by one. He also had perseverance, which was good, because the number of agents who promised to come down and see us but then developed a puncture en route to Dorking was unbelievable.

Finally, at about the time we were thinking of leaving the cottage, Pete got us an agent called Terry King who booked us for some London shows. (He had found Terry by looking through the back pages of *Melody Maker*; we'd look at the listings and find out which enviable bands had five shows in a row, and then try to find out who their agent was.) Although Terry was good at getting us gigs, some would be at nightclubs and Genesis were not a nightclub band.

At the Revolution Club off Berkeley Square we'd have to play three sets an evening. The first set would generally go okay and we'd go out to the pub afterwards. The second set would usually go okay again and we'd return to the pub, by now feeling that life was pretty good. The third set would be at one in the morning and all the pubs would be shut. Because we couldn't afford drinks in the nightclub – they cost more than we were getting paid – we'd bring in our own cider and beer and have it in the dressing room. This meant that by the time we left the stage at 2:30 a.m. we'd be rather tired, very depressed and extremely drunk.

It was worse at the Blazes, a smartish nightclub on the Cromwell Road where we'd have to play to a crowd of guys looking for girls and a couple of dancers on stands, gyrating.

The Blazes' stage was designed for a nightclub band with an upright piano, not a big organ. By the time we'd got all our gear on to it, the only place for me was on the floor by the side of the stage, which would have been fine except that I now had a cello, given to us by Brian Roberts's granny, on which I would play a song called 'Pacidy'. (I used to put paper frets on the neck, which always fell off and I would have to find them by torch in the dark. However, as a band our attitude was always that the more anyone could bring to the table musically, the better. Pete's flute tuning was always a bit interesting but, still, it brought texture.)

You knew there was going to be a disaster eventually and, sure enough, one evening at Blazes I was playing 'Pacidy' and swept my bow straight between the legs of the girl at the nearest table. I think we got halfway through the song before there was a scream.

Not all the venues we were playing were so smart.

I'd seen the Cream play at the Roundhouse in Chalk Farm in December 1966 when the floor was just rubble: you'd try to move and you'd fall over a brick. By the time Genesis played there in March 1970 they'd at least got rid of the bricks and put in temporary seating, but it still had a concrete floor and the sound was crap.

We performed there at the Atomic Sunrise Festival, on the same bill as David Bowie and Hawkwind. Bowie was a bit unapproachable (quiet, kept himself to himself) whereas Hawkwind would always make you feel at home. Especially if home was the Kasbah in Tangiers. The smell of joss sticks and hashish backstage was overwhelming.

We hoped when we left the cottage that we were doing something special, that there was nothing else quite like us around. Genesis often got lumped together with Yes, but they were more about virtuoso playing than we were. One night we all went to see them at the Usher Hall in Edinburgh – they were brilliant technically but the music didn't move me. Jon Anderson's lyrics sounded good but weren't really about anything. Yes wouldn't touch humour with a barge pole, whereas we always did have a sense of fun.

Steamhammer were more heavy rock than us; Carl Palmer and Atomic Rooster were darker. The Strawbs, Pentangle and Fairport Convention were a bit similar but they were playing traditional chords, whereas that was what Ant and I were trying to get away from. Without sounding too grand about it, Genesis were different: each song was a folky, fanciful story set to music. You had to listen and follow it. You couldn't carry on drinking and chatting, and just drop in for a couple of bars.

This meant that, from an audience's point of view, it was probably quite painful to understand. If we'd been playing more traditional music and they hadn't liked it, at least they would have known what it was they didn't like: soul or R&B or blues. We weren't any of those things. As a result, our audiences in the early days tended to be of two sorts: those that loved us and those that didn't know what the fuck was going on. Sometimes they didn't know that there *was* anything going on. Drums rarely appeared for the first twenty minutes of our set, which is why half the time no one knew we were even playing.

One of the places that helped us to survive was the Friars in Aylesbury. The crowd there were always into music, open to seeing something different. Dave Stops, the guy who ran it, was a great supporter of ours. We also managed to get a residency at Ronnie Scott's, which impressed my parents. I couldn't quite bring myself to tell them that we were upstairs at Ronnies, i.e. in the dodgy bar-and-disco bit where we played to an average of six people, three of them usually friends or friends of friends. Those that didn't know us personally often heckled in the intricate bits, and during one particularly bad night Tony – who's the kind of guy who takes it all until he suddenly blows – sprang up from behind his keyboard.

'We are no ordinary rock band!'

Being a classically trained pianist, 'rock band' was a label that particularly used to annoy Tony. He'd even thought the organ was a bit heathen at first.

When we played at a pub in Hemel Hempstead, Tony refused to go back on to play an encore. He was miffed because he thought the audience didn't appreciate us enough. The rest of us couldn't believe we were being asked to play an encore in the first place – a few weeks earlier we'd played to an audience of one. Pete had carried on for a bit then asked if there were any requests.

'Don't be so bloody silly,' I said to Tony as we walked back down the corridor from the stage to the dressing room; but Tony can be incredibly stubborn. Eventually, I'd had enough. There were wooden chairs stacked all down the corridor so I picked one up and went for him. Then I kicked him all the way back to the stage. We all knew how to push each others' buttons terribly but our fights were only one step up from the playground. When we supported Ginger Baker's Air Force at the Revolution, Ant and I were standing outside the back door before the show when Ginger's partner arrived. A few minutes later, Ginger kicked her out: 'Don't you fucking come in here when I'm rehearsing!' This was a bit of an eye-opener.

★ ★ ★

Our breakthrough came in February 1970 when we first played the Marquee Club.

Backstage, the Marquee could have been any other club: it smelled horrible – beer, cigarettes, sweat – and the dressing room was teeny. But it was such a figurehead of a venue and, for me, the realization of my dreams. Even going in the back entrance with the gear as opposed to queuing at the front was a buzz. And then to be getting up on the same stage as my heroes . . . suddenly it felt like we were the real thing.

It was also at the Marquee Club that Strat – Tony Stratton-Smith, the owner of Charisma Records – began to take notice of us. We were supporting another Charisma band, Rare Bird, who had two keyboard players, one of whom was Dave Kaffinetti (who later appeared in *This is Spinal Tap*) and no guitarist. Instead, Dave would play an electric piano through a fuzz box. They were so good that both Tony and I came away from watching them feeling completely deflated: we thought there was no way we could compete with that. For some reason, however, not only did Rare Bird like us, but their producer, John Anthony, did too. John knew Strat well and managed to persuade him to come out of his drinking hole, Le Chasse, and round the corner to watch us at the Marquee Club.

It was one of our better nights – there must have been at least eleven people in the audience. Strat arrived in a suit, handkerchief in his breast pocket, wearing a tie and he was slightly sweaty round the collar.

Before going into the music business Strat used to be a sports journalist. He'd been booked on to the plane that crashed in

Munich in 1958, killing many of the Manchester football team, but had survived because his plans had changed at the last minute. He was a larger-than-life character – jovial and a big drinker, but able to handle his drink well – and he also loved music. When it came to Genesis, what he loved was the emotion and power of our classical chords. And, like Jonathan King, he was impressed by Pete.

Our early shows were tough for Pete: he had a voice but he didn't know how to be a front man. At some point he'd got a bass drum, which he'd furiously bang in the instrumental sections and which acted as a safety barrier between him and the audience. It was out of time mostly but John Mayhew was louder so it didn't bother me. Pete also had a tambourine and at the end of 'The Knife', a driving, dramatic song that we'd use to close the set, he'd thrash around and bang his drum. With a strobe light going as well he'd usually look a bit demonic. You'd often see his tongue sticking out of the side of his mouth, he'd be concentrating so hard on what he was doing.

The problem for Pete was that neither the drum nor the tambourine were any use to him in the gaps between the songs, and the gaps between the songs were as much a part of our set as the music: it used to take Ant and I forever to get our guitars in tune. Pete was never someone who could banter with the audience so, out of sheer desperation, he started telling stories.

He was always slightly not-of-this-world and the stories he'd tell were the same. He'd often take a character from a song and spin a mad, whacky, surreal tale about them, all completely deadpan. I'm sure they were great but, to be honest, I can't say I ever paid attention. I only realized he was doing something different when I didn't feel his panicked 'What do I do now?' rabbit-in-the-headlights look boring into my back as I was struggling to tune my guitar.

★ ★ ★

Charisma's offices were above a dirty bookshop in Old Compton Street, but the label had a classy feel, a family feel. As well as Rare Bird, they had the Nice, Van der Graaf Generator (an interesting, progressive, keyboard-based band) and Lindisfarne. Strat wasn't in it for the money, either, although he must have been happy when, having signed us, we all went for a meeting to discuss our wages and John Mayhew argued him down to £10 a week from an opening offer of £15. I think John was always a bit less enamoured of Genesis than the rest of us were.

Our first proper album, *Trespass*, was recorded at Trident Studios in July 1970. Trident was in St Anne's Court, a seedy, narrow street that always smelled of urine because that's where all the drunks ended up, and there'd often be the odd, rather dodgy hooker knocking around as well. Queen were signed to Trident and because of that got free studio hours in the downtime; they'd go in at midnight and work until eight in the morning.

We'd been playing *Trespass* live for a long time before we went into the studio and as a result it felt like performing, not creating. The feeling of freedom on every album since has been wonderful by comparison.

The real problem, however, was the material itself. Because none of us really knew how to write a song, we'd each write bits. We'd then go and fight the others about which bits we should use, always arguing that our own bit was 'for the good of the

On Whale Island, Portsmouth Harbour, with Mum, Dad and Nicky.

Dad, aged six, fishing in Cape Town.

Me, aged three, at Morris Lodge Hotel.

Just moved up North!

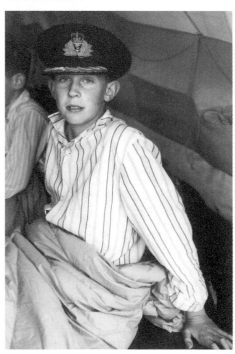

At scout camp in Wales. Still
considering the Navy…

Ascham St Vincents 2nd XI Xmas 1919

Matches played   Won   Lost   Drawn
11   11   0   0

G. Dermot .   A.H. Taylor .   W.F.Mc Rutherford .   E.P. Merritt .   C.A. Brownlie .   D. Bittra .
                                                    (goal)
              H.R.D. Clarke .   F.R. Scott .   M. Field .
                                          (captain)

Dad in the 2nd XI football team (back row, 3rd from left). Eleven matches: eleven victories.

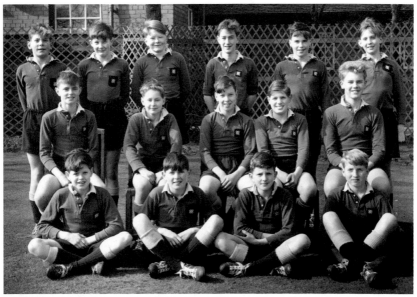

Me in the 2nd XI rugby team (back row, right). The highlight of my brief sporting career.

(*left*) My father on gunnery manoeuvres.

(*below*) Me on speeding manoeuvres, Texas 1976.

Brazil '77. About to collapse onstage with food poisoning.

Dad looking for inspiration.

My father's standards never relaxed.

Backstage, trying to convince Phil and Tony to do it my way.

1986. On my way to work.

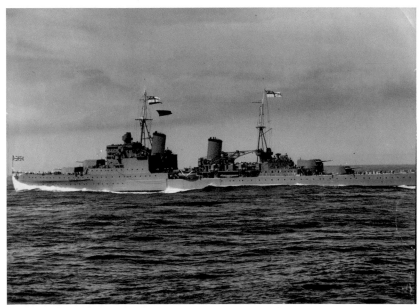

HMS Newcastle, 1952–3. My father's preferred method of transport.

Captain William Francis Henry Crawford Rutherford, C.B.E., D.S.O (1906–1986).

band' (we were still just devious schoolboys at heart). One for all and all for one, but mostly every man for himself.

This was one of the reasons why our early songs were so long: we'd just keep adding bits. Long songs might appear clever and hard to write, but for us they were easy. We'd just take bit A and bit D and segue them together. What we didn't realize was that it was generally better if you didn't try to use the whole alphabet every time.

A prime example was the opening track on the album, 'Looking for Someone'. It started with Pete's idea and began with just simple piano chords and voice – such a Pete thing. If I had it now, it'd be a fabulous song as I could make something out of just the first couple of bits. Back then we rambled on with another eight minutes, throwing in bits and pieces. We were determined to prove ourselves and, while Pete always realized that space in a track was important, the idea that less is more was completely alien to the rest of us.

'Stagnation' was another example: we should have limited ourselves to two guitars but instead we used about ten. The result was that they all ended up cancelling each other out on record and the final thing sounded so muted you couldn't hear anything properly.

It would be a long time before we sounded any good on record. For years the sound would be a bit wishy-washy. John Anthony, who produced *Trespass*, had an infectious, cheerful aura and did a good job of lightening us up. The infuriating thing about him was that if you wanted to re-do a part, he'd insist that you sat through the whole song waiting for the right moment. You couldn't simply fast forward to it and drop it in as John thought that it would cause a click on the recording. I thought that was absolute crap. Given that some of our songs were nine-minutes long, it made for some rather long days.

★ ★ ★

'Have you got a minute, Mike?'

Lines like that have always worried me. In 1974 Adam Faith would make a film, *Stardust*, in which he'd play a music manager, and whenever he wanted to fire someone his character would say, 'Fancy a pint?' When Ant came up to me one night before a gig at Richmond Rugby Club and said, 'Have you got a minute, Mike?' I knew it wasn't going to be good news.

Rich, Ant and I got into the van and drove out to the middle of the rugby pitch, and that's when Ant told me that he wanted to leave the band. I can still picture the lights of the rugby club hall in the rear-view mirror: it was dusk and the hall had big glass windows. We'd set up our stuff and were just having a break until showtime.

You know when your heart drops when you're on a plane that's taking off? It was that feeling. The blood drained.

Ant had told me before about his stage fright but it hadn't really gone in. I was so busy doing what I was doing I just didn't have the time and energy to worry about other people. It wouldn't be the last time I made that mistake.

'Fine, Ant, whatever you want to do,' I said. 'I understand.'

I didn't understand, if I'm honest. We all got nervous, but I also thought that stage fright was a luxury we couldn't afford. But the truth was also that I wasn't as close to Ant as I had been. I didn't really understand what had been happening in his life.

After leaving the cottage, Josie and I, together with our cocker spaniel, had moved into a flat in Hampton Wick. It was the coldest, dampest flat I've ever known. In the bedroom we had a mattress on the floor and a paraffin heater, which stank, and we'd have to walk the dog in Bushey Park to warm up. If I'd have been single, I probably would have taken more notice of Ant – not just his stage fright, but also his break-up with Lucy and the bronchitis he'd had over the winter. Ant was quite fragile and, when I thought about it, I realized he'd often been ill while we were making *Trespass*.

But it was only now that I saw just how much he'd changed.

The summer before we went to Christmas Cottage, Ant and I had driven all over the country looking for somewhere for the band to rehearse. We'd find places advertised for rent in the *Lady* and then rock up with a yarn about needing a place to study for exams. (It was when we found out what a week in Wales would have cost us that we began to appreciate the use of our parents' homes a bit more.)

Back then, Ant had always been laughing, sitting in the front seat of my Ford Anglia strumming his acoustic guitar and wearing his pith helmet. We'd be in the middle of Herefordshire, miles from anywhere on a grey, wet day, and he'd get out of the car at a petrol station still wearing his helmet, his school scarf wrapped round him, his jeans semi-tucked into his thick-soled boots, and he wouldn't be in the least bit self-conscious. He was an extrovert but he wasn't really worried about being part of a cool set. He just wanted to achieve stuff.

Now I could see that he'd lost weight and was in a terrible way. The stage fright was more than just fear, it was terror. He was upset about letting us down, too, although none of us were angry. You could see he really couldn't do it anymore.

It now seems incredible that the option never arose to wait for Ant to recover, but we were all ambitious: we were just starting to get somewhere and the thought that we could last three months without things falling to pieces was inconceivable. It was my first real insight into how tough you needed to be get anywhere. It was also the most traumatic split of my professional career. There would be other partings of the ways but none would ever affect me as much as losing Ant.

Our last gig together was in Haywards Heath: we played to twenty-five people. Not bad. I got into Pete's Hillman Imp to go home, feeling that at least we'd least bowed out on a high.

In my mind, I had no doubt that Genesis without Ant were finished. Pete and Tony were irreplaceable members of the band, but Ant to me was more irreplaceable than anyone. From the start he'd been the musical inspiration, the creative driving force. Without Ant's drive I'm sure Pete would have gone off to film school, and without him in the band now I wasn't sure that I wanted to carry on. We had been such a close unit.

However, there were fifty miles of country lanes between Haywards Heath and Pete's house in Chobham. It might have been around Leatherhead that I started to reconsider. By the time we got to Chobham, and Pete and I had finished talking, we'd both realized that if we wanted to make it work, we could. It wasn't that we didn't still believe in 'One for all and all for one'. It was more that we were developing a new philosophy to go with it: 'Let's try it and see.'

CHAPTER SIX

In 1970, Phil Collins was a face on the scene in Soho: a friend of Strat, a regular at Le Chasse and the drummer in a band called Flaming Youth. Given that we were in Surrey, not Soho, that didn't really mean a lot to us.

Phil didn't know much about Genesis either, although when he'd seen our adverts for a drummer in *Melody Maker* he'd tried to fast-track his way into the band via Strat. However, Strat had told him that we were pretty fussy and he'd have to go down to Chobham for an audition. Phil arrived from Hounslow and Mrs Gabriel – we called her Mrs G – served tea.

It was summer so we'd pulled back the rug in the living room, set up on the parquet floor and opened the French windows to let the breeze in. Phil always reckoned that I was wearing a dressing gown when he first saw me, and I might well have been: I don't think I was trying to be ostentatious but we were all in relaxed mode. Anyway, Phil had arrived a bit early so while the drummer before him was finishing, we sent him off for a swim in the pool.

By the time it came to Phil's turn, he'd already heard and

memorized the part we were using for the audition and, when he sat down at the kit, you just knew. He had confidence. All the other guys had fiddled around, moved the cymbals, shifted their seat about a bit, but Phil simply changed the snare round because he was left-handed and got on with it.

You never felt anything was a big deal with Phil. Because most drummers don't write, they live to play. As a breed, they're never into the intense, emotional stuff: they just want to get a good groove. Being very much English folk-rock at this point, a groove wasn't something Genesis had until Phil came along. For a start, apart from Pete, we all played sitting down.

In theory we were a very democratic band but really it was whoever shouted loudest that usually got their own way. The rows would be exhausting sometimes: you'd be right in the middle of one and suddenly realize you'd stopped caring half an hour ago, but the thing was, because you were committed, you couldn't just stop. You had to carry on.

Tony was the worst (or the best, depending on how you looked at it). He'd go on so long that in the end he'd just wear you down. Eventually, in later years, I found that if you let him go on long enough he'd suddenly say, 'But then again, you may be right . . .' and start arguing the other way. You had to catch him at just the right moment.

My mind was on the guitarist who'd come to audition with Phil – Ronnie Caryl, his friend from Flaming Youth. The thing about Ronnie was that he was a blues guitar-ist. I could tell he didn't have a feel for our folky, harmony, tinkly guitar stuff, so if I had any reservations that day it was probably because I was worried that Ronnie and Phil might come as a job lot.

Fortunately, they didn't.

*　*　*

It had been Ant's leaving that had made us decide that, as well as a new guitarist, we really needed a new drummer to replace John Mayhew. But although we'd now solved one part of the problem, we were still a man down. That summer Genesis played quite a few shows as a four-piece, Tony playing lead lines on his Hohner Pianet that he put through a fuzz box and me playing guitar and bass pedals. It's a forgotten era now but it was an important time for the band: the moment when Tony and I began to get closer together musically. We were the chords in the middle, Tony and I, the core of the Genesis sound. Even on *From Genesis to Revelation* you can hear it: the repeating riff with the changing chords laid over the top, and Tony responding to me or vice versa.

This didn't mean that things within the band were all that harmonious. Soon after Phil joined in August 1970 we moved into The Maltings in Farnham to rehearse and row full time.

The Maltings was a vast building, a huge expanse of dusty wooden floorboards that had once been a maltworks but now only had pigeons in it. And pigeon shit. We would set up in one corner of the place on some rugs and in the morning our gear would be completely covered. It was always a surprise to find Rich, who stayed there and slept on the floor as security, had escaped the bird droppings untouched.

Perhaps it was because Tony and I had effectively found our workload doubled that it was such a tense period. We were also driven not so much to succeed in terms of fame, but to achieve what we wanted to musically. The arguing was a terrible waste of time, but we were worried about getting it right, making our ideas work. It must have been violent, though, because the first few times we started rowing, I could see Phil thought we were breaking up, it was all over. Then after a few days he got over the shock and I could see him thinking: 'It really doesn't matter, guys!'

We weren't quite on the same planet as Phil. He always had a bloke-next-door, happy-go-lucky demeanour about him: let's have a drink in the pub, crack a joke, smoke a cigarette or a joint. Life is good. I think that's one of the things Pete liked about Phil: the fact that Phil wasn't from the same background, hadn't come from the same rather narrow world as us. Pete was always less stiff than Tony and me, much more in touch with emotions and feelings, much more interested in the wider world.

There was a musical bond between Pete and Phil too: because of Pete's sense of rhythm, he and Phil seemed to lock in from day one. They were both intuitive about music in the same way. It wasn't cerebral, as it was with Tony – with Pete and Phil it came from the gut. Plus, Phil, having joined later, wasn't part of our old playground dynamic, which was why there was often a bit more respect for his opinion. And why he was often left twiddling his drumsticks while the rest of us fought.

Among the songs we were working on at The Maltings was 'Musical Box', which to me was 'Stagnation' one stage on. It was a quirky, fantasy fairytale story that started quietly, built up and, at the end, had a huge dramatic finish that would be one of our best bits for a long time to come. Even today, when I hear Pete sing 'Now, now, now, now, now' it raises the hairs on the b[...] my neck. It's almost annoying: as I'm not a singer, I could n[...] do something so simple that would sound so emotional.

Maybe that's not quite true.

The Maltings had a terrific echo and I found that, if I left my guitar plugged in when I slammed it down in the middle of a row, it made a tremendous noise. And Tony would make sure his keyboards were turned up to full volume when he whacked them and stormed out.

The Maltings wasn't far from Hill Cottage so Phil and I stayed there while Tony stayed with Pete. It felt good, like a new beginning, to have Phil around, and my parents liked him, too. I think they always found Pete a bit of a mystery, but they could relate to Phil more.

They moved the dining table out in to the hall where there was more space and then Mum did what most mothers do and tried to stuff us. The more we ate, the better job she'd done, so there'd often be starters and a main. I didn't really see much of Dad in that period – he'd pass through and he was glad we were there, but he'd quickly take himself off to read the newspaper. I think my parents were pleased to see how hard we worked and how obsessed and committed we were, and they were happy to support us in any way they could. I had thought taking me to my first gig aged ten was as good as it was ever going to get.

Phil stayed at Hill Cottage, in my sister's old bedroom, for a week or so and then we swapped over and Tony came to stay with me while Phil went to stay with Pete. The idea was that it would allow Pete to get to know Phil better, but no one ever told Phil that. He always thought it was because I didn't like him and

ung up Pete to complain: 'Oh, for God's sake, Pete, you have
n for a while, he's a right pain in the arse.'

It didn't matter to Mum who she had staying, and both my
parents thought Tony was very polite. Tony and I did miss a meal
one evening when Mum nearly set fire to the house.

We were sitting chatting when we heard a voice from the
kitchen.

'Um, fire. Fire, Mikey, fire.'

This was in her normal voice. Then it got a little bit louder.

'Um, Mikey, fire? Fire, Mikey?' she said again as though there
still might be some doubt about it. I went into the kitchen and
flames had completely engulfed a saucepan, licking up the sides
of the thing. I had to rush it out to the garden and dump it in
a flowerbed while Tony watched. (He's never been one for the
front line of the action.)

★ ★ ★

Before the Second World War, the Navy was the largest public-
relations organization in the world. The idea was that trade
followed the flag, which meant my father was often part of what
were called 'hurrah cruises', meant to win hearts and minds and
show taxpaying members of the Commonwealth that they were
getting value for money. It was a social whirl, as Dad discovered
in South Africa in 1929:

> Ball suppers were held in basements where at trestle tables on
> wooden chairs we washed down ham, tongue, jellies and blancmange
> with South Africa's more light-hearted and acidulated wines.
>   The stay always included a ship's dance, children's party and

being open to visitors who wandered all over the place, and I found a family one afternoon standing raptly at the wardroom door gazing at the not-very-attractive picture of one of the watch-keeping officers taking a post-luncheon forty winks in an armchair.

Mother was saying, 'I say the poor boy is tired but your father says he's drunk like all sailors. But we can't have a bet on it as it wouldn't be right to wake him up and find out.'

To be fair, it was an exhausting schedule:

I still have the programme of a four-day visit to Accra where all not on duty lived ashore each with a suitcase packed according to a list like a new boy at school. We moved from function to function, the only stable element being where we slept the night, provided that we could remember where it was.

In 1970, Genesis played over a hundred gigs. We moved from pub to club to college and the only stable element was Rich's food, although it was less ham and tongue, more sausages and baked potatoes. At the cottage he'd always pack some food before we set off in the bread van because we simply couldn't afford to eat out – and anyway, where else would you put a hard-boiled egg if not a hamper? But that didn't stop other bands from expecting a scene from Henley regatta whenever we rocked up.

If anything, I felt Charterhouse had actually given us a better grounding than most for life on the road. We'd been beaten down and got used to living quite basically in a tough environment without home comforts. What's more, while our peers who had gone on to university were continuing to live a rather bubble-like, privileged existence, we were learning about life in the real world, where everyone seemed to be against us because of our background. In our case it felt like everyone was doubly against us because our music was so odd.

We had to pay our dues like every other band, lugging our equipment around, earning the respect of roadies and crew. Where things got a bit strange for us was when paying our dues also meant entertaining our contemporaries at their Oxbridge May Balls.

It seemed weird to be back in a world of arches, cloisters and stone pillars again in such different circumstances, but if the setting brought back memories of Charterhouse, then there was absolutely no comparison in terms of the audience. At Charterhouse you'd always be cheered – not so much because of what you were playing but because the masters obviously hated it. Putting them through pain made it all the more pleasurable. May Balls were just painful for everyone: us and the audience. The big act would be on at midnight so by three or four in the morning when we were on we'd be fighting to stay awake – it was so late that we would have got pissed, got over the hangover and got sober again. Those left in the audience that weren't comatose on the floor, throwing-up drunk or acid-ed out were very, very few.

Around the time Ant left the band, the bread van passed its sell-by date and we began to rent a transit van from an East End guy named Reg King, who had a link with Strat. The good thing about Reg's vans was that if anything went wrong with them – which it always would – you could drop them back at Reg's base where a burly mechanic would come out with a sledgehammer, take a swing at whichever part you thought wasn't right, charge you £20 and send you on our way. The bad part about Reg King's vans was dealing with Reg King, which was Rich's job.

Reg was Andrew Loog Oldham's chauffeur – Andrew Loog Oldham as in the Stones' manager and 'chauffeur' as in minder. The first time Rich met Reg was in Reg's office in Soho Square. There was a trail of blood up the stairs, the result of Reg's previous appointment. Reg rang Gail Colson, Strat's assistant at Charisma, afterwards: 'Rich has just left. He's a bit freaked out. He saw the claret.'

We never knew if we were going to make it to a gig in a Reg King van. There was one show in Aberystwyth when the van broke down four times on the way from London. We got there so late we missed our booking and had to turn round and start the drive straight back home. Whereupon the van instantly broke down again. This was in the middle of nowhere and the middle of the night: we managed to call for help from an AA box but then everyone fell asleep waiting.

I woke up to this strange whine – a kind of 'Neoooeeeooo' sound. The funny thing was, it seemed to be coming from the AA box. I got out of the van, went over to the box and opened it up nervously, not sure what I was going to find inside. What I found was Pete. He was sitting inside on a shelf, wrapped in a towel to keep warm, playing his oboe.

If we weren't in one of Reg's vans then we were piled into someone's car, which wasn't much better. Driving anywhere was always a source of friction: as a driver Tony was so slow that journeys would go on forever, but Pete was too erratic. He'd be talking away and completely forget about changing gear – you'd end up shaking so much you felt like you were leaving body parts in the road. When he suddenly remembered that there was such a thing as fourth, you'd feel the car breathe a sigh of relief.

This meant that I would make a dash for the driving role, but Tony didn't like that because he didn't trust me not to fall asleep. He'd start by singing Beatles songs to keep everyone awake and then, when they'd all tailed off, he'd just keep on prodding me. The flaw in his plan was that sometimes he couldn't stay awake either, and when that happened I did occasionally rest my eyes in the shut position.

When I fell asleep and went over a large roundabout, I could pass it off as a just a large bump in the road. It was more difficult when I fell asleep on the M4 and drove over an oil drum that was marking some roadworks. Sparks were flying everywhere – it was like a rocket re-entering orbit – and the noise alone was enough to convince me that we were going to die. Even worse, we weren't in one of our vans at the time. We had borrowed Lindisfarne's vehicle, which was a brand-new transit and had smart airplane seats with headphone sockets. It wasn't quite as brand-new when Lindisfarne got it back.

Naturally, all this driving meant that service stations were an important part of our lives. We're probably the only people ever to have looked forward to getting to the Blue Boar on the M1 at Watford Gap. It'd be 3 a.m., you'd be cold and shivery, and your body would almost go into shock at those horrible fluorescent service station lights – but God, the taste of a greasy full English breakfast would be great.

* * *

It was after we left The Maltings that we found our next guitarist: Mick Barnard of Princes Risborough.

Mick had a Binson Echo – a great delay sound, very novel at the time – and was a really nice guy. We really weren't very nice to him.

To get to gigs, Mick would always drive part of the way from Princes Risborough to meet us, park his car somewhere convenient, such as a service station, and then wait for us to pick him up in the van; on the way home, we'd do the same thing in reverse. The incident that really sticks in my mind is when we were driving home on a horrible, cold, wet winter's night when there was no one around and Mick had been having problems with his car. We were on the opposite side of the motorway from the service station car park so Mick asked us to wait until he'd crossed over the footbridge and made sure his car would start before we drove off.

''Course we will, Mick.'

We didn't exactly bugger off the minute his back was turned, it was more that we sort of instantly forgot about him. And then the next thing we knew, we were a mile down the road. It turned out to be a long night for Mick.

Maybe we were so awful to him because we felt he wasn't quite the one, but I still feel guilty about that night now.

In truth, I was too set on finding 'the son of Ant'. I still missed him, although it wasn't as though he'd vanished from my life completely. He came to a couple of shows – it was a bit frosty, but not that bad. There was a great sadness for me, though, because I knew it'd never be the same between us. He would never be able to share the memories and the jokes that the rest of the band were going to share.

For Pete and Tony, however, it was much less complicated: we needed a new guitarist, simple as that. And so when I fell ill with a stomach ulcer, they simply went and got another one to replace Mick.

★ ★ ★

You don't usually get a stomach ulcer at twenty, but the Blue Boar 3 a.m. fry-ups and lack of sleep had taken their toll. Having now finally split up with Josie after several unhappy attempts I went home to Hill Cottage to recover.

I'd worried and fretted about breaking up with Josie so much in advance but when it came to it, it wasn't as terrible as I'd feared. It was just a relief to both of us to finally acknowledge that it wasn't working. Meanwhile, Mum loved having me back. 'You should stay in bed till you're right,' she'd say, and then I would hear her go downstairs to Dad. 'I don't think he should leave till he's better.'

But while I was laid up in my old teenage bedroom – still with the same green bed cover, the same orange lampshade, the same psychedelic UFO club poster on the wall – Pete had seen an advert in *Melody Maker*: 'Imaginative guitarist/writer seeks involvement with receptive musicians determined to strive beyond existing stagnant forms.' This was Steve Hackett, who was then living in Pimlico.

By the time Pete and Tony brought Steve down to Hill Cottage, I think they'd already decided he was in the band but were still a bit worried about getting it past me. I sensed it was a slight ambush: 'Catch him while he's weak and in bed, he's bound to say yes.' In any case they waited downstairs while Steve came up to my bedroom to meet me. This time I was definitely wearing a dressing gown.

Steve didn't look like us. He looked like an art student. Black corduroy jacket, black jeans, black scarf, black shirt. And black hair and a black moustache. For years Steve was all black. 'He's very quiet, isn't he?' Mum said when he'd gone. But he wasn't quiet or shy on the guitar. Mick had a lovely, warm sound but he wasn't brave sonically, whereas Steve had lots of weird effects boxes. But what was unusual about Steve was that he liked acoustic guitar too – until now, all the replacement guitarists I'd found were either electric or acoustic, not both. Straight away I felt as though we understood each other – although I'm not sure Steve, seeing me in my dressing gown, felt the same.

As we found over the years, Phil had a huge capacity for taking alcohol and not showing it. Steve's first gig, at University College London in January 1971, was one of the exceptions. We'd been for a few pints beforehand but no one realized that Phil had drunk a few more pints than everyone else and was pissed. Phil was such a good drummer that he could pull most things off, but that night he went for his big fill and nothing happened. Silence. He'd played it perfectly, but he was just six inches to the side of every drum.

Poor Steve: it was his first gig, he was nervous and we'd got a drunk drummer. Tony and I gave Phil such a hard time afterwards, which didn't bother Phil, but Steve unfortunately thought that we were arguing about him: we hated him and wanted him out. As usual, it never occurred to anyone to tell the newcomer what was really going on.

Soon after this we set off on the Charisma Records Six Bob Tour. It was like a little Charisma hurrah cruise and one of Strat's best ideas: take a musical package tour around the country, introduce people to three different Charisma acts and charge them virtually nothing (six bob was peanuts) for a ticket. The other two bands on the bill, Lindisfarne and Van der Graaf Generator, took it in turns to headline, but we were the junior partners so would go on first and get the seats warm for when everyone arrived.

Van der Graaf were dark, heavy and moody: a thinking man's type of band. Peter Hammill was a bit like a wild poet, punching the air during songs. The trouble was they had no idea how to put a set together. They'd put all the up songs in a row and then all the heavy, ponderous ones together, and by the end it'd be so dark and you'd be so depressed you wouldn't know what to do with yourself. I learned how not to structure a set from them.

Van der Graaf had been the biggest act on Charisma for a while but then Lindisfarne had a huge hit with 'Fog on the Tyne', a really quirky, stompy, clap-along song. They were all characters and would sit in the back of the tour bus with their Newcastle Brown (they could be really drunk but still perform). When we got to Newcastle it was like turning up with the Beatles. I can remember wanting to go on stage and say: 'Hello Newcastle! We're friends of Lindisfarne! They like us!'

This was before we'd borrowed their brand-new van.

One of the nicest things about the Six Bob Tour was staying in hotels. We didn't have to drive back home after each gig. The thought of getting to Newcastle and not driving back was unbelievable: a bed! Not a very nice bed, but a bed! For us, even B&Bs were financially out of the question at this stage. If the gig was really too far to drive there and back in a night, we'd sometimes be allowed to sleep on the headlining band's floor. Caravan, who had a house in Canterbury, put us up several times.

It was purely because I needed to stay awake to drive that I started taking cocaine: it wasn't recreational, it was just better at keeping me awake than Tony singing Beatles songs while I drove us to Cornwall and back.

Drugs were not something that Tony or Pete ever did. Phil, Rich and I could always enjoy a spliff, but although everyone always thought Pete was completely out of his head, he never even drank much. He used to have one beer and get smashed. One glass of wine and it was all over. And Tony couldn't bear the thought of being out of control so he never took anything, but that didn't mean he was safe. There'd been one weekend at the cottage when Rich had invited some of his friends down so that they could all take acid together while the rest of us, including Tony, went off home. When one of Rich's friends, Bill, offered to drive Tony to the station in Dorking, Tony accepted, completely unaware of the fact that Bill had dropped some acid first. He must have been a bit surprised by how lovely Bill thought Dorking high street was: 'Man, look at the lovely lamppost!'

★ ★ ★

In the summer of 1971, Strat rented an old country house in Crowborough in East Sussex for us to use while we wrote our next album, *Nursery Cryme*. We didn't see him much, but at the weekends he'd come down and get in the bath at 10 a.m. and stay there till lunchtime, reading the papers. So we still didn't see him much.

We didn't take criticism very well in the early years of our career. We were probably quite overbearing in our knowledge of how good we thought we were. We'd hand Strat the tape of an album when we'd finished recording and that would be it – we'd never ask, 'What do you think?' There were times when I'm sure we would have benefited from a second opinion, but Strat believed in us, too, which rubbed off. When we saw him for meetings at the Charisma offices we'd come out feeling great: uplifted, confident. 'Dear boy, it's tremendous!'

As individuals we weren't very confident but we had confidence in our music being strong and different. Plus, you had to be a bit cocky: it was the only attitude you could have if you wanted to succeed. Without Strat, however, I don't think we would have got anywhere. Our first three albums with Charisma were basically an apprenticeship. We learned how to play our instruments properly, how to play live, how to record, and creatively we were given a completely free rein to an extent that you couldn't imagine today. We would never have A & R men or record company execs coming in from outside and commenting on what we were doing: people knew that they shouldn't ask to hear a record until it was finished.

Nursery Cryme wasn't an easy album to write. Maybe it was just the new dynamics that made it feel so difficult by comparison. If Ant had been around I'm sure it wouldn't have been so slow, but we needed to find our feet without him to get to the next stage. This was especially true for me: I wrote one song, 'Harlequin', where I tried to play both my guitar part and Ant's on a single twelve-string guitar by tuning the pairs of strings to harmonies. It was pretty dodgy. Not my finest moment lyrically, either: 'There once was a harvest in this land / Reap from the turquoise sky, harlequin, harlequin'. 'Harvest' is a word I've learned not to use in songs.

Besides 'The Musical Box' we had one other song already up and running before we got to Crowborough. 'The Return of the Giant Hogweed' had something for everybody in the band: fast drumming for Phil, triplet stuff with Tony and Steve playing harmonies together, and a quirky lyric from Pete about a plant that'd escaped from Kew Gardens.

'Seven Stones' was very much Tony's song. It was a great example of what I've come to call Tony's cabaret chords: his big, schmaltzy, music-hall chords which Phil and I struggled with but he loved. In the end we had to make a rule: Tony could have three or four per album and no more. (We always wondered what happened to the ones we'd turned down. Then in 2011 Tony released a wonderful classical album and we found out.)

'For Absent Friends' was Phil and Steve's song. I could have done without it on the record, but because it was something that the pair of them – the new recruits – had written together it seemed right to have it there. Plus, you listened to anything that Phil brought in. Pete, Tony and I would bring something we'd written in and then argue our case, whereas Phil never felt the need. His attitude was always, 'This is it, guys. Take it or leave it.' There was never any ego with Phil.

Steve was different. He hadn't known us for long, so didn't quite know how to play the game like the rest of us and fight his corner, but there was another problem, too. His real strength was doing the most amazing, unique, quirky-sounding things on guitar – he brought something to the band that Ant never would have done and I fully appreciated it. But Steve didn't get satisfaction from that: he wanted to be a writer.

★ ★ ★

By this time, Pete had married Jill, who was the daughter of the Queen's private secretary, in a ceremony at Saint James's Palace. The story got around that Rich had got there early and sat on the Queen's throne before anyone arrived. Pete and Jill were now living in a basement flat in Wandsworth, which is where I had to go one night to tell Jill that Pete had broken his ankle during a gig at the Friars in Aylesbury. She saw me on the doorstep and thought I'd come to tell her he'd died, but Pete had just had a 'We are one!' moment with the crowd and leapt off the stage to be embraced. The crowd had their own 'We are one!' moment and got out of his way. Fast.

At the time we didn't believe Pete had broken his ankle, and we definitely didn't believe he couldn't play an encore.

'It's just a sprain! What are you talking about? You'll be fine!'

We only allowed Tony to drive him to hospital after we'd made him finish the gig.

The next few weeks after that – playing shows with Pete in a wheelchair – were slightly surreal. He didn't get any sympathy from us, although you'd see people in the audience who didn't know he'd only broken his leg thinking: 'Ah, how brave! Poor guy . . .' But we were terrified when he started charging up and down the stage: there were real cambers on some of them and it was a worry whether he'd stop in time. You'd just about breathe a sigh of relief and then he'd start waving his crutches around like he was possessed: quite scary, actually. But the show went on.

At the time, Tony had met his future wife, Margaret. As for me, things were a bit more complicated.

I first met Angie Downing when she was seventeen years old and she was going out with my old Charterhouse friend John Alexander. Before I split up with Josie, we went to his house in Chelsea one day with our cocker spaniel. When Angie opened the door it struck me how gorgeous she was – she captivated me. Unfortunately Angie didn't seem to have the same bolt of lightning. She remembers opening the door and thinking how much Josie and I resembled our cocker spaniel with our Afghan coats and long hair with a middle parting. Never mind the doleful look . . .

John Alexander looked more like a rock star than the actual thing. He had long black hair, a swarthy look, snake hips and a cool Chelsea wardrobe. He used to cruise along the King's Road in either a Mini Cooper S with dark-tinted windows or his sporty looking Marcus. He also had all the equipment – guitars, that is – and that's where I came in . . . I borrowed them.

He had it all, including the girl of my dreams, which really pissed me off. As far as the girl was concerned, she'd have to wait – I needed to figure a plan to impress her. It looked like it might take a while as I was still driving around in a crappy Mini Traveller.

CHAPTER SEVEN

Belgium liked us! Thank God for that!

Trespass had reached number 1 in the charts there, whereas in the UK it had only got to number 98.

This meant that sailing over to Brussels in January 1972 for our first European gig was incredibly exciting. For me, and although I wasn't aware of it at the time, it was also the start of a lifetime following in my father's footsteps.

In 1932, Dad had sailed over to Brussels for the funeral of the Belgian king, Albert I, as second-in-command of the British naval guard that had been sent for the occasion. The ceremony:

> *entailed a long wait on a chilly day and while old stagers like myself had 'dried out', no liquid intake since the previous evening, some of the younger men had neglected advice and some of the older ones found that their internal plumbing was not as good as they thought.*
>
> *A stage was reached where about half the guard needed urgent relief or might suffer real injury and no public lavatory in sight.*
>
> *To our Belgian Army Liaison Officer there was no*

problem. Brandishing his sword at the spectators he opened up a lane disclosing the entrance to a dismal little public park with a few blackened trees and bushes but no sign of any convenience. Indicating the inner face of the four-foot brick wall surrounding the park he announced that it would be 'très convenable' and the afflicted trooped through the entrance like footballers taking the field and, lining up, began shamefacedly to do their thing.

England was then a puritanical country where mere exposure of the person in a public park would bring park keepers and police and lead them to an appearance before the beak, a sharp fine, a stinging rebuke and a few lines in the press placing the defendant forever in the category of a disgrace to his family. 'Queer feller – had up for exposing himself in the park – no real breeding on that side of the family' and so on. Permissiveness and full frontal nudity were still years ahead.

This, however, was the Continent where it was quite usual for men's urinals to be situated on the route to the ladies' toilets so that a gentleman while controlling operations with one hand could use the other to raise his hat in courteous salutation to passing ladies of his acquaintance.

Far from being affronted, the spectators repositioned themselves for a better view. Children were hoisted on to the wall and the operation explained as clouds of steam arose and there was even a hint of muted applause.

Dad could have been describing the view from the stage at most of the festivals I've ever played. You'd be standing there and great clouds of steam would rise up off the crowd whenever the sun broke through, the effect of both the mass of bodies and what had come out of them as well.

At the Black Cat Club in Brussels the problem wasn't the lack of loos but the lack of safety exits. It was downstairs, there was no back entrance and the crowd were all sitting cross-legged on the floor. Smoking. Given that we now had a mellotron, which we'd bought from King Crimson and which was the size of a table with two huge double keyboards, a quick escape wouldn't have been easy.

A few days later we appeared on Belgian TV. This wasn't our first experience of public broadcasting. In February 1970 we'd recorded a live session for the BBC's *Night Ride* radio programme, which was produced by Alec Reid and was the only early recording of ours that sounded any good. We played several songs that hadn't made it on to *Trespass*: 'Pacidy', 'Going Out to Get You' (which was twenty minutes long) and a song called 'The Shepherd', which Tony sang. My hunch is that because it was an hour-long show, no one minded Tony singing, but I think to this day Tony thinks his voice is better than it is. In terms of vocal abilities I would say we were about the same and I have a pretty realistic opinion of my voice, but Tony always thought his was better. I tell him to his face sometimes that it isn't, but I don't think he quite believes me.

A few months after *Night Ride* we'd made our TV debut on *Disco 2*, a late-night BBC2 programme which was like a precursor to *The Old Grey Whistle Test*. We'd played 'The Knife' against a blue-screen background, which had war footage projected on it, and the technicians had also put a blue card under my bass strings – all pretty corny. In Belgium the TV studio had a white backdrop, until we'd all walked across it and set up and it wasn't really white anymore. They had to paint out our trails before they could start filming.

There were always technical problems with TV shows in those days. We tried to do what we could to stop them being a disaster – but knew that they were never going to be any good. The technicians also had a completely different mindset to the roadies, who just want to get the job done. TV technicians only seemed to be concerned with getting their teabreaks. This meant a lot of waiting around, or 'hurry up and wait' as it's called: you'd arrive at the studio, go into make-up and then sit around for three hours wondering what you were doing there.

We were successful in Belgium but we seemed to be even more popular in Italy, where *Nursery Cryme* had got to number 4. It would be the start of a long love affair because our romantic, emotional songs felt right in Italy. Rome was always a good city for us: the feeling of age, history and grandeur worked as a setting for our music. Within a very short time we started playing arenas and stadiums, but in the early days we'd just play at little local discos to audiences of fourteen-year-old schoolgirls. The shows would always be in the middle of the afternoon on a Sunday because the kids had to get home in time for bed.

We were playing up in the mountains one night when Tony got food poisoning. We battled on for a bit without him but it was like being in a car that had lost a wheel, and we had to finish the set early. Because we hadn't managed to sell many tickets, this meant that the promoter had just the excuse he was looking for not to pay us. Rich wasn't having any of it and got a bit of aggressive. The promoter got a gun. We didn't get paid.

Our early years of European touring often felt like one long drama. In the early seventies it felt like touring round a bunch of different countries whose main aim was to search us as many times as possible. There was one occasion when we'd flown to Switzerland and were detained at Geneva airport: Steve was taken in to a side-room by Customs and I remember clearly the moment when the door swung open, revealing Steve in his underpants looking very forlorn. The Swiss didn't like long-haired bands in those days: we always knew when we got to the Swiss border we were going to be done over.

Sightseeing wasn't really possible given our schedule, but Rich could never drive past a lake without taking off all his clothes and going for a swim and getting us to do the same. In Naples we also discovered another therapeutic past time . . .

Ending a tour with a band row was traditional. The unusual thing about our end-of-tour-row in Naples was that there was a funfair round the corner from the hotel where we were staying. There came a certain point when we were all so sick of each other that we decided the only thing to do was get on the dodgems and bash the hell out of each other repeatedly. I have to say, I've never known an atmosphere cleared so well.

★ ★ ★

After Belgium and Italy, England felt like a pretty dour place. It was also still largely indifferent to us. *Nursery Cryme*, which had got to number 39 in the UK, had moved things on for us a bit in terms of sales and profile, but not enough for a second album. Strat was determined to keep us in the fold, and if he hadn't supported us, Gail Colson, his assistant, would happily have given us the nudge. She'd once called us 'posh public schoolboys', which was funny because she was posh too. Her husband, Fred Munt – a Jack-the-lad, sorter-outer type – didn't like us either. He was the Charisma tour manager and, for a PR guy, incredibly honest: 'Ah, it's rubbish, mate. Rubbish.'

Fred had organized the Six Bob Tour. One night he'd convinced us that we were going to be mobbed leaving the band hotel and that the only way to save us from our public was to climb out of the window and over a ladder on to the waiting bus. We went along with it, but of course when we drove round to the front of the hotel there were only four people there. All of them looking for Lindisfarne.

Security was something that was never around when you needed it in the early years of our career. By this time I'd already been beaten up by a bunch of Hell's Angels at a horrible club somewhere: the stage wasn't very high and there was a bunch of biker boys in the front row who'd start smashing beer bottles on the ground during one of our quiet moments. When the broken glass started coming on the stage I put my guitar to one side and said, 'Fucking well shut up and listen.' Or something to that effect. As the Hell's Angels launched themselves at me, I looked round for backup from my friends and compatriots. I've never seen four guys leave the stage so fast.

There was bit of a mêlée in which I got a bit bruised before I managed to limp off after the others. Even after that we didn't come up with a policy as to how to defend ourselves en masse. So obviously it was only a matter of time before it happened again.

There was always an awkward moment of negotiation as we drove back into London late at night after a show. The issue was who got dropped off first. Was it quicker to go via Earls Court and then central London or to come down the A1? Often it would depend on who was driving, and on this particular night it was Pete, which meant that Tony and I were dropped off at Hangar Lane Tube station while the others carried on into London.

Hangar Lane was never the best part of town. Tony and I were just sitting on the platform waiting when a couple of drunks came up and started the old 'What are you staring at?' routine. I was tired, fed-up and gave a bit of stick back, which is when one of them headbutted me. After that things got hazy, but I do remember that Banks, my cohort, was nowhere to be seen. The story goes that he was found outside on the North Circular trying to wave down cars and shouting, 'Help! They are killing my friend! Stop!'

No one ever did.

★ ★ ★

As a band we'd found a formula for writing music: short pieces that we'd join together into a single song the length of which (fifteen to twenty minutes) would allow us to do something brave and interesting. 'Supper's Ready', the song that took up the whole of the second side of our third album, *Foxtrot*, was a great example.

The intro was Tony's, who had come up with it while we were waiting to play a gig in Cleethorpes. We were in a gym with a lovely big echo when Tony picked up a guitar, and suddenly, there it was.

'God! Tony, that's fantastic!'

'What? What did I do?'

Half the art of writing is to know what's good. Coming up

with the stuff is one thing, but recognizing it is another. Tony is the same on keyboards. I can walk into the room and he will play for a couple of minutes. I'll hear some amazing chords and get excited that this could be the setting for a new song, yet he has no real idea what he just played. It was probably because Tony doesn't normally write on guitar that he found the chords in the first place. It was just three notes and not a shape that a guitarist would ever play. (I never did feel territorial about Tony playing the guitar in the way that Tony felt territorial about his keyboards. I thought it made for quite a nice image on stage: three acoustic guitars together.)

Foxtrot felt an easy album to write, as though we'd found our way a bit. We wrote the majority of it in the basement of the Una Billings School of Dance in Shepherd's Bush (Phil's mum ran the Barbara Speake Stage School in Acton and had connections). One song, 'Watcher of the Skies', had been written while we were in Italy a few months before. We were playing the Palasport in Reggio nell'Emilia near Parma, a huge, crap, echoey place, when in the middle of the soundcheck Tony played the opening two chords on his mellotron. They sounded incredible, although, once again, I'm not sure he knew just how good they were. The lyrics were then written by Tony and me together, sitting on the roof of our hotel in Naples while we imagined the world had ended. Quite odd, given that it was a pleasant, sunny day.

Pete always understood how to make words flow. Sometimes he'd try to cram in too many, as he did on 'The Battle of Epping Forest', but his words always sang well. Tony and I, not being singers, didn't have the same understanding. 'Watchers' was a prime example of the fact that you can write great lyrics that read well but are hard to sing: 'Watcher of the skies, watcher of all / His is a world alone, no world of his own . . .'

Our music was always so quirky and unusual sounding that it needed equally quirky lyrics. Tony and I were very much into sci-fi, and we'd all studied Latin and mythology at school, influences that bubbled into our words. But it's also true that we hadn't got the confidence to write something as simple as 'I love you, babe' at this point. It was such a direct emotion, not something that you could say if you'd been to public school and had learned to hide your feelings. It wouldn't be until much later on that I felt I could write a love song.

★ ★ ★

In July 1972 we took a day off from writing the album for Tony's wedding to Margaret in Farnham. We then generously allowed him another day off for a honeymoon driving to Dartmoor and back.

When Margaret married Tony, her life became the band. She was a home person, but if the road was home, that was fine with her. She always came everywhere with Tony and I don't think he would have lasted otherwise. We've dragged Tony round the world complaining for the last forty years and he's loved it all, but if he hadn't been in a band and married to Margaret I often think he wouldn't have travelled so much.

Steve had also met his future first wife, Ellen, a few months before at the Zoom Club in Germany. We'd played a gig and flown back to England the next day, by which time Steve had inherited Ellen, and Phil had inherited a girl called Kiki. Kiki was definitely one for the bands – great fun, a lot of makeup, a lot of hair – whereas Ellen had a dark, German side. Given that the idea was that you finished a tour and got away clean, it always seemed a bit ironic to me that both Steve and Phil came back encumbered as a result of the very last night.

By now Angie had broken up with John Alexander. Even when they were going out together, I would take her for dinner. John had asked me to look after Angie when he was in Norfolk. Yet I still didn't feel it was the right moment to tell her how I felt. We were friends, and I hated the thought that I could lose her friendship if it all went wrong.

She was at Lucy Clayton's in Knightsbridge. While her friends jumped into their boyfriends' sports cars, I would arrive in the transit van. Angie had quite a rebellious streak and rather enjoyed clambering in and driving off with the band to a gig in Hastings. In many ways we were quite similar. She had gone to boarding school, and like me, hadn't particularly enjoyed it and resented the discipline. She did, however, manage not to be kicked out and became Head of House, at which point she banned fagging. That's just how she was.

When she finished college she started modelling in London, but was soon persuaded to go to Paris and Milan for work. This meant that she only needed a part-time base in London and, as I often left my flat to drive to a gig at 2 p.m. and didn't arrive back until the next morning, I offered her my bed. The only snag was that there was only one of us in it at any one time.

At the time I was living in Earls Court, which I couldn't afford. I'd therefore moved into the smallest bedroom, at the back of the flat, and let out the front bedroom, which had big bay windows on to Redcliffe Gardens. Gay Tom, as we all called him, wore very high silver platform shoes, mauve trousers and big hair, and always had some dodgy bloke in tow. He was also Australian.

Sadly, Gay Tom couldn't really afford Earls Court either, so he had to share the room with a sound-man called Bruce who worked for Clair Brothers audio systems and was not into gay people. Like Angie and me, Bruce and Tom were ships in the night most of the time. When they weren't, Bruce would be kicked out to sleep on the sofa while Tom had his way with whomever he'd brought back from the gay club.

Gay Tom still never had any money, though. Eventually it got so bad we agreed he could pay me his rent in cocaine.

★ ★ ★

In May 1972, Pete appeared on stage at the Great Western Festival in Lincoln with a reverse Mohican: he'd shaved a strip down the centre of his head and was also wearing white facepaint, eyeliner and a jewelled collar.

You had to admit, it was a look.

Festivals were often places where we died a death. It would be hard to create an atmosphere and our moody songs never did well on a sunny summer afternoon. Nevertheless, they were exciting to play. I was nearly beside myself when, after we'd played Reading in August, the guy making the announcements had come on at the end and hurried us off: 'That was Genesis: I'm afraid they've got to leave promptly because of touring commitments.' At the time I hadn't yet understood that, if you were in the middle of a bill at a festival, you didn't do an encore: you had a slot and kept to it. 'No, no, we've got time! Really – we've got time!'

At festivals, Pete was left with an even bigger responsibility on stage. Our songs were often story-driven, but no one could hear the words because the PAs were never very good, so as the band's representative he had to make the connection with the crowd and get across the sense of the songs. Also, he was still the only one of us standing up.

We must have seemed very intense and studious, but it was never a conscious decision to stay sitting down: we just weren't natural stage people, and by sitting down could hide behind Pete and the music. I'd wanted to be a songwriter, that was always my plan. I've never been one of those guys who yearns to be on stage. I loved playing live, but it was more about the playing – the feeling when it clicks – than the crowd reaction.

When Pete unexpectedly appeared wearing Jill's red Ossie Clark dress and a fox's head to play the National Stadium in Dublin in October, it was shocking. We couldn't stare too much because we were so busy trying to play our own instruments, but we were dumbstruck that Pete had chosen a small, scruffy, unfriendly Irish boxing venue to give that look its debut appearance. It was about as provocative as you could get.

We had no idea of what Pete was going to do in advance – he knew if he'd run it by us we would have stopped him. After that, it was almost as though we all agreed to ignore Pete's stage look. He'd appear before a show in full makeup and pretend everything was normal, and we'd do the same: 'Hey up, Pete.'

The funny thing was that, outside the band, Pete could talk to anyone about anything. He'd always be referencing world affairs or human rights or social inequalities – even then he had a strong sense of justice. His ability to communicate was a skill and he could turn it on or off when he wanted. If he walked into a room of people he didn't know, he'd go up to the nearest one and say, 'Hello, I'm Peter Gabriel: what are you up to?' He would get physically tired but he never seemed to get mentally tired. He was always writing stuff down and he could always be engaged to discuss things. With the band, however, the old, argumentative schoolboy dynamic made us all sensitive to each other and so Pete, knowing that there'd be a row, simply decided to keep silent and bypass it.

I confess we did grumble slightly after the Dublin gig. But the next week we were on the cover of *Melody Maker* and our fee doubled overnight, so any resentment went away.

CHAPTER EIGHT

In December 1972 Genesis played a Christmas show at Philharmonic Hall (now known as Avery Fisher Hall) in New York, organized by Strat at a cost of £10,000. What we didn't know was that this was our money – the realization that we'd have to pay it all back only came afterwards. At the time we were too busy loving America.

Manhattan was somewhere that we'd lived through the pictures: the big skyscrapers; the long avenues; the taxis; the noise; the bustle; the steam rising off the streets from the subway and pipework. Being there was all my film fantasies come true. It didn't matter that the hotel we were staying in, the Gorham off 57th Street, was a complete dive. The rooms were incredibly scruffy but even that seemed exciting. English scruffy was just scruffy; New York scruffy was cool.

Everything had a feeling of Hollywood, including the moment when, on the first night, the telephone in my room rang. It was reception calling to warn us that a man with a gun was wandering around the building somewhere. I'd been in my room for less than ten minutes and could barely contain my excitement. Just imagine – an Englishman in New York and an actual gunman on the loose! So it was a bit disappointing when, after the police had arrived in a blaze of sirens, the armed man went off peacefully following a minor kerfuffle in the corridor.

I doubt New York would have missed us that much if we had gone down in a hail of bullets. Our first ever American gig, which had been in Boston the day before, had been a complete disaster. It was so amateur. We were playing in a cafeteria at Brandeis University at lunchtime – people had been wandering in with their sandwiches. We hadn't realized that Tony's organ wouldn't work because of the difference in the power supply. We were only saved by the fact that Brandeis specialized in science and engineering: one of the university technicians managed to build a Heath Robinson transformer that just about did the job. By then the gig was doomed anyway: we limped through as best we could and then left everybody to enjoy their lunch in peace.

Our New York debut was nearly as bad. The Rickenbacker bass I was playing had a horrendous buzz on it: I couldn't hear a note all night. No one else could, either, and I was convinced we'd blown it. There was a lift up from the side of the stage to the dressing room, and after the show I got in and flung my bass on the floor in a fit of dramatic swearing and cursing. But then, almost the next moment, Strat swept into the dressing room completely ecstatic. 'Dear boy, they loved it! It was fantastic! You've conquered New York!'

Charlie Watts always said, 'If it's crap on stage, it's fine out front.' I've learned the truth of that over the years. And, sure enough, a review appeared in the *New York Times* the next day:

Genesis is a quintet that blends perversely fashionable theatrics with complex, often ingenious arrangements . . . The visual focus is Peter Gabriel, the lead singer, who center-parts his hair to the crown of his head, changes costumes frequently (from clinging pants suits to dresses and back again) and is clearly working hard to project androgynous demonism. He succeeds, especially when helped by fireflash and smoke bombs set off on the beat at the climax of the act. Mr Gabriel sings well enough, but musically Genesis is most notable for its hammering, heavy ostinatos and luxurious organ playing. Occasionally things get mired in pretension, or lose their rhythmic grip. But the climax worked, and climaxes are what rock is all about.

The gig had been followed by an after-show party at the Tavern on the Green, and by the time I'd calmed down and was crossing Central Park in a chauffeur-driven limo, chatting to journalists, I was feeling rather important. It was my first gig in New York, my first after-show party . . . only one thing seemed to be missing.

It turned out her name was Carol.

Carol wasn't my first groupie, although my first groupie hadn't actually been a groupie. She'd been a hooker who had been staying at the same hotel as us in Naples earlier in the year. The city was crumbling and beautiful and romantic, this girl was petite and dark haired and, all things considered, I was well placed to enjoy my night.

As for Carol, I didn't choose her, she chose me. In fact, she had a long history of intimate relations with UK bands, which she proceeded to list by name over the time I knew her.

In America, English-accented acts were definitely top of the
list for groupies, although I always thought it was more than
just the novelty of hearing us speak: they liked our look, too.
American guys had the long hair but the effect was a bit too
studied. We looked like we didn't care because (apart from Pete)
we didn't. If you were in an English band, your music was your
calling card. I figured that, for the groupie, the prospect of being
put up in a hotel for three days added to the appeal, too.

When we arrived in America for our first tour, everything
was so new and different. I just couldn't get enough of it. We
landed in LA, hired Mustangs, put the roof down with Crosby,
Stills & Nash blaring from the radio. I was twenty years old and
life couldn't get better.

We were staying at a run-down hotel called the Tropicana,
near Sunset Strip, but even that felt part of the Californian story.
We played the Roxy for four nights. After one of the shows,
the guy from Atlantic Records came backstage with his sister in
tow. She was an attractive woman and seemed very friendly. The
only thing was that she was twenty years older than me. I don't
know whether it was because I'd recently seen *The Graduate*, but
I didn't see a big problem with this. After all, shouldn't everyone
have a Mrs Robinson at some stage of their life?

I moved from the Tropicana into her house in the Hills.
Although I was slightly concerned about her having two
teenage children – I felt more in their camp than hers – my
newly found confidence allowed me to throw caution to the
wind and march confidently into her bedroom. She was from
England and used to make me English breakfast tea and roast
dinners, lit by English Rose candles. I'm not sure how homesick

she was, but everything in her house was English. And then there was me . . .

* * *

There's a shot of us in Central Park taken on our first trip to New York. With the boating lake just behind us and the Upper East Side behind that, we felt almost like pioneers or preachers, spreading the message of English music.

However, when we flew back for our first proper tour of America three months later, in March 1973, we found out that New York had completely forgotten us. So much for conquering the place.

America was somewhere you had to break state by state, as we learned. Chicago and Cleveland were first to get us (there was a leading radio station in Cleveland that had broken David Bowie a few years before, so that was an important city to crack). Eventually, New York followed suit. Canada was much quicker to take to us and touring there was always a boost: we actually sold tickets in Canada, probably because we already had a following in France. We weren't helped by the fact our American record-label guys in those early days were hopeless. They just couldn't understand what these weird-looking kids from England were all about. Worst of all was Jerry Greenberg, who was the chairman of Atlantic Records.

'I wan' that song ta be shorta. Shorta. That's too long. Ya gotta make it shorta.'

There's missing the point and there's missing the point.

Before Atlantic we were with Buddha Records in the US, who had an interesting, odd mix of people: Donna Summer,

Richard Pryor and Monty Python, who were also signed to Charisma Records in the UK. All of us loved Monty Python – we could quote bits at each other till we were blue in the face. So when Nancy Lewis, the Buddha Records PR, arranged for us to meet John Cleese while we were in Manhattan, it seemed quite a cool thing.

The record execs weren't the only ones who didn't know what to make of us.

One evening we appeared on American TV to perform 'Watchers' and were introduced by Steve Miller, the cool American blues guitarist who was about to have his biggest hit with 'The Joker'. Pete wore his usual costume – cape, bat-wings, UV eye makeup – and you could see that Steve Miller was totally lost.

When we played live, American audiences, like the ones back at home, would be split. Half of them would be fascinated: we were like a bizarre circus coming to town and they couldn't keep away. The other half would shout 'Boogie!' or 'Rock and roll!' whenever we got to a long acoustic section. It was annoying – it only took one voice to completely ruin the atmosphere.

We were playing Princeton University one night and, unusually for me, I'd had a joint before the show. Pete was telling one of his stories in a gap between songs so it was all a bit chilled out, a bit hushed, and somehow or other I just nodded off. That was the thing about sitting down to play: it was technically possible to fall asleep. I came round after a moment or two and looked about to see if anybody had clocked me – no one had – but I had come pretty close to just falling off my stool.

I was determined to pack in as much of America as I could.

Tony, Pete and I were good tourists, Steve perhaps less so, and Phil was interested when he could be bothered to get up. On every day off, we'd hire a couple of cars, put the tops down, turn the music up and speed off somewhere.

One afternoon in Florida, Pete and I went to visit a place we'd heard about that was funded by some West Coast hippies who were researching dolphins. Pete and I wanted to play some music to them – the dolphins, not the hippies – so off we went, me with my guitar, Pete with his flute.

It didn't feel odd at the time. After all, in our first summer as a band we'd often played outside, sitting in a circle in someone's garden, although I don't know how the dolphins felt about it. They lasted the day at least. But the thing that did feel weird was seeing these beautiful creatures in their tiny concrete pools just a few yards away from the lovely, blue, open ocean: I came away feeling that the hippies hadn't quite thought that one through.

On another occasion we were due to play in Mississippi and Louisiana, but when the dates were pulled, Rich, Tony, Margaret and I decided we'd drive down to New Orleans anyway. It's a unique place: the jazz clubs, the narrow streets with the balconies hanging over them. It has a darkness to it, an exciting edge. While I was there I also tried oysters for the first time, having heard about their aphrodisiacal powers: I ate twenty-five of them and then threw up. The Russian chocolate incident had obviously taught me nothing.

But perhaps our best road trip was when Tony, Margaret, Steve and I decided to check out the Grand Canyon and Vegas en route to LA. Pete had flown on ahead but the rest of us hired cars, booked a Travelodge and set off.

Having got to the Grand Canyon we decided we'd do it properly and hire mules to take us right down to the bottom. Steve stayed at the top – he was even less adventurous than Tony, if that's possible – but Tony came down with Margaret, despite having a fear of heights and being less than au fait with his mule. I've got an album full of photos of beautiful Californian scenery, with Tony looking unhappy in the foreground.

That evening we drove into Vegas, which, in those days, was extremely seedy. I've always quite liked gambling and hit a winning streak at the Dunes, but there was definitely an edge in the air: you half expected to be escorted out with a gun to your head. It all made for a kind of Rat Pack charm, though.

The West Coast was one thing, but arriving in the South felt like arriving from Mars. We probably looked like aliens to the locals in our velvet flairs, with Pete in his black jumpsuit and his hair shorn down the middle. Even off stage there was always a definite 'What the fuck? Goddamn hippies!' reaction from the police whenever we got stopped – which, in my case, happened often. It took me some time to realize that the speeding laws were different in different states. I'd just about worked it out when, in 1974, a flat 55 mph limit was introduced. When you were trying to drive across America on huge, dead-straight highways in the middle of the desert, this was a joke.

As time went by I developed a bit of a spiel that I would deliver every time I was pulled over: it was the first time I've ever been in America, the cars were just so good, I hadn't realized how fast I was going and so on. Plus, the accent helped. To their ears, you only had to open your mouth to sound sorry.

These occasions were also when I discovered the wisdom of one of the few bits of advice my father ever gave me: ask for someone's name in a sticky situation and always write it down if you can, as it changes the power dynamic. I've often used that tactic when I've had trouble with unhelpful customer, service departments. Nevertheless, I regularly had to backtrack by a couple of counties to pay a speeding fine: 'You gotta go back and see the judge in Gainesville' is a phrase that particularly lives in the memory. And America isn't short of Gainesvilles.

★ ★ ★

Just before the war, my father had also visited New York. Like me, he was impressed by the food:

> a roast beef sandwich at 'Jimmy Kelly's' . . . a many layered affair tackled with knife and fork and very different from the dreary ones wilting under glass on English railway buffets.

This was in 1939, but English food in 1974 was still pretty basic, even if you weren't eating in a railway buffet. My memories of the time seem to be mostly of Berni Inns, Berni Irish coffee (10p with whiskey and cream) and Berni gammon steaks. American food – pastrami, gherkins – was a revelation.

Dad had come to America from Australia, where he'd been the Gunnery Officer of HMAS *Sydney*. When his relief arrived, after he'd been promoted to Lieutenant-Commander, he was given the chance to travel back to England via the Pacific, Canada and America for $50.

My father left Sydney in a heatwave of 48°C in the shade;

by the time he'd sailed up the Pacific to Canada and joined the Canadian Pacific transcontinental railroad, it was -16°C.

On our first platform stroll, a friendly Canadian asked if we were English, saying that he thought so as our ears were obviously freezing which he could tell as they were drooping like tired flowers. At the next stop we bought ear muffs.

At the same stop we found the international boundary post between Canada and America in the middle of the platform and crossed and re-crossed from country to country twenty-four times before the whistle blew.

Arriving in New York, my father visited the Empire State Building, the Rockefeller Centre and Harlem. Then, when his Cunard liner home to England was cancelled, he was offered an upgrade: a premium cabin on the Queen Mary.

The first class passenger list read like a mixture of Debrett's and Who's Who, some names carrying the additional information that the personage was accompanied by a manservant or personal maid.

An E. M. Wagner, 'bon-viveur and epicure', also kindly introduced Dad to 'snails, frog's legs, caviar, plover's eggs and many other delicacies against a backdrop of carefully chosen wine'.

Five days later, my father arrived back in England and a country rearming for war.

I'd often think, as the band set off on tour, that Dad must have felt the same buzz, the same sense of adventure that I did every time he sailed off somewhere new. You'd try to pretend touring was work, just part of the job, but the excitement was intoxicating: I never did understand bands who said that it was all such a big drag.

The downside was that England always seemed so far behind to me, coming back from America. Everything was better and less expensive there, Americans were naturally get-up-and-go positive, which I liked, and success wasn't a bad thing, whereas in England people only liked you if you were struggling. Added to that, in the UK we were originally thought of as public school-boys; in America they weren't really interested in that kind of thing.

Perhaps the biggest thing for me, though, was that in America you'd hear rock on the radio all the time and in cars all day long. I used to have a little tape recorder that I would just leave on for half an hour and the range of music would be fantastic. I've still got some of those tapes. Even the sound of the radio was better: English radio at that time was still very flat, whereas every American station would have a compressor, which they'd crank up. It would automatically make what you were hearing more exciting.

I would come back from every American tour full of energy: confident, charged up, on top of the world and feeling a bit all-powerful, thinking I could get away with anything . . .

Dad always told me if ever I was in trouble I could call him, whatever it was, and I usually felt I could. But there's trouble . . . and then there's being busted at Heathrow Airport with a huge bag of grass nearly a foot square. I didn't call him, naturally, partly because I didn't want to cause him any worry, and partly because I just felt stupid at getting caught.

It wasn't that I'd forgotten I had drugs in my suitcase. The grass in America was much better quality than anything I'd had in England and I'd wanted to bring some back. It was more that, having just finished a tour, I was feeling a bit invincible and couldn't for the life of me imagine anything going wrong. Then the customs officers asked me to open my bag.

My initial reaction was to deny the grass was mine and insist that I had no idea how it got there, but given that the package was nestling between my socks, and given that the officers were glaring at me doubtfully already, I decided I had no choice but to own up.

Strange as it seems, I still wasn't worried at this stage. Even when I was arrested by the two young police officers it was hard to take them seriously. Walking from the airport to the car, you could almost see them thinking: 'Hey up! We've got a live one here, Bob! First blood!' They sort of bounced.

It was only when I was charged with possession and flung into a cell at Hounslow Police Station that I came to my senses.

I had a night to contemplate my actions, looking at the dreadful graffiti and scratchings on the walls, imagining the guys who'd been there before me – by the morning I was convinced that this would be my future and I was a lifer. It was so depressing and claustrophobic I vowed I'd never end up behind bars again (although at this point I was still wondering if I'd ever get out).

I was allowed one phone call the next morning and there was no way I was going to call my father. Instead I called Charisma, who fortunately sent a lawyer to get me out before anyone forgot about me and threw away the key.

The drugs laws were much stricter in the early seventies.

There was no differentiation between whether you were in possession of drugs for personal use or whether you were going to sell them – but to my relief I got bail. However, when I left court a couple of weeks later with a fine, I still wasn't out of the woods. Quite the opposite. With a criminal record, getting a visa to travel to America would now be impossible. I would have to leave the band.

But while the drugs laws were stricter in the early seventies, global security was laxer. In fact, it didn't really exist. This meant that when I filled in the visa form I would simply write 'No' to the question: 'Do you have a criminal record?'

Over the years, I must have developed quite a convincing poker face.

★ ★ ★

I've always thought that politics and music should be separate. If you bang people on the head lyrically, it's not as effective as making suggestions and painting pictures. Protest songs have rarely worked for me. Although our fourth album, *Selling England by the Pound*, had a Labour Party slogan as its title and was partly about increasing commercialization and the sense that something was being lost, our music was still more about moods and atmospheres. Perhaps that's why we've always connected well with northern, industrial towns. You might think we would be university-town material, with our thinking man's lyrics, but in fact it was the towns with industrial histories – Bradford, Leeds, Hull, Halifax – who took to us most. I often felt our music was a form of escapism.

The album was difficult to write because *Foxtrot* had been so successful. We wrote *Selling England* in Chessington, in the big, old country house of a doctor. There was a massive oak tree in the garden outside the window – the leaves hanging down, the boughs sagging – and every time I saw it, I had a little moment of recognition. It seemed to be a mirror of how it felt to be making the record.

Our songwriting methods had come on since *Foxtrot*. Instead of writing bits and joining them together, we were now writing more out of improvisations and group jams. The trouble with *Selling England* is that the jams never really fired up. When you'd jammed all afternoon and you'd got nowhere, it'd get a bit demoralizing. Which is probably why I spent so long staring out of the window at that bloody tree.

Selling England wasn't my favourite album but 'The Cinema Show' was a real standout moment. The second half of the song was the start of a new phase between me and Tony. The rhythm was 7/8, which feels different but doesn't sound clever–clever. I'm moving around chords, Tony's reacting and improvising over them, and between the two of us we're coming up with something that would go on to be the essence of the Genesis sound for the next twenty years. And the drumming's great, too.

When we played the song live, Pete and Steve would leave the stage at the end so it was just me, Tony and Phil. It was so strong and it was just the three of us. Although I wasn't conscious of it at the time, I think that must have been something I stored away in my memory: the knowledge of what the three of us could do.

'More Fool Me' was a song that Phil and I wrote, and which Phil would sing on stage. It was the first thing Phil and I had written together, and although Phil had come into the band with no desire to write, it felt easy, intuitive. Nothing was ever laboured with Phil: he'd work fast, he'd write fast, he'd record fast. He was completely opposite to the rest of us. The first time Phil came out front from behind his drum kit to sing, he put on a white jacket which, because he was wearing white dungarees, made him look like a painter, but from the word go people liked him. Before he even sang a note, people cheered.

God knows how, but we also ending up writing a hit single, 'I Know What I Like (In Your Wardrobe)', which got to number 17. Suddenly – only four years late – *Top of the Pops* came knocking.

We turned them down, of course: we were an album band, not a singles band, and there was no crossover at all in that era. *Top of the Pops* was for singles bands like Mud, Sweet, Pickettywitch and all that kind of sugary stuff. It would have felt so wrong for us to have appeared with Pan's People prancing about in the background. We didn't mind the track being played, but we didn't want to go on TV and look cheesy.

Strat freaked out, poor guy. It was our one chance to sell records, to get known, and what did we do? I think my parents might have liked us to appear too, although Mum made the best of it: 'Mikey's been on *Top of the Pops* – nearly!'

★ ★ ★

In 1974 we played *The Lamb Lies Down on Broadway* at Wembley Arena. Seeing as it was a respectable venue I decided to invite my parents along. Angie was back from Milan for a few weeks, so I thought it would be a good idea for her to come and accompany them. She hadn't seen us since we were the warm-up act for the warm-up act. When my parents arrived in the lobby they were dressed as if they were going to the Opera House: my mother in sequins, my father black tie. Angie didn't have to look too hard to find them amongst the mêlée of Afghan coats, though I think it was the sight of my mother clutching virtually everything she could buy from the merchandising shop that caught her eye. (I suppose it's just something only a mother would do.) Having taken their seats, my mother had made sure that most of the rows in front and behind knew who she was, pointing to my photos in the programme in case they didn't know who I was. Pete's grand entrance was to crawl through a phallic symbol, which started from the back of the stage and ended up right at the front. My father adjusted his ear plugs and settled back in his seat, only to be targeted by a thirty-foot inflatable penis.

By the time we were touring *Selling England*, we were mostly playing theatres, which suited us. We always did better in them: the old, fading velvet seats with cigarette burns in them had an atmosphere that matched our music. Plus, people were sitting down in seats, which made a big difference from our point of view. Unlike in the early days of our career, they couldn't just bugger off in the quiet bits.

We had wanted to go further with our staging and it was our production manager, Adrian Selby, who had helped take us to the next level.

Adrian was a friend of a Charterhouse friend: big-faced, big-boned, big-bodied, blustering . . . but in a nice way. And quite fearless, too: he could blag like anything, which is how he'd ended up with us. He came somewhere with us once, just to help out, and then suddenly he was running the show. He was just making it up as he went along, and you always felt he was thinking, 'Phew! Got away with that!' Which he did. He even got away with organizing one of our American tours and keeping no receipts. The taxman was after us for years after that.

We were about to play the Rainbow Theatre in Finsbury Park when Adrian suggested that we buy a massive gauze curtain to form a backdrop to the stage and illuminate it with twelve UV lights. It sounds like nothing now but it was pretty revolutionary at the time. Suddenly, we'd created a platform. It was a slightly ghostly, surreal setting that showcased our songs, and it was definitely more atmospheric than staring at great big Marshall stacks, especially with Pete's UV-sensitive eye makeup glowing in the light.

For me, it was a special gig for another reason – along with the Marquee Club, playing the Rainbow Theatre had been one of my ambitions since I'd seen Jimi Hendrix there in 1967. He'd been on a bill with the Walker Brothers, Cat Stevens and Engelbert Humperdinck. Peculiar combinations like that would turn up all the time back then.

The *Selling England* set consisted of big, weirdly curved screens and we also had explosive flashboxes for the end of the show. Pete, however, decided he'd add a bit of extra drama by flying up from the stage on wires at the end of 'Supper's Ready' – which, given that performing 'Supper's Ready' was already a drama in itself, probably wasn't the best idea. I would often see chaos out of the corner of my eye as Pete went backstage to do his costume change mid-song. It was always touch-and-go whether he'd make it back out in time.

Once we were committed to an idea, we saw it through no

matter what. That night at the Rainbow, we dutifully pressed on, the epic finale came, all the explosions went off, Pete cast his black cloak to the ground and up he soared, singing away. Fine – except that what then happened was his wires began slowly, slowly crossing. Very gradually he was being spun round to face the wrong way, leaving the audience to stare at his back.

Pete spent the rest of the song trying to sing and twist round at the same time. I know because from where I was standing all I could see were his feet paddling in mid-air.

★ ★ ★

Tony Smith was a big guy with a big beard that made you think of Father Christmas. He'd worked in concert promotion alongside his father and had promoted tours for the Rolling Stones, the Who and Led Zeppelin. He'd first seen Genesis on the Six Bob Tour, which he'd worked on with Strat, but he now realized that we could really do with some help from someone who knew what they were doing.

The final straw was one night in Glasgow when we played Green's Playhouse. We'd played there before, a gig I remember mostly because of the absolutely deafening silence that followed our first song. The stage was high at Green's – this being Glasgow on a Saturday night, you had to be out of reach – and, looking down on the silent crowd, you could just hear a nation deciding: 'Do we like them? Are they crap?'

After about a decade of silence – I exaggerate only slightly – everyone went completely mad: they loved us. But it did occur to me that it would have only taken one drunken 'Fuck off! Rubbish!' and the bottles would have been flying.

No one needed to bottle us off the second time we played Green's because we never got on. Adrian Selby was in charge that night, 'charge' being the word: every single truss on stage was live. There was no way we could have played without electrocuting ourselves. Tony Smith, who was promoting the gig, obviously felt sorry for us because a few days later he agreed to meet us at the office he shared with Harvey Goldsmith on Wigmore Street.

Smith is someone who has the ability to calculate exactly how many people there are in an audience or how many ticket stubs a box office has collected with a single glance: his eyes will take a snapshot and the degree of accuracy will be uncanny. He was always quite direct, but when we asked him to manage us he took his time. 'I think I'm prepared to give it a try,' he said eventually.

He then worked out we were £400,000 in debt to Charisma. No wonder he was hedging his bets.

We never really knew how we were doing financially because to us Charisma was a bank: we understood that they were lending us money against future earnings, but as long as we got our wages and could play our music we were happy. None of us even handled cash. Rich, our road manager until this point, would get the per diem – what bands call their living allowance – keep our receipts, go back to the office and return with more funds. The rest of us wouldn't give it much thought.

That's probably why Gail Colson and Fred Munt thought we were a waste of time, actually – they saw the money going out and nothing coming back in. And it was a lot of money going out, too. Although all the bands on Charisma had overheads, they were nothing like ours. Now that we'd developed our stage production and set, we were very protective of it, and so when we started touring America, we refused to support other bands. Our thinking had been that as long we were the only act on a bill, we would have complete control over our own lights and show. What we didn't realize was that (a) the support-band role was how you cracked America, and (b) that entirely funding our own shows was losing us a fortune. The more we toured, the more we were getting into debt.

With Smith at the helm the chaos slowly began to recede; it also helped having someone who'd fight our corner. I never saw his temper first-hand but he could put it on if required. Backstage he could be talking to me and then go next door and start screaming down a phone. The record labels were all a bit scared of him – although with us he took a softer line. He'd just say 'It's up to you' in such a way that we knew it wasn't up to us at all.

Now that we were getting an increasingly large crew of our own, my father would often find a way of drawing parallels between his life and mine. In his mind we were like a ship's crew: everyone pulling in the same direction, everyone committed to producing the best result and ensuring that equipment worked, schedules were kept, standards upheld.

And it's true that it did feel like that on the road, surrounded by roadies and technicians. But when it came to making music, Genesis always felt to me more like a Venn diagram: the music came from the place where we interweaved and overlapped. Tony had his feminine Rodgers and Hammerstein chords, Phil and I were the engine room of rhythms, Steve had his original sound. And Pete ranged across all of us.

It was a way of working whereby the goal was shared but each of us would be pulling our own way, trying to get what we wanted. The result would always be a compromise but to me that was fine: that was what being in a band was about. I felt that, as long as you were getting back more than you were giving up, it was okay.

But we all had our limits.

CHAPTER NINE

Headley Grange in East Hampshire was a huge eighteenth-century country house that had fallen on hard times. Then it had Led Zeppelin living in it while they recorded *Physical Graffiti*, which hadn't helped. When Genesis arrived in June 1974 to write *The Lamb Lies Down on Broadway* there were rats everywhere, it was barely furnished and Rich, who'd been down before us to suss it out, said he'd found ropes on one of the beds.

By this point I was living in a flat in Weymouth Street, which runs across Harley Street. I'd left Gay Tom and his silver platforms in Earls Court but Bruce, my other flatmate, I couldn't shake off. We could only afford one bedroom between us so the rota system continued, but Bruce minded sleeping on the sofa less now he knew it was just me in the bed, not Tom and one of his random blokes.

I was first to arrive at Headley Grange and took the nicest bedroom, which had a carpet and an en suite. Then when Tony and Margaret arrived, rather than do the decent thing and offer it to them, I pretended not to notice, so they ended up in a tiny little room up in the roof. (I like to think I'm more generous now, but I did once make Margaret toss for a hotel room in San Sebastian: I'd got a big room with a nice view and Tony and Margaret were overlooking a car park at the back. A straight swap somehow just didn't occur . . .)

The *Selling England* tour had only been finished for two weeks when we all moved into Headley Grange. The tempo of the business was much faster back then and I personally liked the quicker turnover: it made starting on an album less of a big deal. You felt it wouldn't be all over if you made one bad record. Having said that, making *The Lamb* was anything but fast — it often felt like pulling teeth.

Selling England had been our longest album to date, but that had made it sound quiet on record: the longer an album was, the more grooves there would be in the vinyl, making the volume lower. For this reason we'd decided to make our next album a double one; this also had the advantage of allowing us to spread out and get more musical variety on. If we were doing a single album then everything had to sound pretty strong, but with a double album we could experiment with moods and atmosphere. Even on our first album for Jonathan King we'd included short instrumental links between tracks — which, looking back, had been pretty adventurous. On *The Lamb* these evolved into atmospheric jams, which we all loved, particularly Phil. Like all drummers, he loved improvising and never quite got that the rest of still had to play A chords or E chords if A chords and E chords were what we'd written.

The idea of having a concept came later when we thought we might as well give the double album a bit of a story. My idea was to use *The Little Prince* by Antoine de Saint-Exupéry, a book I'd studied in French at school and which I have a fascination with even now. I loved the fact that it was a children's story that was actually for grown-ups and was quite profound. If we had a basic storyline, my thinking went, we could go to town elsewhere. I could see how it would work visually too, with the book's simple graphic cover and illustrations. However, instead of a sensitive, otherworldly blond prince, we ended up with Pete's idea, which involved a greasy Puerto Rican street kid called Rael.

Pete came up with many different versions of the storyline for *The Lamb* and I didn't buy any of them, if I'm honest. It was a journey, really, not a concept, but it never did hang together in my mind. I read the principal version of the story all the way through without making much sense of it at all (as I told Pete). But what was so fantastic about it was the imagery: the lyrics gave you the freedom to jump to the most amazing places musically. The only issue then was whether we'd get to these amazing places and back in time for us to tour in the autumn.

We didn't have huge, noisy rows at Headley Grange. From the start we realized we'd got a big job on our hands and knew we couldn't waste a lot of time arguing. It also became clear very early on that we'd only get the album made if Pete was working on the lyrics full time while the rest of us were working on the music. This bothered Tony more than it bothered me, but Pete's mind was elsewhere. His marriage had been in difficulties and Jill was also pregnant with their first child. This meant that Pete was coming and going a lot, and when he was around there was often a sense that there was something unresolved going on between him and Tony.

When Genesis had started out we'd been two pairs: two guitarists – me and Ant – and two keyboard players, Tony and Pete. Pete wrote on piano but, because of Tony's sensitivities, he wasn't allowed to play it as part of the band – which seems a real shame. Pete wasn't a fast, technical player, he was a feel man, so he and Tony would have complemented each other rather than the reverse.

In some ways, Pete grew up faster than we did. He'd got married very young, which was itself a strain. He and Jill had met as teenagers so they'd both had to go through the painful process of discovering who they were at the same time as being in a relationship. And then when Jill gave birth it was touch and go with the baby. Phil was a father too by now, but Tony and I were too selfish and wrapped up in our careers to understand what Pete was going through. Looking back, we were horribly unsupportive – there was no hint of sympathy for Pete – and nearly losing his daughter must have put the band in perspective. I'm sure he felt then that something would have to change.

William Friedkin, the director of *The Exorcist*, called Pete while we were still working at Headley Grange. He'd read a quirky story that Pete had written, which had been on the back of the *Genesis Live* album (it had been about a woman on a Tube train who unzips her skin) and he now wanted to engage Pete as a writer and ideas man in Hollywood.

Ever since Ant had left, we hadn't been forced to consider a major factor that might disrupt us as a band. When Pete came to tell us about the offer, we were quite prickly. As with Ant, if this moment had happened later in our career I'm sure we could have found a way forward and allowed Pete a few months off. But we still weren't at the stage where we realized that was really feasible and, what's more, we knew we were committed to touring in the autumn.

Pete's the most wonderful bumbler. It often looked like he would never decide on things – but for all his 'ers' and 'ums', he usually knows exactly what he really wants. Eventually, the rest of us began to get a bit fed up with his indecision and gave him an ultimatum, and at that point Pete left the band.

Afterwards, I drove Tony down to the red phone box in the village to discuss the situation with Strat. He always believed he could talk anyone round – 'Pete, dear boy, come and talk to me' – and he probably could have done, too, but Pete wasn't around to be talked to. And after that, strange as it may seem, the rest of us just carried on writing: it was a way of escaping from worrying, of not dealing with the elephant in the room.

We jammed for hours, recording everything we'd played – Phil was the keeper of the cassettes, being a collector by nature – and then listening back to what we'd done each evening. That was how we found the start of 'Carpet Crawl': I was sitting in the kitchen one night drinking beer, playing back one of the jam tapes of the day, and there it was – one of those bits that at the time we hadn't really rated but, with renewed perspective, was potentially quite interesting.

I knew we'd got a great, strong-sounding album, and Pete's leaving had left me feeling completely deflated. The songs had such effective moods: 'Back in New York City', which was aggressive and crude; 'In the Cage', which was claustrophobic and suffocating; 'Fly on a Windshield', which had real size and power. To have written songs like that and then to have lost our singer felt like a real bummer – so when Pete came back three days later the feeling was mainly one of relief.

What had happened was that when Pete had told Friedkin he'd left the band – 'I'm free now!' – Friedkin had put the dampers on it. He liked Genesis and didn't want to break us up, and his plans for a collaboration had also been much vaguer than Pete had realized at the time.

But while Pete's return wasn't something that any of us gloated about, at the same time we knew it would never be the same again. For the first time we felt that someone wasn't pulling in the same direction as the rest of us. It wasn't 'one for all' anymore. We didn't put it into words but there was a feeling that, if Pete wasn't into the group in the same way as we were, something fundamental had changed.

The most pressing issue, however, was that we were now incredibly behind schedule. The music was on course and we even had a recording date booked, but Pete's lyrics were nowhere near ready. Things got so bad that Pete eventually had to ask Tony and me to write the lyrics to 'The Light Dies Down on Broadway'. He gave us a brief so what we produced was much less flowery than our usual style, and I felt it ended up being quite in keeping with the album. Obviously, it was a token contribution, but at least we could feel we'd done a song and wouldn't have to live with an album that had 'All words by Peter Gabriel' written on it.

Having finished writing the music, the next stage was to record, which we did in a converted barn in Wales, the idea being that we'd sound more real in a space like that than in a sound-proofed studio. But while it should have been quite an idyllic country interlude, having to hang around for days waiting for Pete's lyrics just left us irritated. By the time we came to mix the album in London, we were so far behind schedule that John Burns, the producer, had to work round the clock.

Island Studios was a converted church in All Saints Road in Notting Hill. There were two studios: a nice big one upstairs and a cheap, depressing one downstairs with chocolate-brown shag-pile on the walls. We weren't upstairs.

In those moments when you're up against it, I think anything is allowed. For example, letting Steve doze off while he was holding a full polystyrene cup of coffee. Not very nice for Steve, but funny for us at the time.

When Pete finally got round to recording his vocals he brought in Brian Eno, whom I'd seen at Roxy Music's first ever gig, to work on them. Eno didn't make a huge difference as far as I could tell – it was just a case of taking a few vocals and wobbling them around – but because he had a reputation for doing odd stuff on synthesizers, people tend to think Eno did much of the keyboard work on *The Lamb*. That annoys Tony to this day. He'll be asked about it and his face will drop.

It was now October 1974 and, somehow, we'd managed to finish the record in time to make our touring commitments. We couldn't believe we'd actually done it, we were going to make it . . . and then Steve cut his hand and the tour was put back by a few weeks.

Steve said he'd crushed a glass in a fit of stress, which I never bought, but at that point I decided I needed some time out too . . .

★ ★ ★

The Surrendell commune near Bath was a bit of a scam. It was for people who wanted to say they were in a commune, getting back to nature, but couldn't face going up to Findhorn in northern Scotland and dealing with that.

Rich had been to Findhorn and he'd also been the one responsible for an earlier macrobiotic phase I'd been through. I was mainly doing it to be part of the in-crowd, the peace–love–man brigade, but Rich was completely dedicated and would even bring a little Primus stove on tour with him for the nights when we'd smoked a bit of grass and got the munchies. Without Rich, I would probably have been ordering out for hamburgers but, given that he was my roommate given that he seemed quite happy to start making brown rice and tahini at three in the morning, I wasn't about to stop him. We'd be in a Holiday Inn somewhere in Texas and he'd unpack his rucksack, lay out his stove and supplies at the bottom of the bed, then start chopping carrots. As we'd both be stoned, it'd be a health and safety nightmare.

Being macrobiotic in America was reasonable enough, and in California the macrobiotic restaurants were good – outdoors, with bamboo fences round the seating area so that you could look out at the ocean as you ate. But then back to England I found myself eating in basements off Ladbroke Grove. There'd always be a burning smell where the material hung over the lamps was starting to catch, and the food was so heavy I would have a job getting back up the stairs to the street afterwards.

I'm not a commune kind of guy, basically, but Surrendell wasn't a commune kind of commune: Princess Margaret and Helen Mirren had stayed there and, although I never saw them, I did see Roddy Llewellyn, who had a pleasant aura. You drank elderflower wine, not beer, which says it all, really. There was a bit of digging in the garden, a bit of building log fires in the evenings, some nice vegetables to eat . . . It wasn't a bad way of killing time, all things considered, but after a few days the cold began to get to me: the cold gets to you in the end in all these places. I stuck it out for a week and then went back to my flat in Weymouth Street, where the heat came free with the rent so it never went off.

★ ★ ★

The Lamb has been viewed as one of our best albums. It's interesting, but I prefer *Foxtrot*. On *The Lamb* the need to tell the story meant that we had to include some sections that worked less well live. Because it was a concept album, however, we couldn't just ditch the weak bits when we took it on the road: we were stuck playing the whole thing. That in itself was a challenge; even more of a challenge was touring it round America before the album had been released.

Considering that we were breaking the number-one rule of touring, the crowd reaction was pretty good – but God, it was uphill.

I think it was Tony Smith's idea for us to save some money by touring *The Lamb* round the US in two beat-up limos. They were definitely back-end-of-the-fleeters: a bit knocked-around looking, the suspension a bit shot. They were also driven by two characters called Joe and Joe, who'd only got half a sense of direction between them.

Joe and Joe were from Buffalo (honestly) and came via another character named Harvey Weinstein. Before founding Miramax and going into movies, Harvey and his brother Bob had a pretty successful business producing concerts, although how they'd managed that with Joe and Joe on their books is anyone's guess. Joe and Joe knew Buffalo like the back of their hand – the rest of the United States was a mystery.

As a band, we didn't do tour buses: we'd tried it once in Italy and nearly killed each other. Buses are defined by the slowest common denominator and, apart from Tony, time-keeping wasn't a strong point, so we would always be late.

My father was the kind of man who would always be looking at his pocket watch even if he didn't have anything planned. I think it gave him his bearings. After his retirement he'd go to London once a week, either to his club or for a consultancy meeting, and always on the 10:10 a.m. train. If he arrived at the station early, he'd let an earlier train pass, waiting for his sched-uled train. My approach was a bit more . . . relaxed. I thought that being within half an hour of an agreed appointment was acceptable but, of course, that annoyed Tony, who'd always be in the hotel lobby on the dot, pacing. And Pete would be nowhere to be seen: he'd be off, doing stuff.

Things would come into Pete's life and he'd get drawn to them. It's the same to this day. People would tell him to visit a certain place or see a certain thing while he was in town and instead of getting up early, he'd realize an hour before we were due to leave that he hadn't done it yet, nip out and not be seen again for ages. Pete always went with the flow more than Tony or me. Even at the cottage in Dorking I'd recognized that, and it was one of the things I admired most about him. He could change, he wasn't stuck in a rut, he had an imaginative freedom. But it could be bloody annoying when you were sitting around waiting for him to materialize.

After the Italy debacle we decided that touring in hire cars was the way forward – it also meant that we could do all the sightseeing we wanted – but even that wasn't foolproof. One of our roadies once left an Avis rental car in a car park in the wrong town somewhere in California, and we only realized what he'd done six months later when the bill arrived.

The drive with Joe and Joe from the hotel to the venue was a little mountain to climb in every town, every day. All you could do was sit back and put your feet up, smoke some grass and drink Southern Comfort, and that would almost dull the agony.

★ ★ ★

For me, the States had lost none of their magic (even if we weren't always in the bit of them that we should have been). I loved the way that every city you drove towards you could see from a distance, with the skyscrapers coming over the horizon. But it was also impossible not to sense the other thing on the horizon: the raincloud that had been developing ever since Pete had temporarily left at Headley Grange. Even as we were setting off for America, I thought, 'We'll do the tour and then see what happens . . .' As it turned out, I didn't have to wait that long.

We were in Cleveland, Ohio, when Pete told us he was leaving the band for good. We were six dates into a six-month long tour.

He explained things to us pretty simply. He was leaving but he'd honour all our touring commitments. And he also kindly agreed that he wouldn't announce he was leaving until the dust had settled and we'd all thought about what we were going to do.

Because we'd had this moment before at Headley Grange, Pete's news didn't exactly come out of the blue, but that didn't mean it wasn't a bombshell. It was a bright, sunny day when it happened, and walking back from the meeting to my motel room felt weird, flat. I felt like it should have been grey and pouring with rain.

Over the next few days, when I was alone with Pete, he'd try to explain it a bit better. 'I hope you understand what I'm doing,' he'd say, and the thing was, I realized I did.

I'd known at the time that *The Lamb* couldn't be a precedent for future albums. Not only had making a double album worn us down, having Pete write almost all the lyrics had made the whole thing less enjoyable. On the other hand, I could see why he wouldn't want to go back to sharing them out between us: Tony and I were writing about aliens, Pete was writing things like 'Fly on a Windshield': 'Lenny Bruce declares a truce and plays his other hand / Marshall McLuhan, casual viewin', head buried in the sand.' Pete was such a strong lyricist and loved the writing side so much that he would never have wanted to go back to our old way of working.

Pete often showed emotion in his face, in his eyes. When an idea started to take hold of him you'd see a small smile start to appear as he tried to convince you that he'd thought of a good idea – whether it was a song or a detour he wanted to take while you were driving. If you said no, he'd always take it with good humour, but you knew the smile would creep back sooner or later – he wouldn't give up.

Talking with him now he had his old, pained expression back: his worried schoolboy look, those furrowed eyebrows. I knew he was torn. He'd had chats with Smith long into the night and Tony had tried hard to persuade him to keep going: Pete was still his mate and they went so far back together. But it was different for me. I've always thought that if someone doesn't want to be where they are, I wouldn't want them to be there either. The worst thing is when someone doesn't share your enthusiasm for what you're doing anymore: the fun just goes out of it.

I remember Pete saying, 'I think you should carry on.' It probably just made him feel better to say it but I think we knew, however hard it'd be, we'd try anyway. In terms of what the way forward might look like, I had no idea but, now that we knew where we stood, I didn't see the point in torturing myself about it. I react funnily to bad news: I worry about situations in advance, but if something's already happened and you can't do much about it, I move on pretty fast.

None of which made me any less sad at losing Pete, obviously. We'd shared such wonderful times and, although we were all still friends, I knew we'd never be as close again. But we also still had two-thirds of a tour left and what were we going to do – be miserable for the next six months?

★ ★ ★

Regis Boff – not quite as good a name as Rivers Job, but nearly – was like a big bear, only from Pittsburgh. He was our tour manager on *The Lamb*. He was, however, not the kind of guy you should play tricks on.

(Knock knock.)

Regis: Who's there?

Me: Police. Open up.

Regis (furiously flushing toilet): I'm coming, sir! Wait a minute! (More toilet flushing.)

Me: No, no, wait! Regis, it's Mike! Don't do that!

Regis: Just coming, sir! Wait a moment . . .

Me: No, really, Regis, it's me! It's Mike! Stop!

Too late. Regis had flushed his stash. Even for a bear he managed to look extremely pissed off about it.

One of Regis's duties was to carry a bottle of eye-drops with him which, when Phil and I had had a good evening, he'd use to get us looking a bit less bleary and red-eyed the next day.

This worked fine for the two of us but our lighting operator, Les Adey, was beyond hope. Les was like a character from a *Comic Strip* sketch: he was constantly stoned, his eyes like saucers in his head and, unfortunately for me, he was also now my roommate.

Rich had stepped down as our tour manager the previous year after realizing that we'd reached a stage where being managed by a mate wasn't really practical. He was always very intuitive and I think he knew his time had been and gone, but we all missed his energy hugely. And, obviously, I missed his late-night brown rice. Now, instead of Rich and his Primus stove, I had Les Adey and his enormous spliffs. Every morning I would see him wake up, roll over and reach for a smoke, which got a bit much in the end.

Les functioned pretty well – just sometimes you'd see his hands shake when he went for a fader – and he also wrote and quoted poetry endlessly. He was a very bright guy, although he could talk himself silly. But there were also moments when he was so out of it that I would really wish he'd just get it together – for example, when we were about to be searched by border guards on the American-Canadian border.

Canada was very free and hippyish in 1974; America wasn't. At the crossing in Toronto there were two small buildings that you drove into, doors would come down behind and then, once you were shut in, you'd be searched for hours.

Knowing what to expect from past experience I made sure to throw my hash out of the window well before we rolled up in our black limos but Les, who was in the same car as Regis and me, was so stoned he'd forgotten where he'd hidden his. Regis and I watched in horror as he started patting himself all over in a thoughtful way as the guards looked on. Pat pat pat. Pause. Other pocket. Pat pat pat. Pause. Regis's face had no colour left in it at all when Les finally started beaming: he'd hit the jackpot.

Why the cops let us off, I don't know – entertainment value, probably – but it was all a bit different to my father's experience of stepping freely back and forwards over the Canadian border twenty-four times in a minute.

Halifax in Canada was a place my father got to know well during the Second World War. His first trip there in September 1939 was on board a ship carrying one million pounds of gold bullion, and after that he joined the North Atlantic Escort Force, which provided escorts for mercantile and troop convoys.

He'd also enjoyed the Canadian hospitality. Local hotels were dry but:

> it was legal to book a room in which to consume our own liquor, the hotel providing glasses, crushed ice and ginger ale . . . if the dining room was raided, hard liquor on the table was unwise but the police would not probe too deeply a bottle coyly stashed round the ankles.

Our tour drinks for *The Lamb* were Southern Comfort and Blue Nun wine. At every hotel we stayed in, a bath would be filled with ice, the bottles put in, and then the lot steadily consumed with predictable consequences. The night I ended up drunk and blindfolded with no trousers on at 2 a.m. in Pittsburgh was one example, although I don't remember what the blindfold was for. Anyway, I was still wearing it when a girl tried to shut the sliding bathroom door in my hotel room while my finger was in the way. She just couldn't understand it: why wouldn't it go? What was making it stick? Clearly the only thing for it was to slam it very hard.

Crack.

It was my left hand, second finger: my fretboard hand.

The party ground to a halt and Regis, who had been having just as much fun as me, managed to sober up enough to take me to the general hospital in Pittsburgh. Once there I also straightened up pretty quickly: the noise and commotion was deafening, with people shouting, heaving and screaming, and weirdos off the street vomiting. Having established that my finger was broken there was nothing much the doctors could do except splint and bandage it, which left me wondering how on earth I was going to play guitar the following day.

I managed it somehow – if you're determined enough, you can find a way to do most things – but my abiding memory of the show was the way that, every time the UV lights came on, my huge white-bandaged finger glowed like a beacon.

★ ★ ★

I never found playing *The Lamb Lies Down on Broadway* particularly satisfying. I felt hemmed in at having to play songs from just one album, particularly when – like 'Here Comes the Supernatural Anaesthetist' and 'The Lamia' – they never connected and would inevitably die a death. For the first time, too, I think we all felt that what Pete was trying to do with the presentation and his costumes was affecting the performance of some songs.

I'd always felt that Pete's best costumes were the ones that tied in to what he was singing: that justified them in my mind. The fox's head had come from the cover of *Foxtrot*, so that was fine by me, and the old-man mask that he had for 'The Musical Box' was obviously the character in the song. (While he was wearing it, Pete would make jerky, geriatric movements round the microphone and it would be incredibly eerie to watch.) But I felt Pete's best costume was the black cloak and orange helmet that he wore for the '666' section of 'Supper's Ready'. It was because it wasn't overly defined – there was nothing that you could put your finger on – that it worked: it was just dark and scary and bizarre. Real theatre.

When it came to *The Lamb*, I could just about defend Pete's grotesque 'The Colony of Slippermen' outfit as it made sense in terms of the lyrics, but the reality was that he couldn't get the microphone near his mouth when he had it on. And during 'The Lamia' he'd be standing in a spinning cone, and he'd get his microphone caught on the edge of the cone, or his costume would catch, or else the whole thing would be going the wrong way.

As far as the press was concerned, however, the costumes were a focal point and increasingly our reviews were focusing less on the music and more on Pete – which was something that bothered Phil most of all. I'm a realist: I could see that there are only so many ways a journalist could write about music. They could talk about the crashing drums, the pounding bass, the whining guitars and the lyrics, but after that, what else is there to say? Writing about costumes and sets is much easier. But Phil was a muso – the music was always the most important thing for him – and both he and Tony would often huff over the reviews.

And yet for all the undercurrents I don't remember feeling that the tour suffered. Pete's decision to leave was something that we could almost put to one side. When you're on tour you can't think beyond the end of it: there's too much work to do in the present to worry what's going to come next. There was sadness, yes, and disappointment, but not animosity. We all even went skiing together – although in retrospect it was a bit stupid to take Les Adey along, too. Pete could ski, Tony and I couldn't, and Les could barely stand in the best of circumstances. We all made it to the top of the mountain and then Pete turned round, gave us a wave – 'Follow me down! Bye!' – and buggered off. No tips, nothing. It must have taken me about half a day to get down that mountain, but I still made it down before Les.

★ ★ ★

Tony Smith had been a bit unsure about *The Lamb* as an album. Nevertheless, when we were on the road, he fully embraced the production – which was just as well because Atlantic didn't get it at all.

While we were touring the smaller American venues, Tony Smith would go back to New York to harangue them into spending money: we had enough of a cult following to keep ticking over but Smith had to work quite hard to keep the whole thing afloat. We were still getting the occasional shout for 'Boogie!', too, which wasn't great.

In Britain we got a better reaction, probably because by now there wasn't a venue left in the country that we hadn't played at least once.

The Lamb was an incredibly ambitious production: as well as Pete's costumes, we also had a backdrop of three screens on which were projected specially shot slides. They never worked properly, these screens – one was always broken or out of synch so that you'd end up with two-thirds of a vista and then some-body's hand – but they were very striking. The whole production was unlike anything else any other band was attempting.

The truth, however, was that *The Lamb Lies Down on Broadway* was not a commercial success. It got to number 10 in the UK and number 41 in America, but we were losing a lot of money on the production. Ironically, if we'd have broken up at this point, the largesse of the Bank of Charisma would have allowed us to walk away debt free.

Smith would always push us to tour more and he'd be clever about it, too. He'd always raise big decisions when there were just five minutes of a meeting to go and he knew we were fading and would say yes to anything just to get out of the room. But you also had to feel sorry for him: it wasn't just that we were in financial difficulties, he'd also only been managing us for a year and we were already just about to be one man down.

In any case, we found ourselves agreeing to go back to Europe for a second stint of touring *The Lamb*, although as it turned out this nearly resulted in the end of Genesis entirely when we blew ourselves up in Oslo.

Like the American power supply, American explosive powder wasn't the same as the European kind: it was about three times stronger. We only found that out when our flashboxes went off at the climax of the encore and it sounded like someone had dropped a bomb. My ears felt like they'd been sucked into my skull, the monitors blew up and there was a piece of the stage missing.

Afterwards, there was a moment of stunned silence and then a little voice piped up from the side of the stage: 'Sorry!' This was a roadie called Peter Hart.

'You're sorry? You're fired!' This was Phil. We were all cross, but Phil was livid. The crowd, meanwhile, had been shocked into utter silence. They all stood there, pale-faced, for the next ten minutes or so, and when they gradually began to file out it remained eerily quiet.

That would have been one way of bowing out, but Pete's final exit was far less dramatic. In fact, we didn't know the show was going to be his last until just before it happened. Smith's plan to claw back some money had backfired and we had to cancel a few dates, with the result that our penultimate date was suddenly our last. Because we didn't find this out until a few hours before, and because Pete couldn't tell the crowd that this was his last show (having agreed with us that it would be a secret for now), the sense of anticlimax was awful.

Afterwards, we all had a few drinks but we didn't want to get drunk and maudlin. I felt dull, rather than depressed, and we were all pretty tired after half a year on the road. The album had never resonated like we'd hoped: it was bizarre and interesting and brave, but it was only later that it would grow to be one of our fans' favourite albums. At the time, most people found it a bit too demanding, a bit much to take in one hit.

Having said that, it probably wasn't a bad thing for Pete or for us that he didn't leave on a high of album sales and rave reviews. The pressure then would have made all our future lives much harder. And perhaps it was a fitting end, too. *The Lamb* had involved more than its share of highs and lows, but the thing that we couldn't deny was that it was an achievement.

CHAPTER TEN

A Trick of the Tail was written in a basement in Acton, Phil's old patch. It was a pretty soulless place – tongue-and-groove pine walls, a threadbare carpet – but sometimes that's what you need when you're writing. In a dead setting, the music can create the images.

Going in to make *A Trick of the Tail* felt to me like the start of an exciting new chapter. I hadn't wanted Pete to leave but I knew we'd been due a change. There's only so long you can carry on productively without shaking things up, and now that he had gone it felt like we were a new band. Our backs were up and we were determined to show the world. I think we all felt a new sense of solidarity – although when we first began work on the album it was as a three-piece. Steve was off working on his first solo record.

Voyage of the Acolyte was a decent album. In fact, Phil and I played on it. I suppose Steve thought he'd ask us because he wouldn't have to pay us (and he didn't). But although we believed in never standing in each other's way, I felt that his timing could definitely have been better: this was a critical point for us and we needed all the ideas we could get. However, as it turned out, those first three days without Steve would set the scene for the next phase of the band.

Writing *The Lamb Lies Down on Broadway* had been like pushing a huge weight uphill, but 'Dance on a Volcano', the first song we wrote for *A Trick of the Tail*, just flowed out. It sounded dark and it sounded big with interesting chords and time signatures: I felt that anyone hearing the intro to that would think it was how Genesis should be going forward. By the time Steve made it back, we'd also written the start of 'Squonk', which was a bit like Led Zeppelin's 'Kashmir', and I knew we were going to be okay. If we could write this sort of stuff, any doubt I had – that any of us had – about carrying on was dispelled.

Seeing our obituary in *Melody Maker* was therefore a bit weird. They'd got hold of the news about Pete before we were ready to announce it ourselves and soon the music press was full of it: 'Gabriel leaves! Genesis to revolution! It's all over!' After that, if you tried to tell people that you'd already got some great new material, they'd just roll their eyes.

Part of the problem was that although we'd always credited the songs to the group, everyone had assumed that they were entirely written by Pete. At the time we'd thought it was a generous and wise move not to have individual credits, but it didn't seem so wise now that most people thought we'd lost the main songwriter in the band as well as our singer.

My parents were worried, too: they read the music papers, as did Jean Granny, who'd take the bus into Farnham from Morris Lodge each week to get *Woman's Weekly* and *Sounds*. (The news-agent would usually mishear her, or else not quite believe that's what she wanted, and she'd usually get given the *Sun* instead. Jean Granny used to get quite offended.)

I felt that it was educative for my parents to read the music press and learn about our world, but the downside was that their perception of how things were going with the band was filtered by the kinds of things that were written about us. That Pete could jump ship – so to speak – was something that made Dad a bit angry too, but he didn't understand artistic things. In his world, if you didn't get on with someone or something wasn't right, you just had to deal with it. Walking away, to him, was unprofessional. But I can remember explaining our 'try it and see' philosophy and after that he felt we were taking a quite sensible and grown-up approach. Plus, the last thing he'd seen of Pete was when he was coming out of a giant penis. Whatever our future held, he knew that at least there wasn't going to be any more of that.

Privately, the question of finding a new singer had been too painful for us to think about since Pete had left: we just didn't go there. Some of the best stuff we were writing for the new album was instrumental, and for a while we thought about keeping it that way. However, we realized that it could get a bit boring without any vocals. But then who would sing them? It seemed an insurmountable problem. Phil could sing, but Phil was the drummer. What to do?

We thought Mick Strickland had the right kind of bluesy voice for us and he also had a low-enough profile to be able to slot into the band. We knew it would have been even more difficult if we were bringing in an image as well as a new face. Mick came in for an audition, but when he tried 'Squonk' it was in completely the wrong key: the poor guy battled through but it was never going to work.

The next day Phil came in with a suggestion. 'Listen, I wouldn't mind giving it a go.' Apparently Andrea, a Canadian girl he'd married in 1975, had encouraged him, but I think it'd been on his mind anyway. 'All right, go on then,' we said. And so he did.

It sounds strange to say now, but Phil's voice then was not the voice it would become. Strat would often be quoted as saying that Phil sounded more like Pete than Pete did, but actually their voices weren't at all similar. It only seemed that way if they were singing the same song, the same Genesis-style melody. What people also tended to forget was that Phil had always sung backing vocals with Pete, so Phil's voice was already familiar – when we played live, what people were hearing was often a combination of the two of them. But the truth was that in 1976 Phil had a pure, choir-boy voice, whereas Pete had an R&B raunch, which was what you needed for a song like 'Squonk'. After a little more unchoir-boy-like living – life on the road, drinking and drugs – Phil got the raunch too, but back then he was still a bit too healthy.

The singing was one thing but the real issue in my mind was whether Phil would contemplate leaving the kit: being the front man definitely wasn't a promotion as far as he was concerned. Drummers generally tend to think singers are the icing on the cake, and not quite the same calibre of musician as everybody else in the band. Even after we'd recorded *A Trick of the Tail* with Phil singing, we weren't sure that he would want to sing on stage or if it would work if he did.

As always there was only one solution: try it and see.

★ ★ ★

It often feels to me as though life in Genesis has fallen into two halves – Pete's years and Phil's years. During Pete's years we were like school kids, fighting our corners, storming around and stomping out. That all changed when Pete left.

It wasn't that Pete wasn't fun – he was – but he was also a big character, and without him there Tony and I found ourselves suddenly needing to be less aggressive, less needing to push to get things to be the way we wanted them. As much as anything it was down to numbers: the less of you there were in the band, the less need there was to score points and the fewer conflicting opinions there'd be. Musically, this also made for a greater sense of cohesion. But Pete's leaving had made us all grow up a bit as people, too, although growing up for Tony and me also meant learning to lighten up a bit.

As Tony and I were ordinarily quite stiff, I always enjoyed making videos. Some bands would treat making a video as though they were making an album but we never took it very seriously. It wasn't as though our performance was going to make a difference. We'd rock up, do what the director told us and cross our fingers. None of the ideas ever sounded so bad at the time, but then you'd see the end results and wonder what on earth any of us had been thinking, like the video for 'A Trick of the Tail', where Phil ended up minimized, hopping around on a piano keyboard.

Our next video, for 'Ripples', was better simply because it couldn't be any worse. Steve, Tony and I seem to be going for a velvet-and-tassels look; Phil is wearing a beanie and may have been making a point. Whatever it was, I'd say it was a good one.

I've been very lucky in my career in having two great front men to hide behind.

Steve had now ditched his black look and took to looking like a cross between a swashbuckling Errol Flynn and Rhett Butler. Tony never did change his look or position once in forty years. If you look at pictures of him on stage, sometimes he'll have his hands out in front of him and sometimes they'll be to either side, but it's essentially the same picture. At least I was now standing up.

I often think how much the guitar maker I asked to chop up my Rickenbacker twelve-string and Rickenbacker bass and stick them together must have hated it. Cutting them up was probably the equivalent of sawing off a limb for him.

I'd taken them into his workshop, put them both on the table and said, 'Can you join them up?'

He looked at me as though I was mad.

'You are joking, aren't you? You've got to be joking. It can't be done.'

When someone says 'It can't be done' to me – to any of us in the band – it's a given that it can and it will be. Sometimes the result wouldn't be quite what you'd hoped: my second doubleneck was made from a Rickenbacker twelve-string and a six-string Microflet bass, which I'd bought in New York and used on *The Lamb*. The bass never sounded quite as good again once I'd had it chopped in half. But the thing about doublenecks was the range they gave me. I'd seen other guitarists with them – Jimmy Page of Led Zeppelin and Rob Townsend of the Family, but they didn't have the range that I had. On stage with my doubleneck I could play bass, twelve-string guitar and bass pedals. Bass pedals went an octave lower than an ordinary bass so they were great for songs like 'Squonk'. People would come out of the gig shaking.

Doublenecks have their downside as well. They're heavy brutes to play and they unbalance you, although I only ever fell off stage once. It was during rehearsals somewhere in the American Midwest and no one realized I was no longer there. I could have killed myself and they would have just carried on playing. 'The Musical Box' had no bass until the pedals at the very end – the middle section was just the low strings of the guitar, filling the bass area in. But as I was lying there flat on my back, pinned to the floor, slightly concussed, I can remember thinking that it would have been nice to have been missed.

★ ★ ★

The *Trick of the Tail* tour began in London, Ontario, on 25 March 1976 – Phil's first show as the lead vocalist. We would always play our first show in the sticks – not that London, Ontario, was really the sticks – and we'd chosen Canada deliberately because there was less history with Pete there than in Europe. Even so, we weren't just worried as we stood backstage, we were shitting ourselves. As was Phil.

In the early sixties, Phil had played the Artful Dodger in a West End production of *Oliver!* and he'd also been an extra in *A Hard Day's Night* and *Chitty Chitty Bang Bang*. We all knew about Phil's stage-school background, but it wasn't something he ever talked about so it had tended to fade from our minds.

Pete had been such a strong figurehead and after so many

years we just couldn't quite imagine how Phil would do it. As soon as he'd made the transition, the history all came back: 'Oh, yes, the Artful Dodger! I remember!' In retrospect it was obvious that he was going to be a success. He came from within the band so there was already love for him from the audience: people were on his side from day one.

On stage, Phil was always a very visual drummer – never flamboyant but very watchable. Even when he tinged his little Chinese cymbals he was a showman. It was noticeable how Pete would always be drawn to standing near Phil on stage, looking over his shoulder to see him perform. But how would Phil translate what he did at the back to the front?

We knew from the start costumes wouldn't be part of it: you only had to look at Phil to realize he wouldn't have been good in a flower mask and, having found a new setting for the band by default, none of us wanted to go back in that respect. Phil only ever dressed up once and that was at a show in Spain when we were playing a bullring: being fascinated by the Alamo, he came out in a cowboy outfit, and you knew the minute he set foot onstage it wasn't going to work. So did he.

But what we didn't know was whether Phil would carry on with Pete's surreal, ghostly stories. He was always more worried about the chat between songs than the singing. So much so that on that first night in Ontario he'd written out pages of A4 notes, reminders of what he was going to say, which I could hear rattling in his hand as he went up to the microphone to say good evening.

I'll always hold that image in my mind: Phil in his T-shirt and long beard and his shaking hand. It was a surreal moment, looking at him in front of me and not having Pete there. An odd moment for everyone. But then you got past it and I can still remember the feeling, after we'd played the first couple of songs, that it was going to be okay. And it was. After that first night he just made up banter as he went along and everybody loved it.

Phil's chat helped us. It lightened the atmosphere between some of our moodier, darker songs. Pete was mysterious and untouchable on stage, which was great, but Phil was always the bloke-next-door to whom you could relate. With Pete's theatrics we never quite knew where we were going. Now the emphasis seemed to be back on the music and us as musicians. Compared to *The Lamb*, I certainly felt a bit more confident on stage now – not that, besides the standing up, anyone watching would have noticed. From now on I would start feeling more comfortable inside myself, more sure of who I was, and my only regret was that I would never again play a whole show with Phil on drums. No one could play drums like Phil – he'd play for the song, not for himself – and I missed that to the end. From the drumming point of view, it was never quite the same again live.

★ ★ ★

When I split up with Debbie 'the dancer' (who happened to be a very good one) my thoughts once again went back to Angie. I was starting to get worried. She was now living with an annoyingly good-looking guy and seemed quite smitten. Fortunately, they had a volatile relationship, so when I saw her after there'd been a blazing row I suggested she come to America with me for a couple of weeks to think things through. To my surprise she agreed. Her boyfriend even dropped her off at my flat. He seemed to be cool about the whole thing, realizing that we were just platonic friends. (My long-term plan belonged to me.) I was trying not to feel insulted that he didn't even see me as some red-blooded rival.

We arrived in Dallas for band rehearsals and checked into the hotel for two weeks. I still didn't feel it was the moment to tell Angie how I felt, and we slept in separate beds. For whatever reason Angie decided not to go home. She hadn't mentioned the boyfriend and stayed with me as we flew up to Canada to begin the tour. I would have thought it would be a difficult transition from 'friend' to 'lover', but somehow it just seemed right one night when we were in New York. (Admittedly, we'd been to a party thrown by Andy Warhol and were both a bit smashed, and our barriers were down.) We finally started sharing the same bed, but unlike Earls Court, this time it was together. Nothing had ever felt so right.

★ ★ ★

Dad never did give me any advice about relationships. I'm not sure how he discovered the facts of life but he was obviously still in the dark as a ten-year-old when his father took him to see a music-hall performance at the London Empire:

> *as we made our way from the dress circle for my interval ginger pop, we crossed the famous promenade behind the circle. I saw many beautiful ladies, exquisitely dressed and usually moving about in pairs. When I asked who they were, my father said that*

they were on holiday. In later years I realized that they were, professionally, very much on the job.

My father always impressed on me the importance of treating women well: always being polite, always pulling out chairs. He was naturally chivalrous, to the extent that during the war uniformed Wrens seem to have been a bit of a shock to him:

I found it odd to be called Sir and have doors opened for me by girls whom I should rightly have been partnering on the tennis court or squiring to dances.

Having said that, he'd always liked my mother's independent spirit. And fortitude. She was:

one of the few people I know to be totally unaffected by a ship's motion however violent. On many occasions in passenger vessels, with the ship standing on her head in rough weather, she was the only person in the saloon at breakfast, leg hooked round the table and ploughing through porridge, fish and eggs, while even the experienced stewards looked a bit wan.

Dad loved a pretty girl and he adored Angie. At family functions he would always seek her out. Angie got my father's dry sense of humour, too. In marrying her I think that Dad thought that I was doing something the right and proper way for once, and I know that he and Mum both enjoyed our wedding in 1976.

I had asked Tony Smith to be best man at my wedding. As

our manager he lived the same life as we did in the band, and if there was a problem we'd always confide in him first before each other. We would always hope that Smith would be able to find a solution and normally he did. He didn't strike me as being the perfect person to organize a stag party, though, but I couldn't see Tony or Phil being up for the best-man role either. As it turned out, Smith wasn't as hopeless as I had feared.

Apparently I spent the night before the wedding at a bar called the Speakeasy, drinking Southern Comfort. I got so drunk I couldn't get the key in the door and ended up slumped on the doorstep until Angie found me the next morning.

I should have realized that the Egyptian honeymoon might not have been as romantic as I'd hoped when I secretly booked the holiday. (*Death on the Nile* hadn't even been shot in Luxor at this point.) The Savoy Hotel didn't live up to its name as we climbed the fire-exit steps to our room, which smelt dank and damp. The single rusty wrought-iron single beds with the lumpy looking mattresses didn't look very appealing either. As for the en suite, the loo was a hole in the floor with an overhead shower. I realized if I didn't take urgent action this marriage might never be consummated. After frantic calls home to our tour travel agent we booked into the Winter Palace Hotel, which had been 'full up'. They now managed to give us the most magnificent suite overlooking the Nile. Things were looking up, and I booked a romantic fishing-boat experience down the Nile that evening. We'd catch our own fish and have them cooked in front of us as the sun set. Angie ended up with dysentery. Her view, for the rest of the holiday, was the black-and-white tile floor in the bathroom. Meanwhile, I was walking around the streets of Luxor in the long kaftan I'd bought in the souk, with open toe sandals, my long hair and beard. I thought I was being followed because they hadn't seen many tourists before. When the name Jesus was being banded about I then realized I had my very own disciples. Mum knew it was only a matter of time.

* * *

Getting married was one landmark, buying my first house was another. It was in Courtnell Street in Notting Hill Gate, which wasn't the area it is now. Courtnell Street itself was okay but the street behind it was a war zone for local drug dealers. I had £4,000 in the bank and got a mortgage – God knows how – for £25,000.

More than anything else I had achieved, it was buying a house that impressed Dad. He hadn't owned a house until he was fifty and a father of two: I was twenty-seven. For my parents it validated their support, and I think it was also a relief to them in terms of the innuendo they'd had to take from aunts and cousins: 'Poor Mikey, what a shame after that education.' 'When's Mike going to get a proper job?' My parents would always defend me, 'Oh, no, he's artistic', but I think they had to be quite strong to keep up the impression that they weren't bothered.

I think Dad was also proud about my ability to do little things around the house, like change a fuse. For all his engineering training he could just about change a light bulb, but change a plug? No chance. Domestic life was another world to him. When Mum, Nicky and I used to stay at Morris Lodge while Dad was still working at Hawker Siddeley, Mum would always leave him a list of instructions: get the coal in (a job we all hated); feed the dog (the dog got proper meat, never canned and, being a spaniel, would always get its ears pegged behind its head with a clothes peg before it ate to stop them getting in the gravy). We came back after one holiday and Dad told us that he'd been getting his dinner and the dog's one night and realized it'd been a toss-up as to which one looked most appetizing.

After a life in official quarters being attended to by a batman, household chores must have been quite bizarre for my father. Neither he nor my mother ever really got into domestic life: both of their homes, Far Hills and Hill Cottage, stayed exactly as they were when they moved in. 'Homes' isn't even the right word: wherever they lived, there was always a sense of transience about the place. Maybe that's why one of my first jobs after we'd moved into Courtnell Street was to repaint. I knew Angie and I wouldn't be there forever, but I was still going to make it ours.

CHAPTER ELEVEN

1977 was the year of punk: it was everywhere. Or it was supposed to be. When you're on tour for seven months out of twelve – as we were that year – quite a lot things pass you by. As far as I was concerned, punk was one of those things: I didn't feel I was really around for it.

Phil's line about punk was always 'shaking the tree': seeing which old bands dropped off and disappeared when you gave them a bit of a shove. Inasmuch as it affected me, I felt the same. I knew punk was in part a reaction to bands like us – the big and grand – and I did like the DIY ethos it brought back. It reminded me of how we'd started in Brian Roberts's attic in the Easter holidays. But I also felt that if you were good enough, what had you got to worry about? And I felt we were good enough. Plus, I liked what we were doing as a band.

Wind & Wuthering was recorded in three weeks while we were staying in a little dormer-windowed house in the Netherlands. This house was in the middle of nowhere and we'd have breakfast in the morning, drive the fifteen minutes to the Relight Studio, shut the door and come out at midnight, by which time the few bars there were had closed. You can get a lot done in three weeks when it's like that.

I'd read *Wuthering Heights* at school and I'd always enjoyed English as a subject, but I'd been too busy resenting Charterhouse to really take it in. Tony was the fan and *Wind & Wuthering* is one of his favourite albums: it's a very feminine album and to me it also felt a bit like treading water after the excitement and challenge of proving ourselves with *A Trick of the Tail*.

There were highlights: 'Blood on the Rooftops', which Phil wrote with Steve, was one of Steve's best songs, and 'Afterglow', which was Tony's, was a big highpoint on stage. We'd have a huge arc of magenta lights behind the drum riser going out into the crowd.

My main contributions were 'Your Own Special Way' and 'Eleventh Earl of Mar', which began with some quite grandiose chords that had given me an image of the Scottish highlands. The lyrics were inspired by a story I'd found about a near uprising among the old Scottish clans.

I knew we'd suffer a bit lyrically without Pete. When you were writing words you'd often be tied by the music to a certain area – but both Tony and I still tended to gravitate towards science-fiction and fantasy-type stories and didn't have the edge of reality that Pete always had. Even when he was at his most quirky, there'd be a harder edge to Pete's lyrics and he'd ground them more in human life and human emotions.

My lyrics mostly fell somewhere between those of Phil and Tony: Phil's were very simple and Tony's were . . . complicated. Tony never did understand how to make words flow. His words are the reason why he'll never write a hit single, although sometimes you have to admire his bravery: he's the only person who could ever get away with writing a lyric about double glazing and nylon sheets and have Phil make it work.

But at the time we didn't really allow ourselves to have any of these thoughts: it would have been too depressing. Neither Tony nor I look back very often – we both tend to operate in the now. And as the years went by we got better at lyric writing too, although long after we were able to be more honest about the quality of each other's songwriting, we still wouldn't comment on the words. We probably should have done, but it was one area where we were all still a little too sensitive.

'Your Own Special Way', which was a love song to Angie, had a simple, straightforward lyric and was a bit of an emotional breakthrough for me. *Rolling Stone* even called it 'a first-rate pop song', but then they never did like us. In 1971 they'd called us a 'new contender for the coveted British weirdo-rock championship' and, five years later, I still didn't particularly enjoy being condescended to by them.

Reviews and the music press in general changed with punk: that was one of the effects it was impossible to miss. When we'd first begun it was quite a friendly scene. The papers might ignore you but they didn't really knock you: there was too much good going on with English music at the time for them to feel the need. But with punk the *NME* in particular got very angry and aggressive.

I never believe people who say, 'I don't care about the reviews.' Of course they care. We all want to be loved, it's human nature. But it was Phil who took our press most seriously. He'd ring up journalists sometimes and defend himself, which I always told him was the one thing you should never do.

However, reviews always mattered less to me than what was happening in the real world. There was one journalist in Toronto who hated us. For years he gave us bad reviews, but the worse they got the bigger we became. That's what I loved about live music: the reaction and feedback from the crowd was spontaneous and natural.

The fact that our success came through live work was one of the things that made us different from the bands that came afterwards. We were popular not because we'd had a hit single (we hadn't, really) or because we'd been on MTV (which didn't exist yet) but because our small cult audience had now become a big cult audience. As soon as we got famous, the initial small cult then felt left behind – as always happens – but the vast majority of the following we'd built weren't going to go away whatever we did.

But it was when we flew out on Concorde to play Brazil in May 1977 that we knew we'd reached the next level.

★ ★ ★

Concorde had only begun commercial flights in 1976 so not only were we one of the first big bands to play South America, we were also probably the quickest to get there.

We weren't quite sure what playing Brazil actually entailed, but the problems began even before we got there. The Brazilian currency, the cruzeiro, was totally worthless in the wider world and there were endless transatlantic phone calls between Tony Smith and the Brazilian promoters, Globo, who finally came up with the brilliant solution of paying us in coffee beans. At that point Tony Smith decided to get on a plane himself.

Payment wasn't the only issue: Tony had heard various stories about the monopoly Globo had over record companies and their ability to impound equipment if things weren't going their way. Given that we had a gruelling European tour ahead of us, Tony wanted a cast-iron guarantee that our equipment would have safe passage out of the country as soon as our shows finished. Globo kept stalling but Tony wasn't backing down, and he insisted on meeting the Globo boss. The Globo boss kept insisting he wasn't available. It was cat and mouse for a while but finally Tony secured a meeting. He was picked up at his hotel by a couple of heavies in a limo who immediately headed for the hills. Naturally, Tony started to get a bit hot under the collar once they'd left the main road for a dirt track – he loved Genesis but I don't think he was quite ready to put his life on the line. When the limo finally pulled up outside a huge mansion on the top of a mountain, miles away from anywhere, he was already picturing the gun that was about to be put to his head.

As it turned out, the head of Globo was like someone from *The Sopranos*: 'Tony! How ya doin'?' He was even from Chicago, although the effect was spoiled a bit by the fact that he was seriously vertically challenged (something even his wingmen couldn't hide). But Tony got his signature on the dotted line and we all thought the fee sounded quite substantial, too – until we realized we were expected to play our three-hour set to 20,000 people not once, but twice a day.

It got worse: as soon as we arrived I managed to get severe

food poisoning. I was so sick I could hardly leave the bathroom, let alone manage six hours on stage, but cancelling was out of the question. Bodyguards were the norm in Brazil but even they might not have been able to protect us from 20,000 unhappy punters with typically fiery South American temperaments, all of whom, I imagined, would be glad of any excuse for a riot.

I thought that if I had a show to do, I would do it, even if I fainted in the process. Which I did. Naturally, the band played on.

In the end the only solution was to get a doctor to sit at the side of the stage with a couple of syringes, and every so often during the set he'd haul me off and jab me in the backside, which is how I discovered I was allergic to the anti-nausea drug Maxolon. (The problem was that it was like a mega-dose of speed: I couldn't stand still and played double time so the band couldn't keep up.)

Tony finally called Angie in the UK. She was three months pregnant with Kate and was enduring her own throwing up sessions so couldn't face coming to Brazil. He told her that it was quite serious and that she should jump on Concorde the following day as it still looked as though I wasn't getting any better.

Angie hadn't really given Brazil, or Concorde, for that matter, a second thought as she'd been so preoccupied with her own issues. When she did finally board the plane it dawned on her that when it broke the sound barrier there would be a G-force sensation. I think she clung on white-knuckled for a while, waiting for the impact, only to be told by the cabin crew that they'd been through the sound barrier half an hour before. The other thing that panicked her was when the captain announced they'd be landing in Dakar in twenty minutes. (She thought he meant Dhaka, Bangladesh, and had got on the wrong plane.) After the refuelling in Dakar I'm not sure how much she loved Genesis. Especially when she arrived. The allergy to Maxolon had been detected and I was on another drug, which had kicked in immediately. I was looking a lot better than her by the time of her arrival.

So much so that I suggested we went to the beach with the others. She sat there quietly while I went out to body surf. Suddenly a large wave threw me back into the sea, and I felt I was in a washing machine and couldn't get out. Every time I came up for air, arms flailing, another wave would take me back down. To this day Angie says she thought I was having a good time as she just waved back at me.

* * *

Despite supersonic transatlantic flights, keeping in contact in the mid-seventies wasn't easy. If you were phoning from the States it meant booking a call through, and the connection was always terrible. I usually forgot the time difference and called Angie at 3 a.m. while I was with the band backstage, drinking, laughing and generally having a piss-up. That never went down well.

With my parents some of the gaps in communication were bridged by tour books: spiral-bound records of the hotels we were staying at, the venues we were playing and all kinds of other information that were put together by the tour manager. These were given to families and crew each time we went out on the road. Mum used to love getting the tour book out each morning. She'd sit down at the breakfast table in Farnham and read it over her toast and marmalade: 'Oh, that's nice! Mikey's in Boise, Idaho, today!'

But for me, showing my parents my touring schedule was also one of the ways I could try to get them to understand what my life was like now.

I was very conscious of trying to prove to my father that it was going okay, even if sometimes I wasn't sure that it was, and so when Angie and I went over to Farnham I would usually bring along a list of the shows we were playing.

Dad would pour Angie and me a glass of white wine – it'd be the same bottle he'd opened the last time we were there – and then put back on the sideboard. (My parents didn't drink wine: that generation liked their spirits too much.) Then we'd sit down and look at the tour books and he'd say things like, 'A lot of travelling involved there,' or, 'A lot of logistics,' but I don't know how much it meant to him really. Ironic to think that, as a teenager, I didn't want him to understand me. Here I was a few years later, wishing he could.

Nevertheless, I felt that looking through our schedule with him was one way of showing him not just the progress we were making, but also the similarities between his world in the Navy and mine as a musician – similarities I was beginning to notice more and more. I showed him photos of us on stage, too: I didn't know about hurrah cruises at this point but I felt that he instinctively understood about presentation, the need to put on an impressive display, and that was very much what we were doing with our live shows.

★ ★ ★

In June 1977 we played Earls Court with a lighting rig consisting of forty-eight jumbo-jet landing lights – a very original look at the time. It was a weird experience for me because I knew Earls Court well from being taken there by Dad to see the Royal Tournament when I was little.

The annual Royal Tournament began in 1880 in Islington and then moved to Olympia and that's where Dad had commanded the Chatham Field Gun Crew in the 1930s. The competition was taken very seriously in the Navy:

Two crews and a maintenance staff went into training early in the year. They had their own training areas and accommodation and were treated as very much an elite with special diets, medical attention, physical training and so on as no one in the barracks wished to occur the odium of adversely affecting their performance.

By the time I was born and my father was Commander of Whale Island, the Royal Tournament had moved to Earls Court. Dad's role was now less active:

I had to take Royal Box duties and ensure that the distinguished incumbent knew when to acknowledge the innumerable salutes from the arena . . . I reacted to the sounds and smells of crews in training and in action like an old war horse to the sound of the trumpet.

It was almost as nostalgic for me being back at Earls Court, except where I'd been used to seeing the backstage area divided up into straw-lined stables full of Army horses, there were now six crew buses, ten lorries and backstage catering. And whereas the merchandise stalls had been arranged with displays of toy tanks and tin soldiers (Dad always used to buy me a set of these), they were now selling T-shirts and fluorescent green plastic necklaces. I shut my eyes and opened them and my brain wasn't quite able to process it, especially as Earls Court in 1977 was full of red, white and blue bunting for the Queen's Jubilee. It took a second to work out which decade I was in.

I felt our light show, with those jumbo-jet landing lights, was increasingly taking over from what Pete had done with his stories. It never really occurred to me to miss his mystique because we were still painting pictures, setting a scene, creating an atmosphere, only with lights not words. In particular, 'Los Endos', the song with which we ended our set, was a huge peak musically and visually, especially with two drum kits on stage so that Phil could go back and play drums alongside our new drummer, Chester Thompson.

Chester hadn't been our first replacement for Phil. Prior to Chester, we'd done one tour with Bill Bruford, who was a friend of Phil from Brand X, a new jazz-fusion band that Phil had been moonlighting in. Bill was up, noisy, direct and humorous. Getting him on board had been a bit of a coup – he was quite a name in America from his time with Yes – but he was a funny choice for a band like Genesis. Bill wasn't a session drummer: he couldn't wear a hat and be someone else. He came from that jazz world where every time you play it, it should be different. That's fine to a degree, but there are certain key moments in certain songs that need to be played a certain way.

Chester Thompson was from Baltimore and he was an incredible drummer. However, he was not a morning man. In London he used to stay at a hotel near Marble Arch, and he'd never be in the lobby when I arrived with a driver to take him to rehearsals. One day, after I'd been waiting for ages for him to show up, Chester finally came down wearing a long leather coat. Nothing odd about that, but when he went to get into the back seat of the car, he suddenly stopped halfway. His body was half in, half out and he couldn't go any further. I was starting to get a bit worried – was he ill? Had he had a stroke? Then I saw that he'd got caught on the car's coat hook. Half asleep, he'd put his coat on and left a bloody great coat hanger poking out the back of the collar. Then when he'd got in the car, he'd managed to hang himself up.

Chester hadn't known much about Genesis before he joined the band (he'd nearly been scared off by a rumour that he'd have to wear a costume) but maybe that was why it worked out so well. It was good to have someone who wasn't too in love with what we did.

With both Chester and Phil playing, 'Los Endos' was a thrilling finale. It was so impressive that I didn't realize there wasn't anyone singing until a few years later, when Elton John pointed it out: 'I can't believe you end the show on an instrumental: what a great idea!' I had to think about it – did we really end on a song with no one singing, no one out front on stage? It sounded suicidal if you put it like that.

Our three nights at Earls Court were when I felt we knew who we were as a band: with two drummers and all the lights it felt as though we were going into battle, all the guns blazing.

When Pete had left, we had wandered around a bit and taken a while to find out who we were again, but I felt now we were planting our flag in the ground.

And then Steve left.

CHAPTER TWELVE

Steve's leaving was strange. It was almost a non-moment. We were mixing our live album, *Seconds Out*, in Trident Studios in July 1977 and Phil, who was in a cab on his way in, drove past Steve in the street.

'Do you want a lift?'

'No, no. I'll see you later.'

Steve never did make it in.

I'm embarrassed to say I didn't realize how unhappy Steve was a lot of the time that he was in the band. We weren't the most sensitive lot and Steve was quite a reserved person, as we all were, but I thought he was quite enjoying himself.

We'd always been guided by the rule that the song was king: the best bits got used, regardless of who had written them. That was the theory. In practice Tony and I probably lobbied a bit more successfully for our bits than Steve did for his. Unlike us, Steve was never an arguer, and because he wasn't as noisy, he tended to get hurt a bit more too.

Steve was such an excellent guitarist but my overriding impression of him as a songwriter is that he always wrote inside the box, which was what we tried to avoid. And when he tried to write outside of the box, it was great when it worked.

I never wrote much with Steve, which was strange. In the beginning it may have been because, in a funny way, I was missing Ant. What bothered me later was that Steve had gone off to make his first solo album just as we were starting to make *A Trick of the Tail*: it was all very well for Steve but the band would have ground to a halt if Tony and I hadn't pooled all our riffs into the album. But then perhaps it was Steve's experience of making a solo record, combined with seeing Pete's solo career also start to take off, that had made him think that he should be going in that direction too. In any case, and as with Pete, I didn't want to sell it to him if his heart wasn't in it.

In terms of my personal Richter scale, losing Steve didn't really register in the way that losing Ant and Pete had. For me, Ant leaving was the worst; Pete was very bad but there wasn't quite the same depth of emotion because Ant had been my partner from the start, whereas Pete had been a unit with Tony. Steve was always a slight outsider. It was true that I hadn't grown up with Phil either, but Tony, Phil and I had developed a strong musical bond.

For some time I'd had a sense of a three-piece bubbling under the surface, that our strongest moments were when it was just Tony, Phil and me playing – now we'd find out if I'd been right.

★ ★ ★

1977 was turning out to be a rather important year. I had become a father. When Kate was born I'd never held a baby before and, like many a new father, I was convinced that she was going to break. When they're that small, that's what you believe: you look at them and wonder how on earth they're going to last the night. Amongst all the turmoil with Genesis, though, I didn't have much time to enjoy those first moments of fatherhood. Angie had been home from hospital for just two days when I flew to the Netherlands to make a new album.

★ ★ ★

'So, tell me: why's the album called . . . *And Then There Were Three* . . .?' I could tell it was going to be a long haul. This was in March 1978 and we were in a radio studio in New York at the start of almost a year of touring. Tony, Phil and me. The three of us. Maybe the DJ had a problem counting.

We'd gone back to the Netherlands and Relight Studios to record . . . *And Then There Were Three* . . . There was always the question when we went in to make a new album: could we do it? We never took it for granted that we'd make another album, ever, but this time it wasn't really the writing of the songs that was the question for me, just the playing. I wasn't in a hurry to play lead guitar and I knew I couldn't play like Steve, but by the time he left we also knew it would have been wrong to bring anyone else into the band to write. There would have been too much history for anyone new to catch up on. In the early days we couldn't paint enough pictures on our own: we needed more of a colour palette, which Steve had brought. But just as a band with four people in it was more agile than a five-piece, so there was a freedom and an ease writing as a three-piece, which was liberating. We could jam together and if someone shot off in one direction, there wouldn't be four others trying to pull him back to somewhere else.

By nature, musicians are always going to be frustrated because there's always something better that you haven't done yet – a better song to write. That's why I've never felt that I've arrived. But, with *A Trick of the Tail, Wind & Wuthering* and . . . *And Then There Were Three* . . ., I felt that the ship we'd been trying to launch finally made it down the slipway.

Having said that, . . . *And Then There Were Three* . . . is a funny album. Because we'd written so much material for *Wind & Wuthering* that we didn't have space for, we decided that on this new album we'd have no long songs. The record suffered for it. Every time we gave Tony Smith an album to play to the record label he'd start smoking again, or drinking again, and with . . . *And Then There Were Three* . . . I had some sympathy for him.

What saved the album was 'Follow You, Follow Me'. I had always found it difficult to put my emotions on paper. Angie, however, had encouraged me to be more open. The song captured how I felt. I was pleased when Pete Townshend said that he liked it: that meant a lot to me, coming from him. It's an up, happy song that makes you smile without being sweet – not an easy thing to achieve – and the lyrics flowed so fast when I wrote them I thought that it can't be that easy. But there's something genuine about them. What's more, it was a song that girls liked as well as boys, which was a first for us. Prog rock was not something that most girls ever really got. Now boys were bringing their girlfriends to the shows: 'You know Genesis: they're the ones who did that song you like!' Finding ourselves with a female audience was almost as big a novelty as finding ourselves in the Top 10 for the first time: 'Follow You, Follow Me' got to number 7 in the UK and number 23 in America. It was by far our biggest hit to date.

★ ★ ★

After leaving the band Ant had gone to music college and become a pianist. I'd worked with him on his first solo album, *The Geese and the Ghost*, which came out in 1977, but even though we still saw each other quite regularly, we never spoke about his decision to leave Genesis. As I had feared, once he'd left he just wasn't part of my life in the same way anymore, which is something I'll always feel sadness about.

I now decided to explore music theory, but soon realized that not knowing anything can make you more adventurous as a writer. When the band were jamming together it was those sonic moments of collision – wrong notes, I think they're known as – which led to our most original and interesting ideas. You write by making mistakes. That's the reason why Daryl Stuermer, our new touring guitarist, wasn't a writer: he couldn't play a wrong note if you paid him. But because we were paying him not to, it worked out pretty well.

Daryl is positive and enthusiastic, and even though he's American, he has an understanding of English music. He shouldn't drink coffee, though: it gives him the verbals. He had an attack at his audition in New York and suddenly it was all pedals and fuzz boxes and footwork . . .

Daryl's guitar playing was just what I'd gone to America hoping to find. There was a level of musicianship in the States that didn't exist in the UK: the Americans just had better technique. I felt that it made them less original and innovative as songwriters (the Clash could never have come from America, for example) but the proficiency was definitely greater.

Daryl wasn't the first guitarist I auditioned. Chester had recommended Alphonso Johnson from Weather Report, who was a lovely guy and a great bass player, but just not good enough on lead guitar. I'd also tried out Elliott Randall from Steely Dan but he was too much of a session guy: when he came in to play 'Squonk' he'd asked me how I wanted it. 'Do you want it rock, do you want it country, do you want it choppy, do you want it jazz?'

What Daryl got and Elliott didn't was that there was only one way to play 'Squonk': you had to play it straight, you couldn't lilt the chords.

The next question was whether Daryl could also play bass: with a bassist, I could finally get rid of the doubleneck. The answer was no, not really, but any guitarist can pick up a bass and play the notes to a song well enough to make it work, whereas that's not true the other way round.

I had always loved bass, the only problem with it being that it's dead boring to play on its own. And with Daryl in the band I often gave Steve's part to him when we played live, while I continued to play bass, although on our newer songs I would tend to play lead. I felt closer to the new songs, they felt more part of me. It took Daryl about five years to become a very good bass player: for the first four he was playing the right notes but he didn't have the groove.

Neither Daryl nor Chester ever could understand what I was saying. Being Americans they had a problem with all of our

English accents, but I might as well have been speaking another language as far as Daryl and Chester were concerned.

My father always had very proper pronunciation but at some point I'd developed a mumble that seemed to get gradually worse by the year. I still have it: I think if I talk fast, I can fit more in. It doesn't work that way, obviously, because I usually then have to spend another five minutes repeating myself.

★ ★ ★

We were on tour virtually non-stop from February to December 1978, although we only played one show in the UK: it was at Knebworth on 24 June to 120,000 people. Looking back it seems unbelievable, slightly mind-blowing. I was only twenty-eight and this wasn't just a festival with a range of big names to draw such a huge crowd. This was our gig, our people coming to see us. But if you were on a roll, as we were then, you rather took it in your stride.

Flying in the day before by helicopter for a sound-check, however, I could not help but be struck by the size of the stage. It was a huge black thing, the biggest stage in the world at the time, and it looked a bit like a fort in the westerns, with the grassy gully of the park leading down to it.

Sadly, that was a view that Tony never saw, because Tony didn't do helicopters. As we soared overhead, he was stuck in traffic on the single tiny road that went in and out of the place. He only just made it in time for the concert, but at least he got there, unlike the singer for our support act, Jefferson Starship. Grace Slick had already been misbehaving in Europe and ended up going AWOL just in time for their Knebworth slot. And poor Talk Talk were heckled: I always did feel that was very unfair.

Knebworth was a big gig in every way and we wanted to make a big impression visually. Instead of just using simple follow spotlights, we'd had the idea to direct beams of light up from the stage into the lighting rig, where they would then be reflected back down via huge, moving, hexagonal mirrors. It was much more interesting and innovative than your average light show at the time, but it was still a bit clumsy and awkward. What we needed was to get the lights themselves to move; it would be even better if they moved and varied their colour, too. But who would ever think to invent something like that?

Knebworth wasn't our only big gig that year. In November we played in front of 100,000 people at La Fête de l'Humanité in Paris, another crowd so huge it was slightly shocking. From the stage all we could see were people, with just a glimpse of the funfairs on the horizon beyond. We hadn't been prepared for that, but we were even more perplexed when we realized that it wasn't a festival we were playing at. It was actually a Communist Party rally.

★ ★ ★

Tony Smith's heart was in live work and he was quite good at realizing that if things were going well and you pressed on a bit, it would pay off. Like my mum when I was at prep school, he also tended to get a bit creative with time when he was talking to me about it. He would pretend to us that every month was only four weeks really, so we'd agree to tour in July and August because that was only eight weeks. Then we'd find out we were playing

Rehearsing in the summer of '68.

'Dear boys, they love you!' Our first manager Tony Stratton-Smith.

First trip to New York – moodily confident.

(*above*) First overseas' trip to Brussels. Feeling a bit queasy on the Mateus Rosé.

(*right*) Pete selling England by the pound.

(*below*) How to kill time when on tour.

(*above*) Phil thought life on the road would be rock 'n' roll all the way.

(*right*) Pegged out after shooting 'Illegal Alien' video.

At least the kids enjoyed Tony's guitar playing.

(*above*) Spitting Image join us on tour.

(*right*) Locking horns with Phil.

(*below*) Playing to half a million people. The last European gig, Rome 2007.

A rather varied bill; Mike + The Mechanics perform variety on the West Coast.

Paul Carrack.   'Chief Mechanic'.   Paul Young.

Angie and I on our wedding day.

Granny and Grandpa with Kate and Tom.

Family photo album.

Before …

After… (Still talking.)

ten weeks of shows. 'But we don't count June because we're in June at the moment.' We'd always fall for it.

That summer of 1978 in America, most of the venues we'd been playing were 'sheds': indoor/outdoor places with 5,000 people under cover and another 15,000 spread out behind in the open air, usually in very picturesque settings. The crowds would bring their picnics with them and backstage we'd often have a barbecue. As the evening came on, it'd be incredibly atmospheric. (The only place for which this wasn't true was Saratoga Springs, where it always pissed with rain. Either they didn't have any other type of weather in Saratoga Springs or they just saved it up for us.)

But while selling out huge venues, we were selling comparatively few albums. Our success as a live band was becoming out of all proportion to our commercial success.

Part of the problem was Jerry Greenberg, the CEO of Atlantic – he had a lot of words, Jerry, but he'd never got our music. Finally, Tony Smith told Ahmet Ertegün, the founder and President of Atlantic, that we were going to try to buy ourselves out with some money that Phonogram had offered us.

Ahmet was the smart, elegant son of a Turkish diplomat and, like Strat, he was in the music business because he loved it. He didn't have rules – he'd been one of the first record execs to pay royalties to black artists, much to the irritation of the other labels. He also believed in giving artists creative freedom, which was why he'd done so well and become so revered. Ahmet was like a god in America.

He'd also got our music from day one. As soon as he heard we were considering leaving Atlantic he got straight on a plane from New York.

'Listen guys' Ahmet said over dinner, 'I take your point. But I'm going to make sure we do this next album right. Please give me one more try.'

We'd always loved Strat's fighting talk in the early days of our career but even at the time, deep down, we knew he was just saying some of those things to make us feel better. But Ahmet's talk was convincing, and Ahmet *was* Atlantic. In those days the head of a record label could go back and inspire everyone else on the label: and if Ahmet was behind you, the whole label would jump. He was also a man of his word. If Ahmet promised that he was going to push a record hard, you knew he would do.

'I love you guys. Please give me one more try,' he said. Put like that, what could you do?

CHAPTER THIRTEEN

'Mr Rutherford, wanker? Wanker, Mr Banks?'

By 1978 I had got married, had a child and felt that all of us in the band had grown up a bit. Which didn't mean that we didn't enjoy making Mr Udo, the extremely polite promoter of our first Japanese tour, yell the word 'wanker'.

What would happen was this: after a show, some of us would want to have a shower, change clothes or have a bite to eat backstage, while some of us would want to get back to our hotel. If you wanted to get away quickly you'd ask to be in the first car, car number one, but in Japan this ended up as 'one car'. Which, of course, came out 'wanker.'

'Who wants wanker? Mr Rutherford, wanker?'

For obvious reasons, the phrase stuck.

★ ★ ★

By the time we toured Japan in the late 1980s, Japanese audiences had learned how to do the rock thing – they couldn't get enough of cat-suited, hair-on-the-chest-type heavy metal. But in November 1978, at our first Japanese show, they hadn't quite learned how to react. The show was at a theatre in Tokyo, but it had the feel of a grand opera house: all the men wore dark suits and white shirts, and at the end of each song there'd be discreet applause.

My father had visited Japan in 1952 when he was commander of the *Newcastle*, which was based at Hong Kong. He was impressed by:

> *The national characteristics of discipline, passive face, austerity and economy . . . nothing was wasted and not a piece of string or empty cigarette package was allowed just to lie around.*

Dad always thought that you should try and glean something from other people. He believed that it was important to keep an open mind, to consider everything that might be put to you and learn what you could. And this must have rubbed off on me because one of the places I particularly wanted to visit while I was in Japan was the Roland music factory in Tokyo. They made some nice guitar effects pedals and I wanted to see what else they had.

The rule of thumb in the band was always that we should learn how to use anything that was available and then choose to use it or not. The electric sitar that I'd bought in New York at the same time as my six-string Microflet bass was a good example: for every album we wrote, I would bring my electric sitar out and try to get it on. Steve had played it on 'I Know What I Like' and I'd tried it on 'Follow You, Follow Me', but sometimes a song just says, 'Thanks, but no thanks.'

Restraint was important. I always thought that Tony was very restrained at a time when a lot of guys were going mad with three-keyboard stacks. The great thing about being a guitarist is that guitars are so primitive – a bit of wood and six strings. That limitation often seemed to me like a strength, particularly when I remembered that, however mad I wanted to go on record, I would still have to figure out how to play what I'd written live.

None of the pedals I saw at the Roland factory that day really appealed to me but I did pick up some drum machines: one for me, one for Tony and one for Phil. Phil wasn't very grateful: 'I'm a drummer. What do I want a drum machine for?'

I was a bit miffed but thought he'd probably find something to do with it. He did. The opening bars of 'In the Air Tonight' were programmed on that drum machine.

Unlike Angie, who came out to Japan for part of the tour, Phil's wife Andrea never came with him. By 1978 it was putting a big strain on his marriage and Phil spent the ten days we were in Japan on a bender – although Phil's capacity for alcohol was such that even then he was still the same lovely, easy-going Phil he always was. He was in exactly this mood when we invited him out for a late dinner in Tokyo one night. We were all talking, eating and laughing when suddenly Phil stopped dead. He looked around the table at us, then at his plate, then back at us.

'Hang on a minute,' he said slowly. He looked at his plate again. 'I ate earlier.'

He'd forgotten that he'd already been out for dinner with Daryl.

To be honest, I think Phil could easily have gone for a third dinner after that if he hadn't realized. So much so that when we all ended up at a club in a funky part of town and he suddenly started dancing, he blew everybody else off the floor. He was incredibly good and incredibly fast.

We always tried to embrace local culture when we were on tour, even if it was a bit of a stretch, such as at the Japanese restaurant where the chefs cooked our dinner in front of us. We'd all watched in horror as they'd thrown handfuls of shrimp – all still alive – on to a hot plate. Even my dad had balked a bit at sushi, although in 1952 it probably did seem a bit more exotic than nowadays:

> *the dishes, delicious to a fish eating nation, sometimes looked like*
> *a specimen from a marine life research laboratory.*

I had shared a car with Phil on the way to the airport when we flew out to Japan, so when we returned to England we dropped him off first before Angie and I went home ourselves. It was only as we drove up to Phil's house that we all realized something was seriously wrong: there wasn't a light on anywhere; it was completely dark.

Andrea had left and taken the children.

★ ★ ★

I often think that the reason Genesis lasted so long is that we never made any plans. We were quite fatalistic as a band and we never thought too far ahead. At the same time, as I got older, I seemed to be developing my father's ability to take the long view.

When Phil told us that he was going to Canada to try to save his marriage, I wasn't sure if he'd come back but, at the back of my mind, I thought that if he did go and live there permanently we'd find a way round it – after all, if you're touring, it doesn't matter where you live.

Phil told us what he'd decided at a group dinner with Tony Smith. Smith always knew everyone's angles and Phil had told him before the rest of us, just as Pete had gone to Smith first when he'd decided to leave.

It's funny, as a band we'd always been so close to each other, and yet not. Tony and I didn't lead Phil but we did set the mood a bit. We could talk about anything when we were together but only if it was within the specific, defined area of our work and our life together. Our personal lives didn't really feature.

Phil's decision was something that we accepted immediately, which seemed to me like a sign of how much we'd changed. In the years since Pete had left we'd finally developed some empathy for each other, and we all knew how serious it was for Phil. He'd always been an organized person – it had started with the cassettes of our jams, which he always kept labelled and ordered, and in the early days he was the only one of us who'd ever know how much was in his bank account. When we were writing an album he'd never feel like he'd started until he had a list of songs – we'd always make him wait a week and by day three he was dying to get his pen out. To have his life turned upside down must have been terrible for him. None of us hesitated when he told us he was going: 'Okay, Phil. Whatever it takes.'

And I genuinely didn't see any point in worrying about the future. It wasn't as if worrying was going to change anything. But there was also the fact that 1978 had been such a good year. Partly because of the success of 'Follow You, Follow Me', for the first time in our careers we could actually afford some time off. Unlike when Ant and Pete left, we were at a stage now where the whole thing didn't feel as though it would fall apart if we had a break.

Anyone was free to leave at any time now – we were more relaxed – but I did think that just walking out, the way Steve had done, wasn't the correct way of doing it. Still, had the graph not changed direction at that moment, our career might never have turned a corner. Maybe Phil's absence, which we hoped would be temporary, would also do us all good by allowing us to take a step back. Suddenly we had some breathing space, some time to take a left turn if we wanted.

★ ★ ★

I wasn't dying to make a solo record but I thought it might be quite fun. *Smallcreep's Day* was based on a novel I'd liked by Peter Currell Brown. It had a *Gormenghast* feel to it, which appealed to me, and it provided both a setting and a story for the music. Unlike *The Lamb Lies Down on Broadway*, though, it also had a plot that you could explain in a paragraph.

One of the nicest things about making the record was thinking about who I wanted to work with: Simon Phillips, a drummer I'd always admired; Noel McCalla, a session singer with a very high voice; and Ant on keyboards. In any other band, working with other musicians would be seen as the start of a slippery slope: 'What's wrong with us?' But Tony was also taking the opportunity to make a solo album while Phil was away, and the bond between the three of us was such that we never felt threatened by anything we did outside the band.

Storm Thorgerson (of Pink Floyd's album covers) had designed several album covers for Genesis and so he seemed a natural choice for the design of *Smallcreep's Day*. I'd decided on an image that I wanted to use and Storm's idea was to spray developing ink over the photograph so that it only came through in patches. When he came down to show me the results he brought six different versions and asked me which one I liked: they all looked pretty similar to me but I liked one a bit more than the rest.

'That one,' I said. Storm looked disgusted.

'No, no, no, no, no. *That* one.'

Storm was very opinionated: that was his strength and his weakness. He was very good at fighting your corner with record labels – getting them to use good-quality paper and things like that – but he would also always try to get you to go to the desert somewhere for a photo shoot and spend a fortune. 'We'll do this over here, and that over there, and then we'll move that sand dune . . .' It wouldn't even be a three-day shoot, it'd be five. I've always preferred graphics to photographs, and this was one of the reasons why: with photographs you can waste ages and spend a bomb on them, and then you'll take a look at the end result and think, 'That's not very good, is it?'

Storm looked like you'd imagine a painter to look – dark clothes, longish hair, cerebral – and had the artistic temperament to match. His partner at Hipgnosis, Aubrey Powell or Po, would then have to come along and made peace in Storm's wake.

Storm would always have a little sketchbook of ideas that he'd show you, and I later recognized some of the ones Genesis turned down on 10CC and Led Zeppelin albums. There were only three or four Genesis covers that I ever actually liked: I was never that mad about *Foxtrot* or *Nursery Cryme*, they were a bit busy for me, although I thought *Selling England* was fantastic.

But in the end the problem with covers was that they'd always end up being rushed. You couldn't decide on a cover until you knew what the songs were going to be about, and then you'd only get a limited time to come up with something before the record was released. A prime example was . . . *And Then There Were Three* . . ., our last Hipgnosis cover. It was definitely one of Storm's B-ideas.

As an album, *Smallcreep's Day* is quite strong instrumentally, but its real value was as a breath of creative fresh air. Unlike other bands, our solo projects were never a reaction to being unhappy with what we were doing as a group. We'd always work on solo projects between albums. It was one of the things that marked us out and made us unusual as a band, and I think it was an important part of what kept us going, too. We learned how much we appreciated the other members of the band and, because we were doing something different and challenging individually, the probability that we would get stuck in a rut was less.

★ ★ ★

Until this point in my life, Friday, Saturday and Sunday nights had always meant a show: I think I was the only person I knew who looked forward to Mondays. Now I was discovering weekends. Strange things: two days when you stayed at home, had a Sunday lunch with your family and didn't work – and also holidays, which were a bit strange too, especially the one Angie and I had in Florence.

I'd been to Florence before: Genesis had played there in 1973 and Rich had scored some morphine. My main memory of that trip is of Tony, who was sitting in the front of the van, turning round to look at Phil and me in the back, raising an eyebrow, sighing, then turning away again.

I didn't tell Angie about the morphine when we went on our holiday, although I did give her a full guided tour. I think she was quite impressed by the time I'd finished. Then we got home and Angie told the Banks about it, and Tony pointed out we didn't play Florence in 1973, it had been Genoa. We'd actually never played Florence. I knew the morphine was strong but I hadn't realized it was that strong.

★ ★ ★

Unlike me, downtime was not something that Phil every really did. Music was his job but it was also his hobby, which I think was part of his problem. He couldn't relax, switch off and engage in family life. His idea of a day off was buying and listening to a stack of records. To be fair, he did have a train set. He kept it in his basement, and every time he took me down for a look I'd nearly beat my brains out on the ceiling. I couldn't really see the appeal myself – but it made him happy.

Phil was always a worker and the one of us who was most drawn by the idea of outside work. When Keith Moon had died in 1978, I know Phil would have loved the job with the Who. They were pretty much revered by everyone and we'd all grown up watching them on the TV. I always think if Phil had joined them we would have found a way to make it work, although God knows how.

In 1979, after it had become clear that his marriage was over,

Phil had moved back to England again. Tony and I were still busy with our own albums, so Phil had gone back to drumming for Brand X, the jazz-rock band he'd been moonlighting with for several years. However, for the first time he had also begun writing his own material.

There was a noticeable difference when we met again to make *Duke*. We recorded it at Phil's house by default: he was on his own, feeling slightly sad and dejected, and I think he probably quite liked having us around. He may not have realized that we'd kick him out of his bedroom, but it was lighter and bigger than his music room, so he just had to sleep in the spare bedroom instead.

The songs that Phil brought to *Duke*, 'Misunderstanding' and 'Please Don't Ask', had a lovely sense of space and ease about them, a feeling of not trying too hard. Tony and I would always try quite hard and when it worked, it was great. When it didn't, it didn't. Phil was always able to let a song breathe; he also had an empathy for what was right musically. Whatever he said, you listened.

It's a question undecided to this day whether Phil also played us the demo for 'In the Air Tonight'. Phil thinks yes, Tony thinks no, and I think it was quite possible that Phil had played it and we hadn't really noticed it. The thing about 'In the Air Tonight' was that it was all about atmosphere: without that famous drum sound I could imagine that it would sound quite plain initially. It was just three chords and all of them probably a bit too ordinary to impress Tony and me, as we're chord snobs. Anyway, we didn't end up with it on *Duke* so Phil had it for his solo album, *Face Value*, and the rest is history.

In terms of my own songs, *Duke* was an album of highs and

lows, the low being 'Man of Our Times', which was my attempt to be a bit Gary Numan. I had a guitar synthesizer for the first time, which allowed me to write songs with string parts. I wasn't a great fan of synth stuff but, once again, I thought it was important to investigate what was on offer. With hindsight it's a song that's best forgotten, like the New Romantic haircuts. They always worried me.

The high was 'Turn It On Again', which came from a riff that I'd had left over from *Smallcreep's Day* and which I always thought was in 4/4 until Phil told me it was in 13/8. Phil was going through his own highs and lows at this point – mostly highs – which may have been why he suggested we speed it up. My only regret now is that the chorus didn't come until four and a half minutes in.

I used bass pedals to write 'Turn It On Again': it was a quite tiring part to play so I used an echo and only had to play every other note. When we came to record it I knew it would sound better played properly so I ended up sitting on the floor, thumping the pedal with my fist. Then when I got tired, Phil took over: that was where his extra energy was useful.

★ ★ ★

'Mike, I really can't live in London anymore, on my own with a baby!'

This was one of those phone calls. I hadn't realized just how unhappy Angie was. She was the first of her friends to have a baby, and she felt isolated living there. She was a country girl at heart, so I agreed she could look for somewhere outside London. I did stress it would have to be the Home Counties, as I wanted to be near to London. She managed to sell the house and find a cottage in Sussex pretty quickly. When I arrived at Heathrow my car wasn't taking me to Courtnell Street but to my new home. It all looked very pretty from the outside, but having knocked myself out on the front door I managed to bump my way across the beams to say hello to my family. Angie looked horrified, as she'd only taken into account the height of the ceilings from her vantage point and not mine, at six feet three. We moved the following year.

I had a problem. There'd be a period of decompression every time I came home from tour. I'd always feel comfortable with the regime on the road. Our days would be completely planned out: a timetable would be slipped under the door of our hotel suite every evening, telling us when to get up and be down in the lobby. We'd be driven to the plane, fly to the next city and then handed a key to our hotel rooms at the other end. It never felt claustrophobic – flying around the world, with people cheering and adoring us every night. I couldn't really complain.

People would always ask if the band hung out together when we weren't working, and the answer would be no. We wouldn't want to go near each other for at least the next six months. It was just that we'd got so close and spent so much time together, we needed a bit of space. The trouble was I didn't quite know what to fill my time with. Suddenly I would have to make my own decisions.

Angie had settled into country life, making friends with other mothers, riding her horse and generally feeling much happier. I, on the other hand, would come back after a tour, feeling rather important and a bit out of the loop, only to see the horsebox disappearing down the drive as Angie headed off to another dressage competition. (That didn't necessarily mean the UK: she went to Europe quite regularly.) I didn't have any hobbies and life seemed to have carried on without me. Angie found a solution when she suggested I take up riding. At first, I didn't quite see the appeal of riding, and if I'd have read my father's book, I might not have agreed with her suggestion:

At occasional large combined services' parades around the Empire the parade orders carried the chilling sentence: 'Battalion Officers will be mounted.' . . . I managed to survive except on one occasion when the Army, having checked that my role required me to ride beside my boss at the head of the column, craftily supplied me with a charger normally ridden by a Second-in-Command whose position is at the extreme rear.

When the band struck up and we advanced my horse made determined attempts to get to his right place so that my entry to the parade ground was like something from the Spanish Riding School in Vienna. My only consolation was that our Second-in-Command, who had been given what should have been my charger, had his own problems and spent his time scattering the rearmost platoon like a mounted policeman dispersing a crowd.

I'd been riding for a couple of months – no chargers – when a friend rang up and asked if I want to compete in a celebrity charity event at Tetbury in Gloucestershire. It didn't sound too bad: a bit of jumping round a little course and then some against-the-clock off-road driving in a 4x4. It wasn't until we were nearly there and I saw the big RAC signs on all the surrounding roads that a bell went off. We were parking the car when none other than Captain Mark Phillips, then married to Princess Anne, came over: 'Oh, Mike! Good man, you're in my team!'

I'd just about trotted over the odd straw bale at home, but as I walked the course at Tetbury, it turned out to be a load of high dry-stone walls and bloody upturned boats. I've never known fear like it to this day. I'd managed to look like the real thing, except my top lip was sticking to my teeth because my mouth was so dry. I was borrowing a horse that I'd never ridden before, and which seemed absolutely huge. Somehow he got me round.

The only problem was that I then had to negotiate the driving part of the event and I couldn't accelerate because my foot was shaking so much. After repeatedly seeing my life flash in front of me over the course of the day, I'd decided eventing wasn't for me.

I missed having the blokes around and the camaraderie. That's when Gordon and Anita Roddick came to the rescue. Angie had been discussing her concerns with Anita and felt I needed a hobby of some sort, as I'd said, 'I'm thinking of moving back to London'. Gordon played polo and invited me along to Terry Hanlon's yard. We all had bacon rolls and coffee, and then played polo, which was more like rugby on horseback, followed by the pub for lunch. At last, I'd found my hobby.

The problem was that I had soon became overly keen and got myself a pony. I'd only been playing polo for about a season when Terry suggested I get a second pony in case the one I had went lame. That seemed like a good idea, so I did. A few weeks later, Terry found another pony which he thought was

better than the first pony I'd bought. However, if I bought this
new pony, pony number three, Terry was sure he could arrange a
quick sale of pony number one. This happened a few more times
as the months passed.

Angie offered to go collect the ponies for me at the end of the
season. I was pretty sure I still only had two ponies, but when she
arrived at the yard, a groom was waiting there with five. Angie
got them loaded in and was just about to drive off when the yard
owner appeared: 'See you later for the next lot?' It turned out I'd
got ten.

★ ★ ★

In 1980 I was thirty. In my mind the past ten years had been
a lifetime: we'd made ten albums, lost Pete and Steve, played
Knebworth, toured Japan . . . Of course, none of us knew that
we hadn't yet gone very far at all.

Touring was becoming an increasingly big deal, and in
America and Europe we'd often find ourselves doing a runner:
a dash from the show to the next town that we were playing.
While we were on stage playing our encore, the tour manager
would be putting friends, families and some drinks in the
waiting limos, the engines would be revved up, and as soon as
we'd finished we'd rush off stage, grab our robes, jump in the
car and off we'd go with our police escort. By the time the
last person had left the stadium we'd already be at the airport
on the plane to the next date. It was always exciting, although
sometimes the excitement would get a bit infectious. We were
in Germany when it all got a bit much for one of our drivers
and he started getting impatient with some slow-moving

traffic. We heard this scraping noise as he started nudging cars out of his path.

After playing such big venues it was always nice to play smaller places again – we were reminded that the music still worked even without all the lights and production – and so in spring 1980 we decided on a 'thank you' tour of the smaller English venues in which we'd begun our career. It would be both a return to our roots and a way of showing the fans how much we appreciated their support.

It was odd being back in the old places. We'd played them so often in the early days that even now I can picture them: Bradford St George's Hall with its tapering balcony and wrought-iron pillars; Birmingham Town Hall with its grand museum-like façade and cramped backstage . . . We even went back to the Blue Boar to see if it was as crap as we'd remembered it: it was.

With Angie pregnant with Tom, and my wanting to be at home more, I drove myself to most of the gigs. The whole tour was filmed by a TV crew who, in the way of all these documentaries, seemed at least as interested in the trucks, flight cases and roadies as the band. Probably more so. I think my parents would have preferred the BBC, rather than ITV, but telly was still telly. As a band there was no danger of fame going to our heads: when we went on to play the Greek Theatre in Los Angeles in May, the security crew wouldn't allow us back onstage for an encore because we hadn't got our passes.

CHAPTER FOURTEEN

Conversations about where we were going musically didn't tend to happen very often. And normally when they did it was because we'd been drinking. Tony's tongue was always loosened by a drink, but you had to catch him between the first couple of glasses and the start of the second bottle, when he began getting difficult. The only problem was that in the old days, by the time you'd convinced Tony about whatever it was, Pete would be so pissed and past caring you'd lost him altogether. I could keep going for longer than both of them but that wasn't difficult.

In 1981 one of the conversations Tony and I did have over a drink was whether we should change our name. You know when you chat about something knowing that you're never going to do it? It was one of those conversations. We still talked about it quite enthusiastically anyway.

We'd now reached a point in our careers where we felt we were in danger of becoming a caricature of ourselves, and with our new album we wanted to break with the past. Not disassociate ourselves from it, but not repeat it, either. We didn't want to make another album where I'd contribute a couple of my acoustic songs, Tony would contribute a couple of his bigger, grander songs, and we'd carry on in the same pattern. This meant fewer long songs, which was an idea that Tony was less sure about than Phil and me because those were more his area, but we all wanted to move on.

In the end I don't think we even got as far as seriously putting forward any alternative names – I can't remember any of them if we did, put it like that. We definitely never mentioned them to Tony Smith: we weren't that stupid. But Tony's great strength is that, even if we had, he'd probably have calmly said, 'Okay . . . let me think about it' – while screaming silently inside – and then come back to us a few days later and said, 'On reflection, I think no, probably not.' He doesn't overreact, Tony. Which is good.

★ ★ ★

We were in the early stages of writing *Abacab* when 'In the Air Tonight', the first single from *Face Value*, was released. It went to number 2; the album was released a month later and went to number 1. Phil came in the next morning and we all looked at each other: 'That's not bad, is it?' We were all quite surprised, Phil included.

The timing was important: had *Face Value* been released during a gap for Genesis then it's possible that Phil might have considered not returning. I'd have understood it if he had moved on – but as it was, the songs we were working on were sounding good and Phil, like Tony and me, was the kind of person who would get very engrossed in the here and now. Plus, I think Phil enjoyed what we did as a band too much to leave. The fact that we carried on making group albums even after his solo career took off seems to me to speak for itself.

Face Value was produced by Hugh Padgham, who had also worked with Pete since he had gone solo. We now brought him in as a co-producer on *Abacab*. Hugh was the first person to make us sound on record like we sounded live. We had real fire playing live but we had never really captured it on record before. Hugh, like Phil, also worked fast. Writing and recording had already got much quicker now that there were just three of us in the band. Two yeses and a no, two no thanks and a yes: done. In any case, we wanted to move faster than Pete. 'It's coming out at Easter,' Peter would always say when you asked him about his latest album. 'Which Easter?' you'd say. (It always struck me as ironic that one of the things that bothered Pete about Genesis was not having enough time to write the lyrics. It was only when he began to make his own solo records that he discovered it wasn't Genesis that was the problem. Lyrics have their own tempo.)

Personally, my own preference would always be to do three albums in the time it would take other more self-conscious artists to produce one. Two of the albums would be likely to be good, and one perhaps would turn out bad, but it would be better to let the songs have their own life rather than labour them and lose the momentum. I've always felt that what we produced was, literally, a record of a certain moment in time. In another year we'd be sounding a different way and be writing different things, so what was important was capturing how we sounded right at that minute.

Phil had used the Phenix Horns on *Face Value* and was keen to try some brass on *Abacab*. Tony wasn't sure, but I was open to the idea and so flew with Phil and Hugh out to LA, where the Phenix Horns were based. Phil had been building them up as an incredibly tight, iconic four-piece and I was ready to be impressed. I soon had to revise my expectations. The first hour and a half was spent sorting out various demands: drugs, food, drink . . . Fair enough, I thought, but then we went in for the first take and it was appalling. I looked round at Phil and Hugh, and Phil and Hugh very definitely didn't look back at me. The second take wasn't much better, probably slightly worse: out of time, out of tune, all over the shop.

Hugh, in those days, had a slightly boyish look and always wore a big, slightly frayed sweater. He'd have a grin that he used to pull out when it was going well – his eyes would light up – and a frown that came out when it wasn't going how he thought it should. It wasn't a mega-frown: just a worried look. Concerned. We'd all seen it when we were trying to prove to him that a bit we were working on was actually okay.

Hugh had taken his sweater off in LA but he was definitely wearing that little concerned look of his. 'Is there a problem?' I asked eventually. 'No . . .' Hugh said slowly. 'They'll get there . . .'

And when they did – and they really did – their sound was unique. But it was a lot of work – a *lot* of work – partly because they were all such characters. Don Myrick, the saxophonist, was eventually killed in a drug bust in 1993. Louis Satterfield, the trombone player, hurt his lip at one point and while he couldn't play, locked himself in a hotel room and went room-service mad to the tune of $5,000 in a single night.

★ ★ ★

I've often thought that the reason why British bands tend to last longer than American ones is that in America it's easy to find yourself surrounded by people who believe your hype. In Britain you can go into a pub and people will fall over themselves not to notice you.

This was one of the nice things about moving to the country, although when the band bought Fisher Lane Farm in Chiddingfold, Surrey, with the idea of turning it into a residential recording studio, the locals weren't best pleased. Chiddingfold is a quiet English village and the idea of a rock band descending caused a bit of a stir. However, the roadies soon ingratiated themselves at Chiddingfold Working Men's Club – especially after they'd discovered the beer was subsidized. After that the policy generally seemed to be to turn a blind eye. The only person who ever caused any bother in Chiddingfold was a guy who thought he'd used his powers of telepathy to write all our songs. Having then communicated them to us subliminally, he'd got a bit annoyed when we started passing them off as our own and now he was after his royalties. He wrote to us quite regularly and occasionally he'd appear at 'The Farm', as the studio became known. One of the roadies would drive him back down the road, plonk him in the middle of the village green and off he'd go until the next time.

The Farm was perfect for what we wanted. It began as quite a funky old building with a barn in which we stowed the gear, and a milking shed that we used as a garage. As time went on we developed the accommodation for crew and engineers and built a stone-clad drum room based on the one at Virgin's Townhouse Studios. Hugh was involved in designing it – drums and voice were Hugh's forte – and that drum room was another reason why we began to sound on record like we really did as musicians.

The process of finding The Farm hadn't been easy, though. Just like back in the days when we had needed to negotiate drop-offs on our way back to London after gigs, delicate logistical negotiations had been involved.

After I'd moved out to the country, I often felt that I'd started an exodus: Tony and Margaret came down soon after, then Tony Smith and then Phil. Phil was just down the road from me: I'd always been touched by the way he rang me before buying his house to check that I didn't mind his being next door.

Phil's house, Tony Banks's house and my house now formed a triangle, but the problem was that it was unequal, meaning that one person's house would always be nearer than the other two to the studio we were considering. The aim, obviously, was for our own to be the nearest, but none of us would ever say that when we were being shown somewhere further away. 'It's very nice but I'm not sure about the acoustics. I think maybe we should keep on looking a bit longer . . .'

We even considered a four-sided farmhouse set round a courtyard with a galleried hall – but it was so nice that the idea of filling it with roadies just didn't seem right.

Not that the roadies ever had any complaints about The Farm, despite its remoteness from London: on sunny days they'd even sit outside on the lawn in front of the studio in deckchairs. Being in a studio with a window was a big plus for us as a band. Prior to this, we'd always been locked away in basements – but there were downsides, and watching the roadies tanning up every summer was one of them. I know they did it to annoy us.

★ ★ ★

Most of our crew had been with us for years by this point: Bison, Pud, Little Geoff and Dale (no one knows how Dale escaped having a nickname: he was Noodlemier for a while but it never took hold). Pud was Welsh and called Steve Jones but there were four other Steve Jones in his class at school so, being small and round, he ended up as Pud. Bison was stocky with thick black hair.

Bison had been part of Genesis legend since the last night of *The Lamb Lies Down on Broadway* tour when he appeared naked on stage as Rael's body-double. Normally, at the climactic moment, Pete would appear on one side of the stage and a mannequin dressed in Rael's leather jacket would appear on the other. On this particular night Bison decided he'd take the place of the mannequin, not only without the leather jacket, but without anything else on either. Full frontal. There was a strobe going and I remember very clearly how every part of his body was an odd grey-blue.

Bison had a fantastically quick sense of humour but you wouldn't want to get on the wrong side of him. A few years after he joined us we were playing a gig in Germany and there was a drunken heckler in the front row. 'Can you have a word?' I said to Bison. I then watched as he walked calmly down to the front of the stage, made his way towards to the troublemaker and Bap! knocked him out cold. I was trying to play but for the next song and a half all I could think about was whether Bison had actually killed the guy. The man's body was now hanging over the aluminium safety fence, waving slightly like seaweed as the barriers heaved.

The crew worked all hours. I've always said that if there was a roadie's union, touring would be impossible, although the work was a matter of pride for them, too. But it was no secret that the only way they could keep it up was with chemical help, and that was where Howie came in.

Howie was from the Bronx. We first met him when he was selling illegal merchandise at the back of a venue. He looked exactly like the kind of guy you'd imagine would do that: a skinny face and you never knew how old he was. He had a bad shoulder, too: he claimed he'd been hit by a stray bullet but you suspected that it might not have gone that wide.

Howie supplied the road crew with the various substances they needed to keep them awake but no one ever mentioned that was his official role. His official position was court jester and he was so good at it that occasionally you'd just have to turn him off. We would all enjoy the patter for a while but then he just wouldn't shut up. Mostly, though, everyone loved Howie. He would interact effortlessly with anyone – fans, crew, the band, the record companies – and then when he'd finished a tour with us, he'd join the Pink Floyd road crew and carry on in the same vein.

Nick Mason, the drummer with Pink Floyd, once told me that when the band were invited to Cape Canaveral to meet some astronauts, Howie was somehow in tow, and he was greeted by everyone there like a long lost friend. And when Genesis played at Atlantic's fortieth anniversary party in Madison Square Garden, an event hosted by Michael Douglas, as soon as we walked into the dressing room it was Howie who was greeted with a load of high fives. Even Michael Douglas seemed to know who he was.

He got everywhere. At the end of one American tour we said our goodbyes and left for England, only to see him a few days later looking very at home at The Farm for the first time. He soon became a regular fixture. Not only that, he went on to play himself in with the locals so well that he even became Chairman of the Chiddingfold Working Men's Club. I'm not sure he was selling his wares to the local OAPs but they always looked very pleased to see him.

Eventually, Howie had to leave us. He was obviously a guy who was used to flying close to the wind and eventually he got a bit too close. Nevertheless, undeterred, he managed to find a job as a postman at the post office in Woking – which, bearing in mind his line of delivery work, I thought showed great initiative.

★ ★ ★

We never intended to own a brothel. I wonder how Dad would have felt.

One of my ploys at the places we visited was to have an outing with the local Provost Marshal to see the types of evening entertainment available to ship's companies – bars, beer halls and the brothels. As regards the brothels, those at places like Singapore were beyond description, Hong Kong better but in Japan they followed the French system.

The houses were properly run and supervised by the police; they were pleasantly set out and presented, the girls in Japanese or western

dress were attractive enough and face was much in evidence in that
for a client to be robbed or done over would be an unforgivable stain
on the house's reputation and most shaming.

Also, in the case of seafaring men, it would mean loss of face
for their clients to be late on board so it was quite a usual sight
in the morning to see girls urging their clients along to the ships,
occasionally looking at the man's wrist watch.

As I did my rounds of several houses it occurred to me that
while it was one thing to be an ageing Captain, accompanied by
a Provost Marshal, making an official inspection, had I been the
young officer of a few years ago with a few quid in my pocket
and a few drinks under my belt, it was a moot point whether my
researches might not have been a bit deeper.

★ ★ ★

The brothel was in Dallas, which in the early eighties was like
lots of American cities – blighted, full of crime and drugs. But
Dallas was also home to Showco, the tour production company
we used, and so that's where we'd spend several weeks rehearsing
at the start of each tour.

At some point someone in governmental office had come
up with a plan for a new rail transport system in an attempt to
rejuvenate parts of the city and increase land prices. One of the
directors of Showco, spotting an investment opportunity, persuaded us to go in with him and so that's how we ended up
owning a car park in Dallas and a small hotel run by a guy called
The Chinaman. Thinking about it, his name should probably
have been a clue, but The Chinaman always paid his rent on

time and in cash so no questions got asked. He had a good run of five years or so before anyone got wise to the fact that he was running a whorehouse.

Since we'd started working with Showco, the days of Les Adey and his shaking hands were well and truly over. We'd always tried to paint a picture on stage and as the venues we played got bigger, production got more important. We wanted to engage every single person who came to see us, even if they were in the highest row of a 20,000-seat arena.

Special effects until this point had still been quite primitive. They also had a fatal flaw in that they were operated by people. One of our early laser operators spent ages lying on his stomach above a laser, only to realize he was facing the wrong way and his beam had been burning a hole in the wall behind him. The laser geeks didn't integrate very well, either: the roadies never did like them and they once left one at an airport tied to a pillar by his own rucksack straps.

We felt that we'd been on to something with the mirrors we'd had back in 1978 for Knebworth (as the *Daily Express* loved pointing out, they each weighed twenty tons, cost £50,000 and contributed significantly to our £25,000 a day running costs – like the TV documentaries, the newspapers couldn't get enough of the figures). But the problem with the mirrors was that the light we shone up at them from follow spots got dissipated on the way back down. Once again, we would have to rely on operators to direct the spots themselves. When we had played at local halls in America with union guys at the controls, this meant we'd inevitably end up with Tony brilliantly lit for my solos and vice versa.

Lights that moved automatically and changed colour were the dream, and one that Rusty Brutsché of Showco shared. Until now, coloured lights relied on gel filters, which burnt out with the heat from the bulbs behind them. The dichroic filters that Jim Bornhorst invented for his new VARI*LITE lighting kept cool, which was not only a technical breakthrough but also a bonus for us, standing under them. It wasn't too bad for me but Chester was bald and sitting on a drum riser at the back of the stage: he'd often complain that he was starting to feel a little bubble going on up top.

VARI*LITE lighting may have stayed cold but they weren't climate-proof: when Rusty came over to The Farm in December 1981 to demonstrate them to us, it was a freezing cold day. We were out in the old wooden barn and the lights took forever to fire up – but when they did start to work, they were fantastic.

The visuals and lighting had always been something that Tony and I loved. At some point, the two of us even discussed making an office version of the VARI*LITE. (The idea was that because VARI*LITE lighting didn't generate extra heat, companies would be able to save on air-conditioning costs – this being an era when empty offices in Dallas still left their lights burning all night.)

Tony and I would often have our differences musically, but when it came to visuals, never: we both shared the same strong sense of what we wanted and what would work. Because Phil was less interested in that side of things, it always made for a natural division of labour when we were rehearsing. We would go back to our hotel each night and Tony and I would work with our lighting director, Alan Owen, on new looks; meanwhile, Phil went to his room to listen to the day's tapes and make notes on the sound mix.

With VARI*LITE, however, all of us saw the potential. We put up a few hundred thousand dollars for research and development, and then spent the next few years as guinea pigs at the mercy of lights that would suddenly start smoking or spinning round like they were possessed. During the whole of the *Abacab* tour, I would be aware of crew padding backwards and forwards across the truss above me to deal with a light that was freaking out: the technicians would either unplug it or take a hammer to it. The funny thing was that both methods seemed to work equally as well.

But as the problems got ironed out, other bands started to see that we were setting the standard. VARI*LITE lighting had revolutionized the industry, and because they weren't commercially available, the only option was to rent them from us. By the early eighties the Stones were hiring our VARI*LITE rigs for their world tours. I'm sure that a lot of cheques made payable to Genesis were written through gritted teeth.

CHAPTER FIFTEEN

For me, the first side of the album *Genesis* is pretty high on the list of the best things we've done.

Duke had been a bit of a rebirth for us as a band in that, although we'd each brought a couple of individually written songs into the studio, the strongest ones were the ones we'd written as a group. (Group-written songs were always the favourites on an album, too, simply because we'd all had a hand in them.) *Abacab* had proved to be a transitional album, but a necessary one. I always felt that one of our strengths as a band was to go a bit too far off in one direction, realize that we had, and then get back on course again. Looking back, *Abacab* was one of our off-piste moments, and maybe that's because even on that album there had been some individually written songs.

All of the songs on *Genesis* were written as a group, hence the title. When we went into the studio in May 1983, none of the songs were already written.

We went in, plugged in, took a deep breath . . . and began to play. Although we didn't know it at the time, this would be the start of a wonderful roll that would last for almost ten years.

The making of *Genesis* would set the pattern for the albums that followed it. We'd go into The Farm with nothing, sometimes having not worked together for a year or more, and plunge into the unknown. Compared to other bands it was a weird way of working, and there'd always be a nice kind of fear about it. What were we going to do? Would it work? But always, even by the end of day one, it felt natural. Better than that, when we were making the next few albums the music flowed out so fast that we couldn't keep up.

I've always felt that the only way to have any integrity in music is to do what inspires you and what you like, and not to worry about what's going to happen when the record comes out. While we were touring *Abacab*, we'd been booed in Holland by a bunch of old hippies when we'd played 'Who Dunnit?'. It was a sonically bizarre, angular song, which we loved and everybody else hated. But what people didn't get was that we weren't trying to be punk: that song was a punk pastiche. Also, from our point of view, our set was pretty intense and quite technically challenging, and 'Who Dunnit?' was simply a bit of a break. I played drums on it and Tony even wore a frogman's mask. And yet those old Dutch hippies still couldn't tell that they weren't supposed to take the song seriously.

There would always be talk of 'old fans' and 'new fans', but in the studio there were no fans. We just went in and jammed and improvised, and the songs came out the way they came out. None of us were in control. Nevertheless, the way the songs came out on *Genesis* – long songs with long, long solos – meant that even at the time it felt like an album that the old fans would enjoy.

'Home by the Sea' was a dark, moody, two-part, eleven-minute thing (the second part was called 'Second Home by the Sea'). It'd got size, it'd got grandeur, it'd got everything. We knew how to do pieces like this by now. It was like a classical piece, and when we played it live the automated VARI★LITE truss would break up into diamond-shaped pieces and descend on the stage, moving around and beaming down green light. This may not sound so special now that VARI★LITE lights are everywhere, but at the time it was one of our most iconic looks.

'Mama', the best song on the album, was seven minutes long. The tune had begun with a drum loop I'd written in the sound-proofed spare bedroom at home. I put it through my Boogie amplifier and distorted it so much that it nearly fell off the stand. That was something an American musician would never do, I always thought. Take a sound and really fuck it up.

We had got the drum pattern playing in the studio and Tony started with his dark, low sustained chords, and then we just jammed on it for half an hour, recording as we were playing. We had known that if we caught the song as it came into being we might catch some magic. This was why we had wanted a studio of our own – to catch that spontaneous magic – and with 'Mama' we succeeded. Quite a lot of the final song came from that first, original jam.

The evil laugh was Phil's idea. He had said he wanted to do something like 'The Message' by Grandmaster Flash. Phil was always more musically aware than Tony and me, and would get out and see bands much more than we did. Tony and I never really left the house musically in the same way as Phil (although our solo albums had cured the agoraphobia: we could at least now go past the front door). I saw our insularity as a strength: when we played and wrote together we realized how unique each one of us was musically, and how unique we sounded as a band.

'Mama' was too brave for American radio, but I was very gratified when it came out in the UK and went straight to number 4. It was such an uncommercial song, given its length, but it really caught the public.

With *Genesis*, I was now achieving what I wanted to achieve without having to try so hard. It was also the first album where I felt I'd got into decent lead playing, purely because I'd been doing it for so long. It was the same as had happened in the early years with Phil's voice: you couldn't go faster than you could go.

The slight shame was that I was now playing a Steinberger guitar, which looked odd on stage. It was tiny – just a bit of carbon fibre and some strings – and it had a small sound too, although that was why I had wanted to use it. If everything on a song is big – big bass, big bass drum, big guitar sound – then you're left with no space. For our music, the beauty of the Steinberger sound was, because it was small enough to fit into the narrow band that was left, it sounded big as well.

It did make me look like I was playing a banjo, though. On stage I used to feel like George Formby. (That's why I designed the MR1 Steinberger: the first to be shaped like a proper guitar.)

★ ★ ★

Genesis went to number 1 in the UK, the same position as *Abacab*. That previous album *had been* our first official number 1, but unofficially we'd probably had several number

1s by this point. The problem was that previously we'd always fallen victim to the fact that sales were calculated according to the returns figures supplied by record shops. Because our cult following mostly raced out to buy our albums in the first week of release, the record shops would be overwhelmed and unable to register all the sales they were making. At least that's what I believed. It was only as barcodes had come in at the start of the eighties that sales figures were beginning to be more accurate.

Between *Genesis* and *Abacab* we'd also released a live album, *Three Sides Live*, which had got to number 2. It was while we were touring this that we reformed with Pete and Steve at Milton Keynes. For one night only.

★ ★ ★

By 1982, Peter had made four solo albums and also started the WOMAD festival. It was a huge undertaking: very well intentioned but a financial nightmare. Pete always had innovative ideas – he was a brave character – but he wasn't very realistic sometimes with the detail. After WOMAD he had ended up so far in debt that he was even getting death threats (although I didn't know about them at the time).

Being honourable, Pete had promised to pay everyone back, personally if necessary, and so when the idea of helping him with a fundraising reunion show came up there was no deliberation. We decided straightaway to make it happen. Given that we were in the middle of a forty-date UK tour ourselves, this was a logistical nightmare – did I say Pete wasn't very realistic sometimes? He wasn't the only one. In the end we had only a few days of rehearsals at the Hammersmith Odeon, playing songs that, in a few cases, we hadn't played for years.

I can honestly say that I wasn't aware of how much the fans would like seeing us all together again. That was one of my main reasons for not wanting the Milton Keynes Six of the Best show to be filmed. In retrospect it was one of my worst decisions.

As a band we were very serious about quality control – rightly so, I think – and I knew at the time that our performance was going to be a bit substandard, purely because of the lack of time we'd had to rehearse. My logic was that if you were there on the night it would be fantastic, but if you saw it again a couple of years later and it looked a bit shoddy and sounded bad, it would spoil the memory.

As it turned out it was special. It was only later that I realized how good it would have been to have a record of it for the fans, and also how special the whole thing had been for me personally, too.

At the start of the show Jonathan King introduced us and Pete came on in a coffin. It was very Pete. We started with 'Back in New York City', which was quite brave – beginning with a bang – and ended with 'The Knife', which was fun. It took us back to those early club days with Pete swinging his microphone up in the air.

It was hearing Pete sing the old songs again that made me appreciate what an amazing job Phil had done – how he now carried them so well. Over the past few years Phil had got a crack in his voice, a throaty rattle, and they were as much his songs now as they ever were Pete's.

Pete was never a match for Phil's drumming, though, much

as it frustrated him. When we came to play 'Turn It On Again', Pete suddenly decided he would play alongside Chester on Phil's kit. Like everyone else, what Pete hadn't realized was that 'Turn It On Again' was in 13/8 time, which made it like a merry-go-round: he'd think he had got to the end and suddenly we would be off again. He spent the whole song trying to work that one out, but I'd much rather someone put some passion in and make a mess than get everything note perfect. Plus, as a band we always quite enjoyed those moments when someone fucked up.

'Man on the Corner' from *Abacab* was a good example: the first beat wasn't in the obvious place. Until Phil told us where it was, Tony and I were lost. Once you knew where it was, the riff felt beautiful, but part of the charm of playing it live was watching Tony trying to work it out in his head: he usually had to get Chester to give him the count. (The one thing about Tony's mistakes is that he'll never hold his hands up if he gets it wrong. I'll always own up but Tony's technique is to look at me over the top of his keyboard and growl so that I immediately start thinking it's me that has messed up. He used to do it to Phil, too, and it was ages before the two of us were on to him.)

Steve joined us for a few songs at the end but there's little else I remember about Milton Keynes. It poured with rain the whole night, and it was my birthday too, so the crowd sang to me. Backstage was a quagmire with everyone in wellingtons, and we all had a glass of champagne to toast the moment, but the whole evening was like a dream, really. It remains one of those things that you look back on and wish you'd taken in more. The problem for me was that life was now so busy there was no time to pause and reflect, which was one of the reasons why I hadn't thought about how much the fans would like seeing us back together again. When you're as busy as we were, it's hard to get outside the moment enough to consider other points of view or even other people. And therein lay a real problem – not that I saw it at the time.

★ ★ ★

The Mama tour for *Genesis* was when we got our first private plane. This might sound great, but somehow it wasn't quite how you might imagine it: this was entry-level jet-setting. The plane cabin was okay but the cockpit was like something out of *M★A★S★H*: everything was khaki coloured. One night we were playing Cincinnati and our tour manager, Andy Mackrill, and I were walking past the bar in the hotel where we were staying. Like half the bars in America it was too dark to see anything properly, but I thought I vaguely recognized a face in the gloom. 'Who's that?' I asked Andy, squinting at a swaying character who was obviously just about to slide off his stool. 'Oh,' said Andy. He did a double take. 'Oh. That's the pilot.'

We were playing New York on that tour, and Angie had flown out to visit and brought Kate and Tom with her. This wasn't unusual, as our children travelled the world from a young age. We thought it was a great education for them, but they also had to learn to fit in with the band rather than vice versa. When we were flying between cities, we'd plonk their Moses baskets at the back of the cabin and they'd just have to stay there and sleep. You can be quite tough with children, really; it wasn't much different from my father making Nicky and I park our tricycles neatly inside the painted white lines on Whale Island.

One night we were due to fly to Washington, DC, in our private plane to catch the Rolling Stones in concert. The kids stayed behind in our hotel with a nanny, while Tony decided to pass up the opportunity. Given that it was dark, it was snowing and the plane was an incredibly small two-prop eight-seater, you couldn't blame him. It was when the wind got so strong that our plane seemed not just to be staying still, but actually going backwards that the rest of us began to wish we'd stayed behind too. I looked out of the window and we weren't flying above the sky-scrapers as we left Manhattan, we were passing them at around the level of the fortieth floor. We would have been able to see people in their offices if there hadn't been a blizzard in the way.

At this point we realized we were just going to have to grit our teeth and drink our way through it, the issue then being that, because the plane was so small, there was nothing on board except miniature whiskeys.

After half an hour or so we'd drunk at least a tray of minia-tures and I was feeling a bit better; Angie, however (not at all unreasonably), was still convinced that we were going to die.

'What's going to happen to the children? We've left our chil-dren and they're going to be orphaned!'

'Don't worry,' I said, the whiskey having started to work by this point, 'Tony Smith will look after them.'

Angie looked at me and went absolutely white. 'Mike, Tony Smith is sitting behind us.'

In the end we got to Washington in one piece but by then we were all too drunk to care, and Keith was in the same state as the rest of us.

It was actually Charlie Watts who I think best summed

up life in a rock band: he said that being in the Stones for thirty-five years boiled down to five years of work and thirty years of hanging around. I never stopped loving travelling and touring, but there were down days when we'd be in Kansas City and it would be pouring with rain and we'd been there twenty times before. This would be decade two or three, and by the end of it we'd begin to feel a bit landlocked.

I did try to work between gigs. I ended up feeling so guilty that I wasn't busy writing songs all the time that I asked one of the technicians at The Farm to design a flight case with a little monitor/mixer, a tape recorder and some pedals in it so that I could record ideas while on tour. In my mind I imagined I'd sit in my hotel room writing and doing great things, but talk about a white elephant . . . Every day the hotel porter would come up to my room, huffing and puffing as he lugged this thing in, and every day I'd open it up, look at it, shut the lid again and send it back down. I never used it once.

We all had ways of coping. Phil had his portable train set, which would keep him amused for hours. Tony went through a phase of weighing himself before and after he went to the loo – he had always liked science. For my part I ended up watching a lot of American television, or rather American commercials, which always seemed to take up more time than the programmes. There was one car dealer on the West Coast who always started his end-lessly repeated ads with 'Hi! I'm Cal Worthington!' I never met Cal, but pretty soon I wanted to kill him.

Trevor Horn, the Frankie Goes to Hollywood producer, also had a quote about life on the road that I always liked: he said that touring bands were like a Viking horde coming to town, raping, pillaging and leaving the next morning, the fires still smoulder-ing. The only thing that fails to convey is that the casualties were usually mostly on the invading side. At the end of one particu-larly memorable tour there was only one roadie left who had been restrained enough not to need penicillin.

★ ★ ★

Rather than a Viking horde, a touring band is more like a visiting circus. In some towns, for the two days that you were there, you weren't just the most important thing that was happening: you were the only thing that was happening. It still felt like we were living in an increasingly strange bubble a lot of the time.

Until the early eighties, PR had mostly meant press and radio. In America, on the late-night radio, you'd often end up chatting and smoking dope with the DJs – their voices would always drop an octave the minute they went on air. We'd choose the songs we wanted to hear and we'd chat away, but it never ceased to amaze me that what we were saying was going out beyond the room we were sitting in. That disbelief was the key to it, really – otherwise I would have been a bit worried about whatever was spooling out of my mouth.

Sometimes some dignitary or other would arrange for us to receive the keys of their city, which was nice but slightly puzzling. Why on earth would you trust your keys to a bunch of long-haired musicians, of all people? But it was when MTV launched in 1981 that my life in the band really began to resemble my father's years of hurrah cruises: PR went crazy.

We put up with the chat shows but, as for MTV, I had mixed feelings. I could understand how exciting it was for fans to learn more about the bands they loved and to see songs coming to life in videos, but at the same time I felt videos took the mystery of the songs away. You weren't free to interpret the lyrics as you'd imagined them.

There was also the fact that MTV fed an insatiable curiosity about bands as individuals, which I didn't think was necessarily a good thing. I had mostly escaped attention throughout our career, but with MTV, image suddenly started to matter for everybody in a group, which was a pain in the arse. During the Mama tour my image mainly involved leather trousers, curly hair and a jazzy red-and-white striped shirt. At least it was better than the Robin Hood look I'd had earlier on, but that's about the only excuse I can offer.

With the birth of MTV, promo became a bigger and bigger part of our lives until eventually we seemed to spend more time in TV studios that we did on stage. There was one day when we sat in a studio in Chicago and from 10 a.m. to 10:15 a.m. we were on the main morning show in New York, then from 10:15 a.m. to 10:30 a.m. it was Baltimore, then it was Philadelphia . . . and on it went round the country, non-stop, for eight hours. I could have shot myself.

Phil was great on camera, which was a big help, but one less positive effect of MTV for us as a band was that our singles were played so much they tended to dwarf the rest of the songs on our albums. This in turn altered the public's perception of us. I'm sure that in America, where we were now playing to huge crowds, a lot of the audience had come to hear the three- and four-minute singles, but live it always seemed to me that the long songs in our set, like the 'Home by the Sea' two-parter, went down just as well.

★ ★ ★

Norbert Gamson was a trustworthy guy: smart, reputable and generally in control. He was our French promoter for the Mama tour, and by the eighties promoters were a bit more professional than they had been in the seventies. They didn't solve disputes by waving shotguns around, for one. Nevertheless, there were still dramas, and one night Norbert was attacked and robbed.

Hard as it is to believe now, this was an era when promoters would still often leave a venue with £100,000 worth of takings to bank in the morning. On this occasion Norbert had taken our £100,000 worth of takings and was walking back to his hotel late at night when he was set upon by a masked figure who, having relieved him of the cash, sped off in a car.

This was all a bit suspicious. Who knew Norbert's plans and where he was staying? Who knew when exactly to catch him with the money? It had to be an inside job, one of Norbert's employees, we thought – and it was. It was also possibly the easiest investigation in French criminal history, because not only had the culprit used his real name when hiring his getaway car from Avis, he'd hired it using Norbert's company account.

The Norbert Gamson robbery wasn't the first time we'd been victims of a set-up. In the mid-seventies we'd played two nights at the Academy of Music in New York, and as the dates were back to back, decided to leave our gear locked in the hall overnight. The next morning I came back and my guitars were gone.

A union security guy had been in the hall all night so there was absolutely no doubt who was behind it, but New York unions at that time were pretty scary. I'd been amazed, the first time we played New York, that Dale couldn't even carry my guitar from one side of the stage to the other: a union guy had to do it. (They'd also always drag their heels setting up so that they could get overtime. Between six and seven o'clock, the stage would go dark while everyone went and had their supper. The union guys would barely even pretend to lift a plectrum until ten to six, and then they'd go into a frenzy ten minutes before they were due their break.

For several hours we were all left wondering what to do until finally a phone call came through informing us that we could buy some of the gear back. We didn't have any choice about it: a deal was done and the guitars were returned – one of them being the Rickenbacker that I'd borrowed from John Al at Charterhouse and somehow never got around to returning. It had stood me in good stead over the years.

★ ★ ★

I knew by the time we were touring *Genesis* that my future was not as a solo artist. Any doubt I'd had had been removed by *Acting Very Strange*, which was released in 1982 and was the first and last album I'd ever sing on.

I had no real desire to sing, but people would always ask if I was going to try it and eventually I decided, what the hell, I'd give it a shot. But it was one of those times when, even before you start, a little voice inside tells you it isn't a good idea. And you end up doing it anyway.

What I had discovered about my singing is that if I drank enough Remy Martin my voice could get a bit of a husk, a bit of character. The key then was getting to that stage and doing my bit before I got entirely drunk. I managed sufficiently to make the album but afterwards I can clearly remember Dad dropping a very polite hint that branching out on my own wasn't the best thing to do. Obviously, Mum thought it was the best record I'd ever made. She particularly loved the video for the single, 'Halfway There' – four minutes with the camera focused almost entirely on me. It was more of a surprise that Eddie Van Halen liked that song too.

When Eddie suggested that we should have a go at doing something together, I don't think he realized what he was getting into – i.e. that my vocal ability was pretty well linked to my alcohol consumption. But then I didn't know what I'd let myself in for with Eddie.

Having arranged a date, I flew over to LA and checked into the Sunset Marquee, looking forward to starting work the next day and prepared for the fact that Eddie liked to get going early. This sounded fine and sensible to me. Then I found out Eddie's early was 2:30 a.m.

If there's one thing I've learned over the years about late-night sessions it's that they don't work for me: your judgement goes. 'That snare drum sounds great there!' you think – and then the next morning you find out it doesn't.

But working like that obviously suited Eddie, so I set my alarm for the early hours and drove over to his place feeling that horrible, gummy-mouthed feeling when you've gone to bed and got up again too soon, in addition to which I was jet-lagged.

I liked Eddie's guitar playing and he liked Genesis, and I still think that, had it not been for his schedule, we might have got somewhere. But after three days of 2:30 a.m. starts I was in bits, and on day four I wandered home again. I'm not sure he knew I'd gone, really.

Even though it hadn't worked with Eddie, the idea of doing something collaboratively still appealed to me. I knew I didn't want to form another band and I knew I definitely wasn't going to sing myself again but maybe, I thought, I'd just try to find some songwriters to work with and see what happened . . .

CHAPTER SIXTEEN

Mike and the Mechanics didn't begin as a group. They began in 1984 when I asked Jon Crawley and Stuart Newton, who ran our publishers Hit and Run, along with Tony Smith, to recommend some songwriters to work with me on a solo project. Phil, meanwhile, was making *No Jacket Required*, and there was a gap in the Genesis schedule. Jon and Stuart came back with a list of ten names, at the top of which were B. A. Robertson and Chris Neil, so that's where I decided to start.

I didn't know much about B. A. beyond that he was a Scottish singer and songwriter who'd had a couple of hit singles with 'Kool in the Kaftan' and 'Bang Bang'. He had also written for my childhood hero, Cliff Richard. Chris Neil was an actor and producer as well as a great songwriter and had previously worked in George Martin's studio on Montserrat. To be honest, though, the whole thing was an absolute punt – their names just happened to be the first two on the piece of paper I'd been given – which meant that it was wonderful to find that the three of us seemed to have a chemistry straightaway.

Chris, B. A. and I spent the summer of 1984 bluesing away

at home and by the autumn we seemed to be drawing near to making an album. Chris has got good ears and could hear something in my noodlings. 'All I Need Is a Miracle' started as three different songs, and it was Chris who took the best bits from each of them and put them together. Even though what we'd got was sounding good there was no master plan. We didn't have a record deal and I had no idea of what we'd do next. I just knew that I didn't want to form another band. So off we went on our separate ways until, on a cold, blustery November day, I got a call from Chris.

'I've been thinking, Mike – why don't we go to Montserrat and record?'

I looked out of the window. It was grey.

'Do you know what, Chris? I think that's a good idea.'

As well as knowing how to pick his moments, Chris had a way of making the atmosphere in a studio fun, which I rapidly came to appreciate. Producers are always first in, last out and quite a lot of the job involves saying things like 'It's sounding great guys! I think you're on to something!' while inside you're dying. I would soon learn this the hard way producing an American band called Red 7 at The Farm. In a band, if something isn't going well or you're not sure about something, you can pass it around like a hot coal and take turns to carry the can. If you're a producer, you're on your own. I also realized that if it wasn't my music, I didn't feel the same passion for it. Chris, by contrast, had natural enthusiasm – or else he was a better actor than he's been given credit for. Given that he'd been in *Adventures of a Plumber's Mate*, that wouldn't be difficult.

We were on Montserrat for three weeks, during which time

we accomplished an amazing amount, partly because of the catamaran that went out each afternoon at 2:30 p.m. American unions might have got themselves into gear at the whiff of overtime, but if you really want to get something done, dangling a boat trip in the Caribbean in front of people is pretty foolproof. It all went well and we came back to the UK feeling pretty pleased with it. Then I realized, 'Oh, Christ, we've got to find some singers now.' There had never been a plan – the plan was to go bit by bit, see what we'd got – but this was still quite a hitch. Fortunately, Chris Neil was old friends with Paul Young, and B. A. brought Paul Carrack down from Sheffield.

Paul Carrack was an R&B singer so on paper he was the wrong choice entirely for 'Silent Running (On Dangerous Ground)', a big, lush, dramatic soundscape of a song with lyrics that were about as un-R&B as you could get: 'Take the children and yourself / And hide out in the cellar / By now the fighting will be close at hand.' They were rougher and tougher and bigger than anything Paul usually sang. In another voice it could have sounded rather pompous; coming from Paul they never did.

Paul Young, who'd been in Sad Café, had a raspier voice than Paul Carrack and would really belt songs out. He came and sang 'All I Need Is a Miracle' and it was obvious then that we'd got two great singers, each suited to different songs, and that both of them should be on the album.

What people tend to forget now is that there are two other singers on the first Mechanics album besides Paul and Paul: Gene Stashuk, who was the singer from Red Seven, and John Kirby, who was in Heatwave and had a soft, gentle voice. As I wasn't forming a band I didn't see any reason not to have multiple singers: I'd got a blank sheet of paper, I could do what I wanted and in my mind this was only ever a one-album project anyway.

Nevertheless, as Tony Smith pointed out, in order to present the album to the world there needed to be the appearance of a band behind it and, first of all, this band needed a name. Luckily this was one thing I had thought about ahead of time: they were going to be called 'Not Now, Bernard!'

In my defence I'd always heard the word 'Bernard' as being pronounced in a Bronx accent with the emphasis on the second syllable: 'Not now, BerNARD!' I still think it sounds quite cool if you say it that way. But when I told Angie, I found out that the rest of the world say 'BERnerd', as in the saint or the dog, which obviously wouldn't have been great. Mike and the Mechanics was Tony Smith's idea and I instantly liked the name. It was a nice, down-to-earth name and, above all, it meant that the American distributors couldn't put a big 'Mike Rutherford from Genesis' sticker on the front of the album. The chance to be judged solely on musical merit, without any baggage, seemed to me to be the most amazing opportunity and it's one for which I am grateful to this day.

It was never a given that we'd get a record deal – I seem to remember Tony Smith's words were, 'We'll try and get a deal,' hedging his bets as usual. But Atlantic liked what they heard and so, in July 1985, Chris Neil and I went into Air Studios in Oxford Street to finish mixing the album, and that's how I can remember where I was on the day of Live Aid. The telly in the recreation room was tuned in and occasionally I'd pass through and see what was going on. Phil was the only musician to appear at both the Wembley and Philadelphia gigs. Although Bob Geldof hadn't asked the band to appear, there was one moment when I looked out of the window at Portland Place and thought: maybe we should have done it. But we were in solo mode and hadn't been very much in touch with each other, plus it would have felt quite a big deal getting Chester and Daryl over from America for just one gig. However, it probably wouldn't have been harder than uniting the Mechanics for the first time. I hadn't seen Adrian Lee, our keyboard player, or Peter Van Hooke, our drummer, since we'd been in Montserrat six months earlier. All four singers had come down to the studio separately to record their vocals, so the first time they ever all met was after the album was finished and we were shooting the publicity photos.

There was a lot of luck involved in the first Mechanics album: I had found B. A. and Chris Neil at the first attempt, and Paul Carrack and Paul Young were perfect for the songs straightaway. It felt almost like it was meant to be. But there was one final piece of luck to come. Originally, the first single from the album was going to be 'Hanging by a Thread', which was a rather obvious and heavy song. Then Andrea Ganis from Atlantic heard 'Silent Running' and chose that instead.

'Silent Running' was striking, six minutes long and a brave choice for American rock radio. It sounded complicated but it was only three chords, and the bass note stays the same throughout the entire song. It was also exactly the right sound for 1985: it went to number 6 in the US. Our next single, 'All I Need Is a Miracle', went to number 5.

Like the first demo tape Genesis had made in Brian Roberts's attic, Andrea's decision was one of those moments of good fortune that sometimes you need in life.

Paul Young lived to be on stage and was a force to be reckoned with. He gave everything in a live performance and in the studio; he was an intuitive writer and a brilliant singer. We had a wonderful twenty-year relationship.

I soon realized that he loved the rock 'n' roll lifestyle a bit too much when we arrived in New York for our promotional trip. The first morning I went down to the hotel lobby ready to do a full day's work of interviews with him. As I was waiting for him, he stumbled into the lobby from the street, completely out of his head on coke, booze and whatever else he'd managed to score in Harlem, where he, ended up. Obviously I couldn't take him with me, and he had to sober up for the evening as we were doing a live performance on TV. So I called Angie in our room and asked her to look after him for a few hours and to keep him away from booze and any other substances. Apparently this was easier said than done. In between diving between the mini bars in both rooms – Angie had managed to get there first – he tried to smash the hotel window with a chair. He was in such a state and so desperate for a drink that he then threatened to jump from the forty-fourth floor. Angie gave in after a while. By then, she had had enough: she slipped a very strong sleeping pill into his drink. I forgot to tell her about needing him for the live performance later.

In fairness to Paul, everything about the first Mechanics tour was a bit surreal. We performed on the same bill as a troop of lumberjacks at a state fair somewhere, and late-night American cable TV also seemed to be showing one of Chris's risqué films on a loop.

I'd get back to my hotel room after a show, switch on the TV set and suddenly there would be Chris's bottom going up and down as he bonked some girl in a canoe. But that all seemed par for the course compared to what happened when we got to Washington.

The idea of Youngy hanging out with a cop from Manchester just didn't begin to compute. The idea of that cop moving from Manchester to Washington and – God knows how – getting a job with the US Secret Service team that looked after President Reagan was pretty mindboggling. But the idea that this cop would give us a private and very unauthorized tour of the White House . . .

From what I remember, the most impressive part of the White House is the façade. I can't remember much because we were smuggled inside in secrecy in the middle of the night; we'd just finished a show, we were tired and all of us, not just Youngy, were stoned. Inside, the place seemed quite bland, almost ordinary. The only really extraordinary bit was thinking that President Reagan was asleep upstairs and we were all tramping through his state rooms. I think the only thing we didn't see was the Oval Office, which actually felt like quite a relief: even stoned, I realized that would have been pushing our luck.

Nevertheless, when we were invited back to the State Department building the following day for an (equally unofficial) demonstration of lie-detecting equipment, we obviously went along.

As well as looking after the President's security, the Secret Service was apparently also responsible for preventing financial crime. Youngy's friend took us into the vaults where all kinds of top-secret files were kept – we looked at a few of them, too. We all took lie-detector tests, which were very unnerving, as you start to feel guilty before it even starts, especially if you were trespassing in the White House the night before.

★ ★ ★

When I married Angie I was a bit of a cold fish and found it hard to express my feelings. She wasn't and didn't, and she wasn't going to wait around while I mumbled incoherently either. She was going to drag my emotions out of me by force if necessary.

Angie instilled in me the notion that sport was a good thing – okay for health reasons, but she maintained it kept relationships together. I'm not sure I quite got it at first: the sum total of my sporting career was loading and unloading gear, and playing the guitar. Once we had our children, she had us skiing (me included, and properly this time), riding, playing tennis, swimming, waterskiing, golf. You name it: we did it.

There had always been such a gap between me and my own parents when I was growing up. They were older parents from another era. I'd often think about how much fun I had with my kids running around and doing stuff, and remembered that the only time I'd every shared anything like that with Dad was the single golf match we'd played together at prep school.

I did everything I could to keep up my bond with my children. Touring could make this hard to accomplish, but Angie was still escorting them across the globe so I could see them as often as possible. However, there was only one occasion that really made me stop and think. It was a winter half-term in the mid-eighties, when Kate was about seven. We'd gone to Mull for the holidays and were all out for a walk. The scene was bathed in that four o'clock winter light you get in Scotland, when you can't help but take a great photograph with any old camera. I've got a lovely picture of Angie and Kate standing in wellingtons in a river, Angie with her arm around Kate. They're both happy, smiling: a mother and daughter. But when I see that picture now, I remember that during that holiday, Kate, whom I hadn't seen for three months, didn't quite know how to act around me. She wasn't embarrassed exactly, but it wasn't natural. It was quite a shock at the time. She saw me almost as a stranger, not her dad. I tried to make sure that would never happen again.

I was less competent in trying to get closer to my own father. Dad was never impulsive enough just to pick up the phone and say, 'Hi, Mike, I'm just ringing for a chat . . .', something that pains me to think about now. If he called me, it was always with a purpose, and he must have sat down and thought about it beforehand. And I suppose it was for that reason that I was less inclined to pick up the phone myself.

But the pace of my life was also now so fast and I was so busy with work that, much as I find it hard to admit, I was also often lazy when it came to keeping in touch with my parents.

'Mike, have you rung your dad?'

This would be the first week that I'd arrived back from tour.

'No, I will.'

A couple of days later: 'Have you rung your dad yet, Mike?'

'No, but I'm going to.'

A couple of days later: 'Ring your dad!'

Unlike Angie, I put things off. My sister would see my parents regularly but I had to be pushed into being a good son.

I'd always been impressed by my dad's sense of duty towards my two grannies, whom he took care of into old age. I had a similar sense of duty regarding Angie and the kids, and to my work. But with Mum and Dad I felt slightly that all the work I'd been doing – the touring, the recording, the constant travelling and publicity – somehow excused me from having to bother putting in the necessary effort. I'd send them on a cruise each year, which they loved – my father would always be looked after and invited to eat at the Captain's table – and I'd kid myself that I'd done enough.

All of this meant that it was Angie who saw my parents the most. She would always be the one who organized Sunday lunch, birthdays, Christmases – the family occasions – and so it was her suggestion that we have a special lunch for my dad's eightieth birthday.

At eighty, Dad was still mentally very sharp, and I suppose that's what I saw when we met that day at the Bush Hotel in Farnham, not how much he'd aged. With hindsight, I should have noticed that he had lost weight, his neck didn't quite fill his collar, his cheeks had hollowed out and he seemed frail inside his double-breasted jacket. But when someone is so familiar, you don't see those changes so easily.

I gave him an engraved Genesis gold disc as a present and it felt like a nice thing to do: a way of thanking him and acknowledging how much he'd supported my career. Because his own career had been marked by medals and ceremonies, I thought he'd appreciate the symbolism of it, too.

A photographer from the local newspaper came to the hotel to take a few pictures, and later a reporter interviewed Dad:

The captain, who lives in Ridgway Road, Farnham, was adamant when we spoke to him last week that he had backed his son to the hilt – and had not even nurtured a private hope that the boy's career might take a more orthodox course.

'We always supported him,' he said. 'I told Michael right from the beginning: "If there is something you want to do more than anything else, as long as it is both legal and viable, we will support you," and we did.

'My wife would have liked him to go into the Navy, and I also wondered whether it would be suitable, but from the very beginning he was so far into music that we gave him our support.

'I did tell him, though, after he started playing the guitar at the age of seven: "If you are serious about the guitar you must at least know which way up to hold it." So I sent him to classical guitar lessons.'

When I read my dad's memoir, I found he'd written a longer version of the Genesis story there:

Getting their A levels, a parental condition for support, they came up the hard way, travelling around in an old bread van, living on motorway egg and double chips and sleeping rough on the floors of the places where they played their gig, as such performances are known.

Despite vicissitudes, they stuck to it and are now 'Genesis', a world famous group, jetting around the globe in Jumbos and Concordes with an entourage of forty managers, administrators and technicians and a formidable array of specialized vehicles. When not on the job they live the active but relaxing lives of country gentlemen in Sussex engrossed in horses and other activities of a healthful nature.

Anne and I have been their fans from the outset attending their gigs with a discreet insertion of a bit of cotton wool in the ears, taking the musical magazines appropriate to their style of music and becoming in-persons in this field.

On one occasion, Anne was outside in a garden chair with her radio going full blast as the programme was playing the group's music and Michael, the Pop Star, in the house composing further tunes, had to come outside and shout: 'Mum – do you mind turning your radio down!'

When I met my father that day for his birthday it never occurred to me, even for a minute, that anything would happen. I thought I'd see him again in a couple of months in the little window I had between the end of the Mechanics tour and the start of the next Genesis one. My father knew what my schedule was like and I always felt he understood: for all the gulf between us, our lives had ended up being similar in so many ways.

But that day was the last time I saw him.

CHAPTER SEVENTEEN

It seemed realistic to me to assume that if you'd got into Genesis in the early days you probably wouldn't be so keen on *Invisible Touch*. Fans are always going to prefer the era when they first discover you and assume that any change is for the worst. It's a problem common to all long-lived bands. But on stage, when we were playing live, it never felt any different at all to me: it was all a continuum.

Invisible Touch isn't the definitive Genesis album but it was probably our hottest moment in terms of commercial success. It was the biggest we would ever get as a band. And, like *Genesis*, it seemed almost effortless to make. My memory of writing it is of going into The Farm and it just flowing. Phil had a little drum machine – a blue mono Akai – and we'd start with a nothing-very-much loop and jam over it. Phil would sing whatever came into his head, and Tony and I would pile in fearlessly with any old chords and noise and racket. And out the songs came.

When we went into the studio to make *Invisible Touch* towards the end of 1985, the three of us hadn't worked together for three years. During that time I'd released *Acting Very Strange* and *Mike and the Mechanics,* Tony had released a soundtrack to a Michael Winner film called *The Wicked Lady* and two solo albums, *The Fugitive* and *Soundtracks,* and Phil had released *Hello, I Must be Going* and *No Jacket Required.*

Had it not been for the fact that we all shared one manager, Tony Smith, then *Invisible Touch* might never have happened. There'd have been so many conflicts of interest – clashing tours and competing publicity schedules. With different managers pulling in different directions, it's easy to imagine that the band would have been pulled apart. As well as having one manager, we were simply three people held together by a thread from way back and, while not ever being demonstrative, we were friends in a genuine way. Plus, for all our solo work, there was still something the three of us could only do when we were together in a room.

The *Invisible Touch* tour ran from September 1986 to July 1987. It started in America, then went to Australia and New Zealand (our first time in both countries), then went back to America, then over to Japan, then up to Europe, then back to America, then back again to Europe and ended finally in four nights at Wembley. We'd been doing pretty well for quite a few years, but Phil's solo success and Mike and the Mechanics had pushed us into a different kind of global visibility. Yet one of the main reasons Genesis were still achieving so much was because we were a very hard-working live act. Live shows had always been our foundation.

It was while we were discussing our touring plans that Tony Smith noticed that I was going to be out of the country for almost a whole year. Prior to the start of the *Invisible Touch* tour in

September, the band would be rehearsing for a month in Dallas, and for the two months prior to that I'd be on tour in America with the Mechanics. 'If you wanted, you could take a tax year out,' he said. If I didn't return to the UK, I would save a fortune.

At the time it seemed almost crazy not to do it. Angie and the kids would be flying out regularly so there wouldn't be any difference from that point of view, and I'd be in the country so little anyway that staying away for a few more weeks seemed hardly here nor there. At the time, it all seemed so simple.

★ ★ ★

While we started rehearsing in Dallas for the tour, I asked Angie to come and join me for the weekend, as I hadn't seen her for a while. I told her that one of the road crew would pick her up at Dallas airport and take her to the hotel. I'd meet her there after rehearsals and we'd spend some time together. What could go wrong?

Firstly, Angie must have picked the only carry-on bag from the cupboard that had a huge joint stashed in a side pocket. (I'd managed to forget about it while I was in Jamaica.) She boarded the plane not realizing what lay ahead. She was sitting in first class with only one other passenger. They exchanged niceties and that was that. When they landed, Angie thought she'd sail through customs as she only had a carry-on bag. She also noticed the Nancy Reagan 'Just Say No' [to drugs] campaign posters everywhere. As she went through customs, she was stopped and searched. The Jamaica Inn matchbox and one large joint were discovered. Thinking this was some kind of joke to begin with, she soon realized this was a very serious situation. She was questioned about who was meeting her – she didn't know – though being the wife of a rock musician certainly didn't help. Her fellow passenger had also been arrested and, while being interrogated, had managed to swallow a bag of heroin. He was promptly whisked away in an ambulance.

Seeing as they had travelled together, the customs officers thought Angie was involved with the man. After being strip-searched and questioned again, she was told she could 'go down' for twenty years. Meanwhile, the roadie who had gone to pick her up assumed she wasn't on that flight. He had come back to the rehearsal hall so I thought she was at the hotel, and just carried on playing. (There were no mobile phones then so communication was terrible.)

Angie was allowed one phone call and telephoned a very good family friend, Nick Cook (who is also known as 'The Commander'). He lived up to his name and managed to get hold of Tony Smith. Angie was released three hours later. The look on her face said it all. It also didn't help that her name would now be logged, which would make travelling to America and Australia very difficult. Whenever she came on tour after that – it frankly was a miracle she'd want to come anywhere near me – she'd have to wait on the plane until the authorities came to take her off. She would always explain to the children that it was because they wouldn't have to queue.

★ ★ ★

Certain bands have certain years and 1986 must have been our year. When *Invisible Touch* was released in June 1986 it went to number 1 in the UK and number 3 in the US; we released four singles from it and each got into the US Top 5, including 'Invisible Touch', which was our first US number 1.

The tour began in mid-September in Detroit, Michigan. It was like we had entered the stratosphere: private planes, police escorts, packed stadiums every night. And everywhere we went there'd be a Genesis song or a Genesis video playing. For the next eleven months it was like being royalty.

People would often say, Don't you get tired on tour? Perhaps what they don't understand is the connection you have with a crowd on stage: the energy you get from 50,000 people in a sold-out stadium is incredible. You're standing there and the noise is just a roar: it's like a battle cry but everybody's on your side.

And then the telephone rings at 3 a.m. when you're on your own in a hotel room in Chicago.

★ ★ ★

When I got that call in Chicago, I sat listening as Angie told me that my mum had just called her with the news: 'Angie, darling, Dad's dead. I've poked him with my stick and he's not moving: he's definitely gone.'

Mum was very immobile herself at this point, and she and my father slept in separate beds, so poking him with a stick would have made sense. It was just the sort of thing she would say so I could almost hear her voice: it was the same voice she'd used when she'd nearly set the house on fire in Farnham while Tony had been staying but she didn't want to cause a scene. 'Um, fire, Mikey? Fire?'

At the time I couldn't think properly. I didn't discuss arrangements with Angie, I was too much in shock. About a year before my father died he was due to have a minor operation. Before he went into hospital he took Angie to one side and told her that if anything happened to him, she should look in the box he kept under his bed and inside she'd find a key for his bureau: the telephone numbers of the doctor, the undertaker and the order of his funeral service. Death for my father, like everything in life, was about correct procedure – he'd even been organized and thoughtful enough to leave some money for my mum in the box. Like the papers, he'd put it neatly in a plastic folder.

Dad may have confided in Angie rather than me, but I think he knew the chances were that I'd be away when his box was needed. Maybe he also knew how hard I'd take it. It saddens me now to think he'd gone through that thought process – but, of course, he was right.

★ ★ ★

The next day, I sat with Tony Smith and planned out how I'd fly home for the day of my father's funeral and then back to LA for that evening's show. Meanwhile, the tour carried on as normal, as though nothing had happened.

It was surreal. I found I could go on stage and get lost in the music for two-and-a-half hours and even enjoy it. I could switch off. The thinking process stopped. But then the show would end and the realization of what had happened would hit me all over again. There was a sense of security, of safety, playing with Tony and Phil, but we never discussed what was happening. Our friendship just wasn't like that – Tony and I just weren't brought up to talk about our feelings. If you've been to boarding school at seven, you've got to hide your emotions to survive so it becomes inbuilt. That's one of the many reasons why marrying Angie and becoming a dad had been so good for me.

Two weeks later, on 13 October 1986, I flew back to England for my father's funeral and then, having been in the country for less than twenty-four hours, turned round and flew back to America to play in Los Angeles. When I stood there playing 'Mama', hoping that I was showing my father how my life had been shaped by what he'd taught me – duty, honour, commitment – I was aware that I had not always demonstrated those values towards him when he was alive. As a teenager I'd been so intent on rebelling, so intent on making sure that I was everything that he was not. Now, I hoped that, before he died, he had seen something he was proud of in me, something of the right spirit. I had many of the regrets that so many of us suffer: all the things I hadn't told him, all the things I hadn't done. I think my father knew I loved him even though I'd never said it, but I'd never even managed to tell him how wonderful he'd been in supporting me all my life – in fact, just what a wonderful person he'd been.

After the show that night I went to bed, and Angie eventually fell asleep as I lay beside her, glad she was there. The next morning she'd have to get straight on a plane again to fly home to look after Kate and Tom. I couldn't sleep, the past twenty-four hours had been too bizarre. I'd buried my father in the morning and then flown backwards in time on Concorde in order to play that night's show. I felt somehow that my father had gone on a journey too, and at that moment in time I wasn't quite sure where either of us were.

★ ★ ★

The morning after the LA Forum show, a dilapidated pink stretch limo had arrived at the hotel to take Angie to the airport. It was such an LA moment – there were flashing fairy lights all round the back window. Watching her drive away isn't an image I will easily forget. While I'd then gone back to the hotel, disaster had struck for Angie when, almost within sight of LAX the pink limo started billowing smoke. Having left England on the spur of the moment, Angie had nothing with her besides her passport and ticket – no money and no way of calling me for help. While she was standing on the inside lane of the freeway wondering what on earth to do, she heard a little tinkly bell – a Denny's hot-dog van. It was going slowly enough for her to be able to flag down the driver, who turned out to be friendly. So that was how Angie arrived at Los Angeles airport: in a hot-dog van, still in the black wool funeral dress she'd been wearing when she left England the day before.

After my father's funeral she started travelling back and forth to Norfolk to see her own father, who was dying of cancer. By this time we were coming to the end of our American tour, before heading to Japan and Australia. Angie wanted to bring the children to Australia for Christmas because we hadn't been together as a family since my father had died, though she was concerned about leaving her father. The hospital reassured her that her father had a couple of months at least, so it was better to go earlier rather than later. Angie flew out to Perth with the children. She'd only been there a day before her father sadly died. Angie wanted to fly back immediately, but the problem was the children were on her passport. This meant she'd have to take them with her: they couldn't remain in Australia with no documentation. (Travelling that far with two young children is hard enough, let alone taking them straight back again.) We managed to get a free pass for Angie to go as long as she came straight back again. Australia and back in three days was tough, but that's what she did.

* * *

If 1986 had been Genesis's year then it hadn't been a bad year for Pete, either. His album *So* had been released in May and reached number 1 in the UK and number 2 in the US album charts. 'Sledgehammer' was a US number 1 single in July, the week after 'Invisible Touch' had been number 1.

That Pete was reaching his peak at the same time as us wasn't a surprise. We had both been working hard at our careers and each of our albums had sold more than the last, so at some stage it was very likely that we'd end up at the same point on our separate trajectories. I don't think either of us had thought those points would be as high as they were.

I never thought of it as a competition between us – after all, it wasn't as though Pete's sales were taking anything away from ours. I sometimes thought it worked to everyone's advantage. In 1986, Steve Hackett was also in the US Top 20 with a single from his band GTR, and Phil's *No Jacket Required* and the first Mechanics album were still in the US album charts, too. It seemed so extraordinary that one band had resulted in so many successful acts that I think it increased the interest in all of us.

The videos for 'Sledgehammer' and 'Land of Confusion', the fourth single from *Invisible Touch*, were both nominated for MTV Music Video of the Year. We lost to Pete and I do think he deserved it, but it always amused me that our video, which was by far our best, didn't feature us at all. It didn't seem like a coincidence.

'Land of Confusion' was the nearest I've ever come to writing a protest song: 'There's too many men / making too many problems / and not much love to go round.' It was intended to be slightly tongue-in-cheek; it was also the last song on *Invisible Touch* to be written, and just as I was about to write the lyrics I'd got a flu bug. I was lying at home delirious, covered in sweat, but was running out of time. Eventually, Phil came over and sat on the end of my sick bed – being careful not to get too close – and stayed there until I'd written them.

The video featured Spitting Image puppets of the three of us: in the nineties my puppet was then recycled as Jesus – big nose, long hair – which delighted my mum (especially after Egypt) but it upset Mary Whitehouse. I don't think Phil and Tony were very impressed either. They rapidly brought me back down to earth if I started claiming any divine rights. The video was taking a satirical look at President Reagan and I have to admit they portrayed him as a rather useless president. The final scene showed him in bed, suffering from dementia, and accidentally pressing the red button to start a nuclear war instead of the nurse's call button.

The President himself obviously never saw the 'Land of Confusion': while the *Invisible Touch* tour was in Washington we were all invited to meet him at the White House. Seeing it properly for the first time – i.e. in daylight, not stoned, and with a clean conscience – it was actually quite impressive.

As a band we were now so big and flying so high that it was impossible not to get caught up in it all. It had been a terrible year for me personally with the death of my father, but it was hard to avoid the elation. America was like a big touring machine – we just got on it and worked. We were such a well-oiled touring outfit that Pink Floyd's David Gilmour and their manager Steve O'Rourke, who was great friends with Tony Smith, even joined us for a few weeks to relearn the ropes ahead of their *Momentary Lapse of Reason* tour (the Floyd had not toured since 1981).

At the end of our tours, our road crew would disappear and tour with another big band for a year, and then come back to us. This meant that we would often end up knowing people well by sight, but we would very rarely know anything about their lives and sometimes wouldn't even know their names. One truck driver on the *Invisible Touch* tour particularly stood out – he always wore a cowboy hat and had a big, long beard – but when we were in France one morning he didn't turn up. It was Andy Mackrill, our tour manager, who found him: he'd had a heart attack and died in his hotel room.

It was such a lonely death and it made me realize how, in many ways, it was such a lonely way of life, too. Only a few of the guys on tour had families back at home, and when we tried to get hold of the dead driver's next of kin we drew a blank. We eventually found a cousin somewhere in the Deep South who wasn't sure what we should do with him, so we had him cremated in Montpellier. We put his urn in a black box, which flew around with us on our plane until we could find a relative who would come and collect his ashes.

It seemed the right thing to do, to keep him with us, and whenever we played we'd always place his little black box at the side of the stage. However, when Kate and Tom next flew out with Angie, we decided it was probably best not to tell them what was in it. Unfortunately that meant they ended up falling asleep on the plane one night with it between them, using it as a pillow. I think it was Jolie Collins, Phil's daughter, who told them what was inside. I've never heard shrieking like it.

★ ★ ★

In April 1987 we had a month off. Because I still couldn't go home, Angie and I rented an apartment in Verbier, Switzerland, for the Easter holidays, so that we could take Kate and Tom skiing. Tony and Margaret came too and it seemed like Angie and I were finally going to get some rest and relaxation when, one week in, Angie was struck by what seemed to be terrible altitude sickness. It turned out to be morning sickness and she was soon feeling so ill that we had to abandon the holiday all together. Worse was to come.

★ ★ ★

Angie decided to meet me in Malaga for a few days. She was now four months pregnant and hadn't wanted to travel much. As soon as she arrived she knew something was wrong, so we called the doctor, who informed us that she had miscarried, and called an ambulance. It seems strange now but I couldn't go with her as I had to do a morning show with the band. When I arrived at the hospital Angie was already sedated, ready for an operation. I asked what the scan had showed. By the look on the doctors' faces it was obvious one hadn't been done. The scan showed a heartbeat and that the baby was hanging on for dear life. For the following three months Angie lay in bed, either in hospital or at home, with the baby still hanging on, while I had to continue the tour and the tax year. Life had become very strained and difficult, especially when I was on the other side of the world.

I then took up residence in a Sofitel hotel at Paris airport. It seemed easiest to base myself there so that I could fly to England whenever we weren't playing. Over the next few weeks I got to know that Sofitel pretty bloody well.

There was a set of double tables in the restaurant, and the same four businessmen would always be seated there, all wearing pin-stripe suits. I'd always wonder what their stories were – why they were also doomed to spend so much time in this Sofitel – and was beginning to think that maybe they were tax exiles, too. By this time I was more than ready to forget the tax plan completely. The decision had already affected our ability to be close at hand following the deaths of both our fathers, and now I was trapped in a hotel, staring at four businessmen, when I just wanted to be by my wife's side. But then I would realize that I couldn't just go home and be with Angie anyway, because I was still committed to another two months of European shows.

The Sofitel plan worked quite well but it wasn't foolproof. I had needed to fly back to London to make a video for 'Anything She Does'. We had got Benny Hill to star in it and, as always with Benny Hill, numerous busty blondes were also involved. My plan was to go on and visit Angie afterwards but the shoot overran, and as I had to be out of the country by midnight in order to comply with the conditions of my tax break, I wasn't allowed to stay the night. I rang Angie from the set to tell her: 'I'm sorry, babe, but I'm not going to be able to make it: we're running behind and I've got a Page 3 girl sitting on my knee.' I find that funny now, but life was beginning to get very strained for both of us. It was horrible to know what she was going through and not be able to be there for her.

★ ★ ★

By the time the *Invisible Touch* tour got to the UK in June 1987 my tax year was finally up. We were now about to play the biggest shows of our career: four sold-out nights at Wembley Stadium, playing to over 300,000 people. It was a record at the time, although sadly not a very long-standing one: we were beaten the very next year by Michael Jackson, who sold out five nights.

Over the years, I'd got to know how to prepare for big shows. Watching a film was always a bad idea – it would take you too far away mentally and you'd struggle to get your focus back afterwards. The best thing was simply to footle around. ('Footle' was one of my dad's words, like 'squiffed': I can hear that word today and picture him instantly at our Christmas dinner table pretending to be a bit tipsy and pulling his paper hat down over one ear.)

I'd got my footling skills down to a fine art over the course of the *Invisible Touch* tour. I'd discovered that you could make going to buy some more shampoo or razorblades last an awfully long time if you wanted to – but on the second of our Wembley dates I footled a bit too much and was late leaving home. Coming off the North Circular, I hit traffic and ended up in the middle of a solid jam stretching as far as I could see.

It could have been a disaster, but fortunately I had a strange new gadget with me in the car: a mobile phone. It was the size of a brick but it got me through to Andy Mackrill, who arranged for a police escort to come and rescue me. I followed them out into the fast lane and we flew towards the venue, although it was one of the hairiest drives of my life. When I got to Wembley my shirt was glued to my back with sweat.

One of the great things about those Wembley shows was the weather: four beautiful sunny days. Even at the time I thought, 'How lucky is that?' And I knew we were probably at the peak of our career, too, as I looked out at all those people waving. But after the year I'd had, it wasn't something I could really savour as much as I should have done.

* * *

Not long after Harry was born I met Chris Neil for lunch in the West End to tell him that there wouldn't be another Mechanics album. 'I really can't do it, Chris,' I said. 'I've got nothing left.'

At the time I was exhausted. I'd had enough. My father had died, Angie's father had died, we'd nearly lost a child, Angie had been bed-ridden for months and I'd been on the road for nearly a year. I was spent. Naturally, Chris looked a bit appalled that I was calling it a day but, just as he'd waited for the right moment to suggest recording in Montserrat, he was happy to bide his time.

'OK, fine, whatever you want to do. If you change your mind, let's talk about it.'

I think he always knew I'd call.

* * *

At the time we wrote 'The Living Years', B. A. Robertson had also recently lost his father and had a new baby. The song was very much his idea and his lyric, but it tied into both our experiences.

And both of us had our doubts about it. Writing a song about death and bereavement seemed crazy when you stop to think about it. If you try for something that's strong and emotionally touching and you get it wrong, it's not just bad, it's horrendous. But 'The Living Years' came directly from the heart and that's why it worked.

We wrote the song in a cottage situated on the way down to the stables at Drungewick. It had a lovely view looking out over the lake and the music also made for a certain type of reflective atmosphere, a different way of experiencing emotions. I hadn't cried at my father's funeral – it had all been so unreal and I'd been too numb – but there was one moment when B. A. and I were working on 'The Living Years' together that we both had to leave the room. Separately, of course. He went one way and I went the other.

Nor were we the only ones on whom that song had an effect. Paul Carrack's father had died in a pit accident when he was young, something that I half knew but, selfishly, didn't really think about enough at the time. It was Chris who reminded me about Paul's father. (Paul was a typical northerner and as emotionally hidden as the rest of us, but the theatre-world luvvie bit of Chris meant he was a much better communicator.) It seemed to me that something of that experience came out in Paul's singing, making his vocal all the more poignant. He sang it like only Carrack could sing it.

When we'd finished recording 'The Living Years', Chris came up to me, shook my hand and told me that working on it had been one of the highlights of his recording career. I wasn't at all sure how well it had worked, though. I was too close to it.

Then Andrea Ganis from Atlantic heard it and rang me: 'That's a number 1,' she said. And it was: in the US, Canada, Australia and Ireland, and a number 2 in the UK. It also won an Ivor Novello award in 1989 and was nominated for a Grammy in 1990.

CHAPTER EIGHTEEN

It's funny: when I write a song, I never really think anyone's ever going to hear it. Occasionally I will walk into my studio, look out of the window at the orchard and be amazed by the thought that what I'm writing on a spring day at home will be heard by guys in Argentina or the suburbs of Detroit. It's not something I ever quite believe.

Songs do touch people, but to have a song that changes people's lives as 'The Living Years' did is something else. I'm very aware that I'm lucky. The number of people that I've met or who have written to B.A. and me over the years telling us how it's affected them continues to amaze me. I've heard from people who have picked up the phone to their father after years of silence, or people who have managed finally to get close to their father as he is dying.

I had so many regrets after Dad died. I wished he'd been younger so that he and Mum could have enjoyed their retirement more; I wished I'd seen them more often; I wished I had done more for them both. It wasn't until I found Dad's notebooks in his trunk that I realized they'd had money worries. If only I'd known, I could have given them an allowance instead of just sending them off on a cruise. But perhaps my biggest regret was that my dad and I hadn't just chatted more.

It was only really after I found my father's memoir that I became aware of all the conversations we could have had and all the questions I could have asked him. I also began to get a sense of what he had done in the war, including the role he'd had in sinking the *Bismarck* in May 1941:

. . . as a gunnery specialist I had probably the best ringside seat of the day.

First came the spine tingling order 'enemy in sight!' followed by shouted orders and the clash of machinery as the turret's crew made the final drill movements. Then a nagging silent wait until the 'ting ting' of the fire gong and the jar and shudder of the first salvos.

There she was in my periscope – a bit indistinct but large and menacing.

As I looked, large shell splashes went up in the vicinity and, as it was too early for them to be ours, 'Rodney' had clearly fired first.

Then 'Bismarck' herself erupted in a flicker of reddish flashes and I recalled that this was not a target practice and that we were under fire ourselves.

It was just like Dad that he didn't take pleasure in the sinking:

Once the excitement of battle was over there was no euphoria. To a professional seaman the sinking of a ship, no matter whose she is or the reason for her loss, is not a matter for rejoicing, his innate instincts being to keep ships afloat and help those in them.

I began to understand what a shock leaving the Navy must have been for him, too.

But Dad's sense of humour also came out in his memoir – something else that I had not really appreciated when he was alive. What I realized, gradually, was that if there were communication problems between us it was to do with me as much as him. First, I was the grumpy teenager and then I was the ambitious musician, and I never really had time to ask how he was. I'm sure I closed him down and prevented him from really talking to me, but that's only something I have come to appreciate since my own children, Kate, Tom and Harry, have started carving out their careers and having families. They don't want to sit down and discuss my life, which is only natural. If I'd been more open, as I am now, I think Dad would have responded. I only realized that when it was too late. One of the most painful parts about discovering Dad's memoir was seeing what he'd called it: 'This Is My Thing'. 'Doing my thing, man' was something I'd often said to him as a typical sixteen-year-old if I felt he was on my case. It didn't really mean much – I was often just saying it for the sake of it – but he'd obviously taken it to heart. Luckily for me, he chose to respond by writing his book. It's the best legacy he could have left me.

★ ★ ★

After *The Living Years* I made another three Mike and the Mechanics albums with Paul Young and Paul Carrack. 'Over My Shoulder', from *Beggar on a Beach of Gold*, was the most played song in Europe in 1995 and the whole album was one I enjoyed. It had a good, up feeling about it, as though the Mechanics had found their place. But then in July 2000 I got a phone call from Tony Smith to tell me that Paul Young had had a heart attack and had died, aged fifty-three.

It was unexpected, but it wasn't a total shock. I had a wonderful twenty-year relationship with Paul but he had his demons: there was a sense that he was always living just on the edge. He loved the music world, he lived to be on stage, he was the king of rock 'n' roll . . . but the trouble was that when he finished a tour he would go home and carry on in the same vein. At the back of my mind I had always wondered how long he could keep it up.

We were poles apart, Youngy and me. I was always quite organized and controlled, and he was so much the opposite. Even today I'm still hearing stories that the crew kept from me at the time. He would always be having brushes with the police or getting caught up in some drama or other. But he was also a mesmeric presence on stage. Even now, I can recall standing behind and seeing how audiences got him, the looks on their faces as they watched him. He'd have the audience in the palm of his hand even when he was just playing tambourine and backing vocals. And his stage smile was never a stage smile, either: with Youngy it was always absolutely genuine because he was up there, doing what he loved.

By 2007, Paul and I felt the Mechanics had run their course, although I never, ever say I've stopped doing something. I just don't say anything. Nevertheless, in 2009 I was writing some songs at home and realized that they sounded like Mechanics songs, although at this point Paul Carrack was busy with his solo career, so I no longer had anyone to sing them.

I asked Brian Rawling at Metrophonic Music who he recommended: he suggested Andrew Roachford and Tim Howar
and, for the second time, it was almost like it was meant to
be. Roachford and Tim were the first two singers through the
door and they both just clicked. Then, of course, I was reunited
with Gary Wallis, followed by the two new additions, Anthony
Drennan and Luke Juby. There'd been no plan, no auditions, we
simply tried it to see what would happen. And it worked.

While I was busy with the Mechanics during the eighties,
Phil had been involved with the *Buster* film and soundtrack and
his . . . *But Seriously* album.

Tony was a realist, like me. The odds that one of us would
succeed with solo projects were slim; the odds that all three of
us would were miniscule. Tony always blamed me for the fact
that he didn't do more film scores after we'd worked together
on a soundtrack for *The Shout*, a 1978 film directed by Jeremy
Thomas. It was never a great film but we quite enjoyed working
on it together. However, when we went to the premiere, the
music we had written was completely drowned out by atmospheric gusts of wind. I was so cross that I got the producer up
against a wall afterwards: what was the point in bloody getting us
to do all that work? Tony always reckoned that my roughing up
the producer had damaged his soundtrack career. But the trouble
is that you need to schmooze to get anywhere in that world
and, by nature, Tony's not a schmoozer. In everything he has ever
done, Tony has been true to himself.

My own career could never be compared to Phil's either,
though: his success was off the scale. But among the three of us
there was never any ego. When we were on stage each night it

felt the same as it had always done – three mates together – and we still appreciated the things we each contributed musically that no one else could. Which is why, in 1991, we decided to make another album.

★ ★ ★

'You're so rich you don't need to work again. Why are you making another record?' was the question that journalists always asked. That question always pissed me off – as if we were ever doing it for the money. *We Can't Dance* happened simply because we wanted to work together again. Which, after all that had happened to each of us in the five years since *Invisible Touch*, felt like an achievement in itself.

We went into The Farm and, like the two albums before it, the making of it just seemed to fly by. On day one we were a bit edgy, a bit nervous – hoping we'd fire up but knowing that it was never a given that the music would come. But then there was just a rush of exciting creativity. We shot the photographs on the inside of the album at Chiddingfold Working Men's club and it all felt familiar again – the band, the crew, the studio – like no time had passed at all.

Sometimes it really didn't seem like we had been away. We were touring the album in America when I thought to myself that the private plane we were using looked quite familiar. It had been repainted but I knew there was a sure-fire way of finding out if it was the same one. Five years earlier I'd left a little stash of grass tucked behind the sun shield of one of the windows. It took a bit of finding but there it still was – a little dry, a little tired, a little old – but exactly where I'd left it in 1986.

The 'We Can't Dance' walk was Phil's idea: it just happened spontaneously on the set of the video, which we made in LA while we were there on tour. It was quite strange, after years of long progressive songs, most of which were spent sitting down, suddenly to be so well known for a silly walk. When the tour got to Earls Court, huge images of Tony, Phil and me were up on the hoardings in the same place that I remembered posters for the Royal Tournament. We looked a bit different from the marching soldiers, though. I didn't mind the walk becoming so famous because I knew it was only part of what we did, but Phil got upset with Roger Waters after he wasn't very complimentary about it. Phil would always want to ring someone up if they had said something rude about him. I would always tell him, 'Don't believe the good reviews or let the bad ones hurt you.' But I'd been saying that for so long now that even I was beginning to realize that he wasn't going to take any notice. So he rang Roger up and gave him an earful.

Phil always had a way of standing between Tony and me, the stiff public schoolboys, and bringing out the humour in both of us: that was what the 'We Can't Dance' walk was about. No one else could have got Tony and me to unbend enough to do that. We couldn't not laugh with Phil around, and sometimes I'd even think it was a shame that Pete wasn't around to enjoy it, too. Pete only ever experienced the early, very intense stuff and never any of the laughter which, given that he had such a great sense of humour, was sad. Pete would have fitted in so well later on – but maybe it was because we weren't together anymore that we were all able to lighten up, Pete included. We all moved in the same direction in our separate ways.

Following my Egyptian adventure and Jesus *Spitting Image* moment, another single from the album provided an opportunity for a further flirtation with being a religious figure. While we were in Dallas making the video for 'Jesus He Knows Me', American evangelists were big news, filling up the American TV channels, and that was exactly what the song was about . . . exposing crooked evangelists. A high-profile evangelist had been on TV on a Friday night saying the Lord's wish was for his followers to give him $5 million by Monday – only the Lord knows how he did it, but he did. This was followed by a huge investigation into the drug taking, affairs with minors and other sordid antics that these millions were funding.

Phil, Tony and I were whooping it up making the video in the guise of evangelists, and having a small insight into their life-style. The filming started with a jacuzzi filled with Californian babes . . . and us, of course. The next scene was of me having a four-hand massage (non-pornographic) with even more babes. The filming took longer than expected, although no one was complaining. Except I did have to call home and say I wouldn't be home as this wretched filming was running overtime. I'm not sure Angie felt too sympathetic once she saw the video.

The *We Can't Dance* tour was a fantastically opulent time. Each night, we would leave the stage in a convoy of limos with a police escort, bath robes over our heads, go straight to the airport and get on our private plane. But the other side of touring was that the bigger we got, the bigger the shows we played and the more serious it got. There's a lot of pressure when you're playing to 70,000 people a night, and Phil felt that most of all. I could play a concert if I was ill and half dead, but if Phil caught a cold it would be a big deal because he was concerned about his voice. We would always have to worry if he caught a chill going to the plane in his robe; he'd have to wrap up, he wouldn't be able to talk, he wouldn't be able to go out for dinner after a show, not that, even in 1986, he could go out much anyway: he'd be recognized everywhere. The voice was like another person on tour – the fourth one of us – and I think that got to Phil. It stopped being as much fun.

Phil would still make us laugh, but there had been a transformation from the laid-back, beer-drinking hippy he'd been in the early years into someone who had gradually become more serious. He'd always been organized but over the years it came out more and more, and he'd be punctual to the minute. I quite enjoyed making a bit of a mess of my room, making it feel like home with a few things lying around the place, but Phil's would be pristine. He'd become very meticulous even with his packing and unpacking, and I don't think maid service ever had much to do. I'm sure it was a coping mechanism – he would try to keep his own life in order in an attempt to help him handle the workload, the pressure and the fame. Looking back now, I see how strange it was for him to have gone from being the drummer to the singer. He did it so effortlessly that I don't think Tony or I ever thought much about it at the time, but it had never been part of his plan.

All of this meant that when we went for a meeting at Tony Smith's house in Chiddingfold one day in 1996 and Phil said, 'I think I'm going to call it a day,' it wasn't really a surprise. The surprise was that he'd stayed with Genesis as long as he had, after all that had happened with his solo career.

And I think I also knew the chances were it wasn't quite the end.

* * *

Do I regret *Calling All Stations*? No: professionally I don't really regret anything. We did it because Tony and I had written some songs together that we liked. We had replaced a singer before, although I was very aware that the hill to climb was pretty big this time around.

Ray Wilson did a good job as the vocalist but he wasn't a writer. Without a third writer, there was no one to glue Tony and me together; we didn't have anyone to pull us back into the middle ground, the centre of the musical Venn diagram. I'd never been aware before of quite how far apart Tony and I were musically until this album. It only hit me then that Phil was the one who had reined us both in, took what we did best and found a setting for it. *Calling All Stations* was released in 1997 and sold two-million copies – not bad – but when the record was released I also sensed that the mood had changed in terms of radio play. We were becoming a catalogue act. Tony and Ray were keen to carry on but I knew we'd have had to bring in another writer. To me it felt right to just stop there – no real harm done.

* * *

In 2007, Tony Smith told us that Pete had been thinking about touring *The Lamb Lies Down on Broadway*. He'd always thought it was a strong, undeveloped concept and he'd wanted to do something more with it. The technical difficulties of the original production had frustrated all of us and we'd had virtually no budget, so the idea of having another go was appealing. Obviously part of the special effects would have involved making Pete look a little more like he did in 1974, and a bit less 2007.

Phil was touring at the time so Tony, Steve, Pete and I all agreed to meet in Glasgow, where Phil was playing. As far as Tony in particular was concerned, we were meeting to discuss the tour we were going to do. As far as Pete was concerned, we were meeting to discuss discussing the tour we might be going to do. As we realized while spending quite a long two hours going round in circles.

The funny thing was, it was exactly like the old days again: Tony and Pete the same; Steve was quiet; Phil was loving the idea of playing drums again. It all came back: the dynamic was just the same. Personally, I felt it would have been great for Phil and me to be back together as the rhythm section. People always talk about Phil the singer, but I still think of him as Phil the drummer who moved to the front rather reluctantly because no one else was going to. But it had never been an easy album to play and, Steve apart, it turned out that we all had our reservations. Eventually, we realized we were getting nowhere and first Pete left, then Steve left and then it was just the three of us: Phil, Tony and me.

And the weird thing is, when you put Phil, Tony and me in a room, we are the band again. We had been together so long that although Phil had left, I'd never actually thought of it that way. On reflection, that was probably why it didn't strike me particularly deeply when he'd told us he was going in 1996. I'd thought that he could say he wasn't in Genesis anymore and that was fine, but I wasn't sure he could really leave. We had been through too much, shared too much; it was like a bond you just couldn't cut. We may not have seen each other very much but it doesn't ever go away.

So there we were in Glasgow, wondering what would happen next, when Phil said: 'If there is going to be a reunion, we should do the three-piece first. The five-piece would be the finale, but the three-piece should come first.'

★ ★ ★

'What are you doing to prepare? How are you getting fit?'

As soon as we'd announced the 2007 Turn It On Again tour, journalists started asking us that. Maybe they thought we were eighty-something, not fifty-something. In any case, the answer would always be 'Nothing'. By the time Tony and I had learned the songs again, we would be fit enough to play them.

It was a bit different for Phil. His voice had dropped over the years and I used to tell him just to sing a different note – you can duck and dive a bit live – but he wouldn't do that, he saw it as a failure. Then, in 2007, after thirty-odd years, Tony and I finally agreed to change keys. He sounded the best he'd ever been.

We were never confident about the tour. I knew we would sell tickets but I didn't know how many, which is why we only did one show at Twickenham. As it turned out, we could have done many more. It was a great feeling, being back on stage with the band.

The show that meant most to me was the concert at the Circus Maximus in Rome. The ancient Roman chariot-racing stadium was about as far from an anonymous arena as you could get, but it wasn't just that: Italy had been one of the first places to get us when we were just starting out.

We were on stage in front of 500,000 people, the biggest crowd I have ever seen. The silhouette of the stage was like a sculpture against the city. It was a warm summer's night, and we came on just as the sun was going down, with the outline of the Vatican just visible . . .

Forty years of Genesis, playing out the highs and lows, from sleeping on floors to private planes, witnessing the changing faces . . . but, of course, nothing has ever been more important than the music. 'Duke's Intro' kicked in as the massive crowd enveloped us in a wall of noise. Everything worked like clockwork that night, something my father would have appreciated

As a young boy my dad was told . . .

'You'll never be as fine a man as your father.'

He was.
I hope I will be too.

ACKNOWLEDGEMENTS

My heartfelt thanks to my wife, Angie, who helped me find my voice, provided the humour for many of my anecdotes and put them on paper. I can't thank you enough.

Andreas Campomar at Constable & Robinson and Matthew Hamilton at Aitken Alexander Associates.

Tony Banks, Phil Collins, Peter Gabriel, Steve Hackett, Ant Phillips, Daryl Stuermer, Chester Thompson, Paul Carrack, Paul Young, Chris Neil, B. A. Robinson, Andrew Roachford, Tim Howar, Gary Wallis, Anthony Drennan, Luke Juby, Richard MacPhail, Alan Owen, Craig Schertz.

Tony Smith, Jo Greenwood, Carol Willis, Robin Moore and everyone at Hit and Run. Tony Stratton Smith, Ahmet Ertegun, Mike Farrell, John Giddings, Doug Morris, Jonathan King, Nicky Pickering, Mandy Swainston, Andy Godfrey.

Dale Newman, Geoff Callingham, Steve Jones (Pud), Geoff Banks (Bison), Hugh Padgham, Nick Davis, Andrea and Rupert Cobb.

John Alexander for introducing me to Angie.

And special thanks to Stephanie Cross, who over many months made sense of my life on paper and gave me the narrative structure for this book.

PICTURE CREDITS